MIDWEST ARCHITECTURE JOURNEYS

First Edition
1 2 3 4 5 6 7 8 9
ISBN: 9781948742573

Belt Publishing
3143 West 33rd Street, Cleveland, Ohio 44019
www.beltpublishing.com

Book design by Meredith Pangrace
Cover by David Wilson

MIDWEST ARCHITECTURE JOURNEYS

Edited by Zach Mortice

Introduction by Alexandra Lange

BELT PUBLISHING
CLEVELAND, OH

Table of Contents

Introduction

ALEXANDRA LANGE

Louis Sullivan and Frank Lloyd Wright, sons of the Midwest, may be among the nation's most famous architects, but the region has always been a fertile ground for builders both Beaux-Arts trained and self-taught. And yet, far too often, the architecture of the Midwest is covered as a novelty—people out there have taste!—or as a ruinous theme park. Both of these formulas tend to cut off buildings from life, and life from buildings.

In *Midwest Architecture Journeys* we take a different tack, if you will, zigzagging between the sublime and the frothy, along the lakeshore, through small towns, and out among the cornfields. More than two dozen architects, critics, and journalists contribute their expertise, their personal histories, and their idiosyncratic sensibilities to the trip.

We stop at some of the region's most inventive buildings by architects including Bertrand Goldberg, Bruce Goff, and Lillian Leenhouts. We pay admission at less obvious but equally daring and defining sites, such as indigenous mounds, grain silos, parking lots, flea markets, and abandoned warehouses.

Look at the cover. Do you recognize that arch? Designer David Wilson was inspired by the People's Federal Savings and Loan Association building in Sidney, Ohio. But it also resembles graceful infrastructure, a cast concrete overpass overleaping the highway. Driving the flat routes that crisscross the region is also an architectural journey, one that most can access within a mile or two of their doorsteps. Neither is better, and they inform each other. Taking pleasure in those miles takes the edge off the anticipation, but it still matters that Sullivan's "jewel

Opposite: "North Christian Church (1964) on October 22, 2014, in Columbus, Indiana." Nagel Photography/Shutterstock.com.

box" building, ornamented with brilliant blue terra-cotta, is an American gem, not a pasty imitation of European architecture.

The common ground is that combination of the daring and the commonplace. You can visit (almost) all of these spots. Design ambition is not reserved for difficult mountain sites or even futuristic scientific endeavors. European modernists were inspired by the anonymously designed midwestern grain silos and so we still are.

To make some of the more obscure byways easier to follow, the front matter includes both a geographic map—so that the reader can see the territory covered—and thematic groupings, so that the reader can identify common preoccupations about the built environment. It is up to you how to move through the literary journey, driving straight through or dropping in over time.

The first section includes different versions of road trips, from ancient mounds to the mounds of other people's stuff at flea markets. The second focuses on work by some of the Midwest's greatest architects, men and women who found inspiration and clients in towns large and small: a Frank Lloyd Wright house of course, those banks, the wildness of Goff, and the sadness of underfunded and undermaintained public housing. The third considers places whose deeper meaning is revealed to the authors over time, through familiarity, popularity, or through loss. The

fourth looks at a new vernacular, from highway rest stops to abandoned warehouses. You could ask what they are doing in a book next to Frank Lloyd Wright, but that's where they are in real life. Even architects have to eat and, as I discovered on my own Midwest journey, it is useful to know how to drive.

❧

My dissertation is dedicated "To Mark, who did all the driving."

My Midwest journey began in July 2003. I had passed my oral examinations and outlined a thesis that was to look at postwar corporate design: buildings, landscapes, logos, products . . . the total package. There were terrific examples in New York: Lever House and the Seagram Building, one freshly scrubbed with its company's soap bubbles, the other the burnished hue of its company's finest whiskey. But they were tall, skinny examples, and the skyscraper was not an invention of the 1950s.

Organization men had flocked in lookalike suits to lookalike cubicles in lookalike towers long before William H. Whyte thought to chronicle them in *The Organization Man* (1956). What was new was the suburban corporate campus—a skyscraper laid on its side, in its simplest incarnation, which required more land, more parking, more landscape, more sculpture. To see examples of those I was going to have to get in the car and retrace, over the course of three weeks, the path of the industries that boomed after World War II—aluminum, glass, steel, automobiles, cleaning products, tractors, oil, engines—and the cities and towns that sprawled with their success.

There was just one problem. I had lived in New York long enough to be nervous behind the wheel. My husband agreed to be my chauffeur, leading to months of "Driving Miss Alexandra" jokes from the extended family.

My list started out focused on a few architects and a few projects, including the General Motors Technical Center and Deere and Company Headquarters by Eero Saarinen, the company town of Columbus, Indiana, and the archives and Design Yard at Herman Miller in Zeeland, Michigan, but once we decided to drive, it was impossible to stop adding additional monuments. As we researched those buildings, it was impossible not to see how each one connected to the marriage of design and business and thus to my thesis.

Isn't there a Frank Lloyd Wright house around there somewhere?

If we're going all the way to Missouri, why not Oklahoma?

When else will we be near Richland Center, Wisconsin, New Harmony, Indiana, Fayetteville, Arkansas?

Our furthest point west was Wright's Price Tower in Bartlesville, Oklahoma. It just seemed wrong *not* to go, when we were seeing his Johnson Wax Building in Racine just a few days before. Arkansas seems close when you've come so far, and we swooped through the corner to see E. Fay Jones's Thorncrown Chapel.

Architecture history slideshows became an extensive printout. The friends with whom we stayed in Chicago remember us unfurling a scroll of paper when questioned about our route.

Our first stop was Pittsburgh, which—as a man from Chicago told me in no uncertain terms—is not in the Midwest.

We saw Harrison and Abramovitz's Alcoa Building and Philip Johnson's Pittsburgh Plate Glass Building, complexes that brilliantly show off their companies' respective products. And oh yes, what was that down the street? SOM's US Steel Building, as dark and muscular as the other two are sparkly and faceted.

Then north to Detroit, where our Volkswagen Passat wagon was the only un-American car in the visitors' lot. Access to Saarinen's automotive Versailles had been hard to get (and no photos were allowed inside—my first experience of corporate paranoia, though it was still pre-NDA). I had a brief moment of fear the German engineering would be held against us. Saarinen designed a sculptural water tower for the Tech Center, as it is commonly known, and it was a rare thrill to see that tulip-like form rising above

"Deere and Company Headquarters, Moline, Illinois, 1956-64. Exterior." Library of Congress, Prints & Photographs Division, Balthazar Korab Archive at the Library of Congress.

the straight road and the low, rectilinear glass-and-steel buildings of the complex. There's nothing like visiting to understand scale, and to understand that the Tech Center was built for the scale of postwar midwestern highways.

Inside the Tech Center the Techni-color glazed, brick end walls felt like a secret delight. The glazes were developed for the Saarinen office by Maija Grotell, his colleague at Cranbrook, the design school a dozen miles northwest in Bloomfield Hills. Cranbrook itself, visited the next day, felt like delight squared, with its lush grounds, academic courtyards, and wealth of handcrafted details.

A story started to assemble itself along our journey. Chicago is always where it starts, as it starts this book: the second-place finish of Finnish architect Eliel Saarinen in the 1920 Chicago Tribune Tower competition, the Saarinen family's move to Bloomfield Hills where Eero, Eliel's son, met the men and women that would give the postwar midwestern world some of its style and many of its details. Big gestures like the water tower speak to the landscape, but inside homes, banks, and libraries, smaller choices about materials make the difference between bland and luxurious.

I've noticed a defensiveness in the framing of midwestern architecture in many publications, most often in those with "New York" in their title. An assumption made that the reader will be surprised to find something ambitious, something intricate,

something world building in a zone that someone, sometime declared culture- and geography-free. I scoff at that lazy lede: Who are you to know what I might expect?

I'm an easterner—born, bred, lived my whole life on the I-95 corridor—and yet the Midwest never seemed blank or bland to me. How could it when I had my scroll? How could it when I reached one of the twentieth century's best buildings, Saarinen's Deere Headquarters, at the end of the long road to Moline?

In a green hollow, reflected in a man-made lake, there is a palace to the tractor made of steel and inspired by Japanese villas. Such a thing could only exist at that moment, in that place. Scale, material, and personal taste came together to make a modern masterpiece, one that doesn't shout, but purrs like a well-tuned American engine.

Each of the essays in this book started with the same itch to explore. How many other such moments are there out there? Label a different set of buildings "jewel boxes" and string them together on a chain. Make your own scroll—they certainly did.

You could start in Pittsburgh, which, if it is not the Midwest, is at least the Rust Belt. In "Under the Big Dome: The Modernist Nightmare That Buried Little Harlem," Dante A. Ciampaglia complicates the heroic narrative of modernism and materials downtown with the story of the Civic Arena. "The Space Age stainless steel marvel of modern engineering where they gathered was built on the ruins of the Lower Hill District, the center of black Pittsburgh known nationally as Little Harlem," he writes. In retrospect, I should have looked deeper than those facades, and at what we can now see as the "urban removal" project that replaced neighborhoods with shiny objects.

Andy Sturdevant's essay "Groundscraper City" describes a different kind of urban erasure, that of the underground building. In the 1970s and 1980s, the utopian arrow pointed down, into the earth, where the dirt would provide an insulating blanket and solar collectors would harness the power of the sun. He quotes architect David J. Bennett, who designed one such structure at the University of Minnesota. "It irritated me that the attitude of landscaping was decorative," Bennett tells him. "The earth was just a platform, and everyone celebrated the objects and forgot the relationship with platform was somewhat tenuous."

The groundscrapers tend to meet the prairie with concrete angles, dark maws that can be either scary or enticing, depending on lighting and landscaping. Such large-scale elemental forms become a leitmotif of Late Modern Midwesternism, turning up aboveground in projects like Bertrand Goldberg's Wilbur Wright College. Goldberg, best known for the

corncob towers at Marina City in the Loop, decided a college needed a pyramid. Zach Mortice, who also edited this book, describes how a new generation of architects is updating the rather rigid ancient form.

But that's just one way to organize a trip, bouncing between big geometric objects. Each of the book's four sections offers alternatives. The first, "Journeys," highlights essays that make idiosyncratic connections.

Jordan Hicks begins "Out of Earth: The Cahokia Mounds and the Radix of Midwestern Monuments" inside the John Hancock Center, gazing across Chicago. The flatness around the skyscraper, once the second-tallest in the city, might seem bland to some (easterners, westerners) but they would be wrong. "This landscape is sublime; it dwarfs you, and it sets off gentle echoes of awe and terror, commingling somewhere deep in your brain," he writes.

Lynn Freehill-Maye celebrates the earlier verticals of the grain silos, standing up in the land of corn and soybean fields "like rectangles of copier paper."

There's something to be said, however, for treating your daily life like a treasure hunt. *Midwest Architecture Journeys* may start on a Hancock Center high but, as Bryan Boyer says, "Look carefully and you'll find [eagles] roosting atop columns, occupying the center of pediments, and contributing their decorative splendor to moments of architectural importance." He calls it "geo-ornithology": "These birds tell us how a city sees itself—or wants to, anyways." Detroit, prosperous in the 1930s, America's peak decorative eagle period, provides a particularly rich hunting ground.

In the second section, "People," architects take center stage.

Allison C. Meier, who grew up in Bartlesville among houses and churches designed by Bruce Goff, only understands later how wild his legacy is. But even in a Goff grotto, the industrial nature of modernism is present. Bartlesville's prosperity is founded on oil. Goff's rounded forms, his glitter and fur, couldn't have been made without wartime experiments with Styrofoam, concrete, and geodesic structures. The "gems" he embedded into the walls were glass cullet, chunks leftover from the production of bottles.

We get another version of living-with-the-visionary from Joe Frank, owner of the Haid House in Evanston, Illinois. Haid is best known as the architect of the Ferris Bueller house—really, the home of Ferris's anxious friend Cameron, brilliantly played by Alan Ruck. For Cameron the gleaming modernist palace is a prison of chilly modernist ostentation, surfaces that look better untouched. But Frank tells us what's good about glass houses. "The house, with its one central room, brings our family together simply because there is no place else to go, unlike the big Victorians and Tudors, where each person in the family can have their own wing."

On my trip, we didn't make it to any of Louis Sullivan's so-called "jewel box" banks either. Milenko Budimir does, traveling to Central Ohio, where the burghers of Newark, their competitive spirit raised by Sullivan's bank in Cedar Rapids, Iowa, hired Sullivan to lift the town's reputation through architecture. Brilliant green tile highlighted the name of the Home Building Association Company. A lion stands watch over the windows.

Today I would rate seeing the Sullivan banks (there are eight total; Owatonna, Minnesota, is usually considered the best) above the many Wright houses, with their Wright-worshipping guides, that we did put on the route. After the fourth or fifth one, I just wanted to shut my eyes when the guide called Mr. Wright a genius or claimed he invented the garage, the gas station, or the open kitchen. Sullivan never gets the genius treatment, which makes the quest to see his work necessarily more personal.

I complain about the tour guides, but I've never been one, as Amanda Page has, resurrecting the legacy of architect Frank Packard, whose fingerprints are all over Columbus, Ohio, at a moment his legacy seems threatened by new construction.

In section three, "Places," the focus turns to more personal stories of architecture.

Sophie Durbin writes of stumbling into Eliel and Eero's Christ Church Lutheran in Minneapolis, "the

"Edith Farnsworth House, Fox River and Milbrook Roads, Plano vicinity, Kendall County, Illinois. Designed by Ludwig Mies van der Rohe." Jack E. Boucher/Library of Congress, Prints and Photographs Division, HABS: ILL, 47-PLAN.V,1-9.

"Washburn Crosby Elevator, 54 South Michigan Avenue, Buffalo, Erie County, NY." Library of Congress, Prints and Photographs Division, "Built in America"
Collection, HAER NY-244-3.

quiet middle child of midwestern modernism," and finding it initially severe. Those who celebrate the major Saarinens in Detroit or Columbus may not even know about this simultaneous design. But light, brick, and a careful preservation of all of the elements of the church's modernist legacy, down to the furniture, eventually convince her that the church has just the right amount of design.

At the Waterloo (Iowa) Public Library, Monica Reida has her first childhood encounter with civic architecture with a capital A, a Renaissance palazzo with 1940 Edgar Britton murals showing a day at the National Cattle Congress. As an adult, she returns to it as a memory palace, soothing herself with a mental tour. The Laura Ingalls Wilder books are there. The Spanish-language, then Bosnian-language books are there. Britton's cows preside.

Architecture didn't play matchmaker for me as it did for Jennifer Komar Olivarez. As resident caretaker of the Minneapolis Institute of Art's Purcell-Cutts House, she invited an eligible bachelor to a cocktail party and he raved about the house. "He visited the house many times, helping with mundane tasks and, like me, drinking in the beautiful details. Two and a half years later we were married there."

The architecture, alas, was not conducive to married life. Still, her daughters have absorbed an interest in others' domestic lives and a sharp ear for tours:

Historic houses are now in their blood, and they have even begun to critique their interpretation on our vacation stops. (A recent observation: On a house visit, my fourteen-year-old daughter wanted to see more historical room displays and less interpretation labels so she could envision how all the rooms were used.)

In the final section, "Midwestern Vernacular," famous names go out the window in favor of ruins, mausoleums, rest stops, and beer. What does it mean, and what should it mean, to build monuments for the Rust Belt today? Maybe architects, and skyscrapers, have nothing to do with it.

Lindsay Fullerton charts the strange twilight history of the 1933 Century of Progress Homes of Tomorrow, once beacons of progress, now stranded like shipwrecks on the Indiana Dunes. Bill Savage stops in at the Hilltop Brewery in New Glarus, Wisconsin, to admire the faux ruins and "Cow Tipper" robot the brewers have installed, building community through a combination of financial, physical, and graphic design choices.

Our last stop—but it need not be yours—is with Corey Smith. In "An Abridged History of the Tallest Buildings in the Midwest," he knits together strange he knits together strange trips, famous people, and personal history, to describe a possible starting point for the whole idea of the midwestern architecture project: the October 16, 1956, announcement of Wright's mile-high Illinois tower, a building that, in the mind of the megalomaniacal architect, was as big as the state, with accommodation for 100,000 people, 15,000 cars, and 100 helicopters. The sketch of the tower alone is twenty-two feet long. (Today, you can even buy a beer named after The Illinois.)

But what of it? Smith writes:

> Tallest buildings get remembered, written up, archived, talked about, and there is beauty in choosing something as arbitrary as *tallness*. But I'm ignoring the most fundamental question— when the tall building gets built, who gets to go in? Who does it serve? Skylines are iconic. But icons are only so useful. Images aren't houses. Myths can't nourish.

Don't let the journey end with the icons—go out and find something better, an architecture that means something to *you*. Even if you have to drive yourself. ✠

ISLAND QUEEN

SUSPENSION BRIDGE, CINCINNATI, OHIO

JOURNEYS

Opposite: "John A. Roebling Suspension Bridge in Cincinnati, Ohio. Taken c.1907." Library of Congress, Prints and Photographs Division, LC-D4-70073.

"View from the Hancock Building." Photo by Gabriel X. Michael.

Out of Earth:
The Cahokia Mounds and the Radix of Midwestern Monuments

JORDAN HICKS

I. Plane

This piece is a reflection on something ancient, but the best way to enter it may be through a more modern experience. Go to the building formerly known as the John Hancock Center, on Chicago's near north side. It was stripped of its name in early 2018, and now goes simply by its street address, but whatever you call it, it is stunning. Designed and built in the late 1960s, it soon became one of the city's icons—its tapered form, its X-bracing, and its resolutely dark anodized aluminum façade remain powerful. Many tourists and school kids come here to be whisked up to the observation deck. Avoid this, with its "TILT" and clamor. You want to be somewhere you can just sit and look. So instead, go the bar on the ninety-sixth floor and sit near the window on the west side. This is where you'll see it: the city's grid stretching further than you can see. It is grid to the horizon, unifying and dominant. If you look for just a moment, it's simply an interesting perspective on the city. But look longer, and the midwestern landscape will well up around you. Moving toward dusk, the light and lights all betray the same thing: It is flat. It is even. It is mathematical in its abstraction—the plains as a plane, infinite. In some corners of the American imagination, this is the landscape of cultural and physical monotony. This place is dull; it's bland; it's the nothing accent of the newscaster. But from this vantage, even before you're a few drinks in, you will see it is not that at all. Rather, this landscape is sublime; it dwarfs you, and it sets off gentle echoes of awe and terror, commingling somewhere deep in your brain.

From other corners, I can already hear the protest: It isn't like this throughout the region; there's hills here and bluffs there and dells and, and, and. Yes. But imagine yourself here centuries ago, facing west, just beyond the Great Lakes and worlds from the Rockies. For many of us this is hard. So here is a statistic: per a 2014 study in the *Geographical Review*, Illinois is second flattest state in the United States, after only Florida.[1] Keep this in mind on a drive south along Interstate 55, slashing southwest across the state. The hills, when you do find them, are not steps up a terrain toward something more dramatic. Rather, they feel like events in and of themselves. Emerging from the plane, they are events as much as landscape. Some conversations about midwestern architecture might start with the Prairie Style, or the Chicago School, or the Homestead Acts, or sod houses, or wigwams. But I think that you can find the radix of midwestern architecture in the landscape above all else. In terrain that is essentially (even statistically) flat, buildings take on a different meaning. In Chicago, they have become our mountains. I have heard this analogy often. People here gaze upon the Sears Tower as Seattleites do upon Mount Rainier. This is not to claim any formal resemblance between the two. Though some architects seek possibility in geometric complexity, and some contemporary design sensibilities might hew towards the biomorphic or the botanical, the history is this: in the Midwest, we built mountains with hard edges and simple forms. We built mountains in geometries that nature cannot yield.

When I say "we," I mean those who build. The first builders belonged to indigenous cultures long since vanished, absorbed over centuries into latter traditions. The names that they called themselves, and the intricacies of their world, are often lost. But they started in the most direct way possible—with the Earth itself.

II. Mounds

Indigenous people across North America built mounds out of earth for many centuries, for many purposes.[2] The heaviest concentrations of these mounds are found in the Midwest and Southeast of the present day United States; if you live in these regions, your state has mounds. Some are protected historical places, some active archaeological sites. Some have been integrated into parks, cemeteries, golf courses, agricultural landscapes. Many have been destroyed by the overlapping violence of looting, development, and neglect. Also: the inescapable racism that undergirds our culture. St. Louis, Missouri, was once dotted with mounds, none of which remain; the last were razed shortly after the Civil War. Until the dawn of the twentieth century, many white people doubted that mounds were the work of Native Americans at all. Instead, they posited tales about Vikings and Druids. Joseph Smith, when spinning the fantasies of Mormonism, claimed that the mounds were the work of a lost tribe of Israelites.[3]

The earliest mound complexes rose from the flood-plains of the Mississippi Delta. The mounds at Watson Brake in Louisiana date to 3400 BCE. The site is an oval, nearly three football fields across. There are eleven mounds here, between three and fifteen feet high. They are connected by a berm, also called a ridge. The complex was built in phases, over hundreds of years.

By 200 BCE, mound building had become common across many cultures in the Midwest and Southeast, but especially amongst people in the Ohio River Delta. Early cultures here—often referred to as the Adena and the Hopewell[4]—built various types of mounds. Some had flat tops with raised platforms for ritual. Others were precisely geometric berms, lines of mounded earth defining a settlement—circles in Detroit, an octagon in Newark, Ohio. Later cultures built "effigy" mounds, like those that may have once dotted Chicago.[5] These mounds are representations, often of an animal. The Serpent Mound in Chillicothe, Ohio, is a 1,300-foot long pictogram of a snake—coiled tail, undulating body—swallowing an orb.[6] From the ground, the entirety of the effigy is hard to discern. It is best understood from a platform high above.

Some effigy mounds marked burial sites, while others did not. But the mounds which archaeologists refer to as "conical" often do. (To me they look more like domes, or half spheres, owing to the passage of time.) Many mound burials are accompanied by rich caches of material goods indicating trade across long distances. Shells from the Gulf Coast are unearthed in the Midwest; mica, copper, obsidian all traveled far. Meanwhile, the details of these burials suggest elaborate ritual. Fascinatingly, one Ohio burial site included a wolf's palate, worn by a person with their front teeth knocked out.[7] Many mounds contain bodies that appear to be ritual sacrifices. Often, mounds were built over the course of many burials. Skeletons become strata. Archaeologists often hypothesize on the belief systems of these ancient cultures. The lineage from ancient mound builders to present-day indigenous nations is not always clear. But, clearly, more input from and collaboration with indigenous people is necessary.

Some conical mounds entomb entire wooden structures. In some cases, archaeologists suspect that these were homes of a prominent individual or clan; in others, the structures seem to be charnel houses where the dead were ritually prepared. Burying buildings has always piqued my interest. Wood structures are temporary by dictate of their material. Like everything organic, they decay. So it is hard for me not to read these mounds of earth as an ancient struggle for permanence. To memorialize, to consecrate, people manipulated the earth itself into a new configuration. Conical mounds, even after centuries of erosion, betray the precision in the minds of their creators. In the best-preserved examples, there is no mistaking mounds for hills. They are too regular in shape. The way they rise from flat ground is too quick, too decisive.

"Hancock Building." Photo by Gabriel X. Michael.

"Modern stairs lead to the top of Monk's Mound, a Cahokia Mounds Historic Site. Cahokia is a pre-Columbian Native American city directly across the Mississippi River from modern St. Louis, MO." PhilipR/Shutterstock.com.

Because of their material and arrestingly minimal geometry, it is tempting to think of the mounds as forebears to the land art of the 1960s and 1970s—Robert Smithson, Michael Heizer, and others. In fact, Heizer built a series of mounds in Ottawa, Illinois, on an abandoned mining site. This is now part of Buffalo Rock State Park. Known as the Effigy Tumuli, the work includes five effigy mounds—turtle, snake, frog, catfish, water bug. Heizer is clearly riffing on indigenous practices here—or appropriating them.

An earthwork is related to, but maybe distinct from, architecture. The material of an earthwork is the same as that of its context. But it is understood as deliberate, and it carries meaning, through its very shape. Earthworks, ancient or modern, rarely enclose space to be occupied (at least by the living). But as an architect wholly disinterested in the rigid categorization of the things that people build, I see these mounds as architecture. In them, I read the same impulse legible in ancient stone architectures from cultures around the world. The mounds are North America's permutation of Stonehenge or Chichen Itza or Luxor—human presence made mineral. That they were crafted from soft earth makes them no less stunning, and it is deeply sad that they are not celebrated like their distant counterparts. The US owes more to the indigenous people of North America than it will ever give them. This is obvious, and sad, and ever urgent. It is important to remember that the mound sites of the Midwest are not just landscapes. They're not curiosities, or relics. They are the first acts of monumental architecture in this place.

By 400 CE, mound building had become less common in the region. But, by 1000 CE, there was a resurgence, with the rise of what we now term the Mississippian culture (for it spanned up and down the river, from Wisconsin to the Gulf states). Mounds were built at a greater scale by societies of increasing complexity and hierarchy. The largest and most prominent Mississippian mound is at a UNESCO World Heritage Site just outside of East St. Louis, Illinois. It is known as Monk's Mound, in a place called Cahokia.

Cahokia is found in "The American Bottom," a region which sits within the Mississippi River flood plains of southern Illinois. The American Bottom spans the confluence of the Mississippi and Missouri Rivers, at the north, and the Kaskaskia River at the south. There are cyclical floods and rich, organic soils. Agriculture flourished and flourishes here, from the introduction of maize to the machinations of Monsanto.

By the fifth century CE, the people of this region settled in agricultural communities, villages. Sometime in the eleventh century CE, people began to concentrate in greater numbers at this specific point. Cahokia became a city. Archaeologists debate its population—estimates range from 3,000 up to 25,000.[8] To those outside of the esoteric and rigorously scientific conversation, the exact number of Cahokians is not really important. What you need to know is this: even at the low end of the estimate, Cahokia was the largest settlement in our hemisphere, north of Mexico, until well after the start of European colonization. But by the end of the fourteenth century CE, Cahokia was largely deserted; only many dozens of mounds remained. Counts vary (as boundaries are ill-defined and history has been cruel) but surpass one hundred. The best way to engage with this history is to visit. The relevance of Cahokia goes beyond historical fact and demands physical presence.

III. Cahokia

I've come to Cahokia many times—first with my parents, on an early college visit. Later, as part of an archaeological seminar focused on the ancient city: its mounds, its palisades, its middens, its culture. In the ensuing years, I kept going there—alone when I needed some quiet, with my partner on an early date. Once with architect friends in town for a wedding, who were quietly enthralled.

In recent years, I've approached from the east, in that long drive across Illinois, negotiating only slight changes of terrain. But when I lived in St. Louis, Missouri, I came from the west. This approach is telling. Try it. After crossing the Mississippi, you will skirt north of East St. Louis and head northeast on Interstate 55 / 70. This route takes you past a pair of contemporary monuments: the drag racing stadium dubbed Gateway Motorsports Park, and the Milam Landfill.[9] You'd be forgiven for mistaking the latter as a mound. It is a grassy hill, tall and long against the highway. Only the occasional scavenging birds, and the protruding vents (which release built-up methane) hint at the trash below. You will keep going, exiting the highway close to the Indian Mounds Golf Course, and drive west on Collinsville Road. You'll pass a small cinder block Mexican restaurant on your right—there is a sizable population of Mexican immigrants in the area. I had my first bite of sesos here in 2003. (I cannot recall what the restaurant was called when I first visited; it was El Gallo Jiros when I visited more recently. I'd recommend stopping in.)

You'll then pass a perfect circle, demarcated by vertical posts, hewn from trunks of red cedar. This is a reconstruction of what archaeologists termed "woodhenge," an astronomical observatory. Standing in the center of this circle, at the equinox, the sun appears to rise over the enormous mound to the east. While we'll never know the details of Cahokia's cosmology, the intertwining of power and divinity is palpable. The enormous mound looms ahead.

That mound is the largest earthen structure in North America. It is Monk's Mound, named by curious Americans who encountered an insular French Trappist order living atop it in the early nineteenth century. (The Mississippi was subject to French colonization since the late seventeenth century.) Without any context, this monument had spoken to the monks' aspirations, too. Monk's Mound is nearly one hundred feet tall, over 1,000 feet long in the north-south direction and covers thirteen acres of land.

The ensuing centuries have softened its edges, but Monk's Mound remains arresting. Briefly, let's consider Monk's Mound as a formal object. In Cahokia's prime, it was a crisp ascension of four platforms. The lowest platform covered approximately the southern third of the mound. It then rose steeply. The second platform aligned towards the west, and the third, much higher, aligned to the east. Cahokia is stringently axial, but Monk's Mound is not symmetrical. The fourth and final platform aligned to the south. We know that wooden structures sat atop these platforms, sites of ritual, and an inscription of hierarchy.

On the right side of the street, you'll find the Interpretive Center. This place is a treasure. But before you step inside, cross the street—carefully, as there's no signal here on this stretch of the old Route 66—to walk up Monk's Mound.

Concrete steps mark the north-south axis of the mound. The proportions of these steps are not gentle and modern, not the seven-inch risers and eleven-inch treads inscribed in our muscle memory. The rake of the mound demands a much taller step. Due to this, walking up Monk's Mound will require more exertion than a comparable height ten-story building. If you're not an athlete, it will be easy to get winded, and on sunny days, your neck and back will heat quickly. On my first ascent, I was sweaty by the summit.

The view from the top is your reward. You can see clear to the skyline of St. Louis to the west-northwest.

Saarinen's arch looks back at you, like a mirror or an answer. The waters of the Mississippi are not always visible, but they are evident in a gap of vegetation stretching from horizon to horizon. It's not as mercilessly flat here as in Chicago, but make no mistake. There is no landform that can even try to obstruct your vantage in any direction. Even if you knew none of its history, you would understand Monk's Mound through your eyes and your lungs and your legs and your sweat. The mound is fashioned from earth, from the Earth, but it is unmistakably the product of human mind and muscle. Monk's Mound was an engineering feat of its era.[10] And it is not comprised solely of dirt. While drilling into the mound's slope for drainage in 1998, engineers hit stone forty feet below the second terrace.[11] The purpose of this stone structure is not yet known, but it was built with significant effort. The nearest limestone is ten miles away.

After lingering at the top of the Mound, you might want to get out of the sun. Cross back to the Interpretive Center. This is a boomerang-shaped building, low and heavy. The walls are brick, massed in smooth corners. Above sits a standing seam metal roof, hipped. The center was designed by Booker Associates and completed in 1989, though its finishes and its material palette are reminiscent of a decade and a half prior—earthy all the way down. It has its flaws, and strange moments, but there is palpable joy and care in its design and construction. The entry doors are bronze, sculptural, heavy with birds and landscape in deep relief. You'll probably enter, though, through the modern glass doors to the side.

Once inside you'll be drawn to a large model on a raised platform, depicting the scores of mounds. The model is an irregular heptagon, with lights and buttons for illustration. From here, you can enter the theater for a brief film. It boasts a gentle electronic score and closes with bird sounds. At the film's end, the screen rises to reveal a full-scale diorama of several small structures, and mannequin Cahokians going about their everyday tasks—grinding corn, working hides. From here you will wander through exhibits and artifacts.

There is more to know about Cahokia than I can possibly relay here. Its residents participated in a ball game, known to us as chunkey, with fevered intensity. This was played on the immense earthen plaza south of Monk's Mound, which had been carefully engineered, graded, and flattened.[12] The people of Cahokia participated in human sacrifice. The excavation of Mound 72 yielded body after body. Some were mutilated, and many met a brutal end. The fall of Cahokia, in the fourteenth century CE, remains the subject of debate. Climate change, internal political strife, and environmental degradation all may have played a role. But for whatever reason, the people of Cahokia dispersed. It is unclear which historical nations can trace their lineage to Cahokia. Caddoan speakers to the southwest; the Osage, Kansa, and Omaha of the plains; the Iowa, Oto, and Missouri: all of these peoples may have Cahokia deep in their lineage.[13]

IV. Building

For a long time, I thought about my interest in the mounds as something separate from my role, my vocation, my identity as an architect. It is only recently that I've begun to understand the influence that Cahokia, and mounds more generally, have had on my understanding of architecture. Somewhere, below my conscious design efforts and day-to-day professional tasks, the mounds take hold. When I'm struck by the clarity and unity of a project that is platonic in its form and monolithic in its material, I am seeing the same qualities that I find meaningful in the mounds. When I find something sublime in the scale of a plaza or the rigidity of an axis, Cahokia is in my mind, too. But more than anything, it is the mound as mediation between flat plane and endless sky.

In my first week of architecture school, an instructor strode into his lecture class silently. He walked up to the whiteboard and drew a long horizontal line. He then drew a short vertical line, centered upon the horizontal one. He announced, "This is architecture," and left the room. Of course, he came back a moment later to explain his diagram and relay its history. (Maybe it was something Louis Kahn had done long ago? I can't remember, and it is not really important.) I liked this instructor, but I remember rolling my eyes at the time. It was all a bit theatrical, a bit precious for my budding taste. But it was also a distillation of a simple truth. I'm not so interested in *tectonics* here—the idea that we take pleasure in

"Collinsville, IL—Jan 5, 2018; Sunset at Monk's Mound with silhouettes of visitors at the largest earthen structure at the Cahokia Mounds pre-Columbian ruins complex in southern Illinois" PhilipR/Shutterstock.com.

understanding structure, in seeing how things stand up. I am interested in how architecture communicates our values, our ambitions—and once all of that falls away, our presence. The vertical line reaches out of the ground, and is made from it. It addresses us—it stands up to be considered. It is telling us something. It is marking something. It organizes us through our shared subjectivity. And it points toward the sky. The mounds enact this diagram of architecture with aplomb, and all the better for their context: a long, flat line stretching from horizon to horizon.

As a white person, the mounds are not mine. But they are the heritage of indigenous artists and designers, like Chicago-based Santiago X. He is a member of the Coushatta Tribe, a nation in Louisiana, who are descended from the ancient mound builders of the southeast. Santiago was also trained as an architect. In his art practice, he iterates on indigenous culture and forms through digital technologies—scripting, projection, drones. These are works of Indigenous Futurism: crisp, bold, colorful, meditative experiences. Santiago is currently at work on a pair of mounds on Chicago's North Side. These are not replicas. They are the first new earthen mounds to be built by indigenous people in hundreds of years. As Santiago explained to me, mounds are not static, historic—they are part of a living, thriving culture. The two designs are contemporary abstractions of a serpent effigy; in one project, under construction along the Des Plaines River in Schiller Woods, the serpent seems to burrow in and out of the ground obliquely,

arching and curving. In the other, along the Chicago River in Horner Park, the serpent coils into a mound. It creates a path, concentric circles leading visitors up, twelve feet above the plains. The two mounds are bookends of a walking trail, traversing the ground of the canoe portage between the rivers used centuries ago. By geometric coincidence, this portage aligns with Irving Park Road, an east-west vector of the unyielding grid.

Santiago's project is multivalent. The twin serpents nod to the joining of the two rivers further south. As effigies, they harken to ancient traditions, but render them in a contemporary formal language. The project will have an augmented reality aspect—visitors will be able to scan objects and symbols with their phones to learn more about indigenous cultures and share their own experiences. In a wonderful irony, the Horner Park mound will be constructed upon land restored by the US Army Corps of Engineers. And the project can be seen as a rebuke of sorts to Heizer's appropriation. Ultimately, these mounds are the start of a much larger project. Indigenous forms and principles, redacted from our built environment by colonialism, can guide architecture and urbanism into a radical future. As Santiago explained, "I think of mounds as a platform to build on."

Elsewhere in Chicago, I'm thinking about the city's legendary architecture, as well as some of my personal favorites. The Monadnock Building. Federal Plaza. Marina City and River City. The Hancock. The

Metropolitan Correctional Center. The Thompson Center. These buildings spring from different lineages and are grounded in different philosophies. But they all harbor a geometric purity, a formal unity and rigor. We read them as precise objects in a flattened field. The origins of their materials are abstracted through the processes of smelting steel, mixing concrete, floating glass, quarrying, and stacking stone. But they are made from the Earth, too. ✾

"Spencer Kellogg Elevator, 389 Ganson Street, Buffalo, Erie County, NY." Library of Congress, Prints and Photographs Division, HAER NY, 15-BUF, 35—4.

Silos, Celebrated and Lonesome

LYNN FREEHILL-MAYE

I. HOME: Central Illinois, 1988

As kids we didn't think our little Illinois towns held anything tall and important except the pointier-than-thou steeple of a church or two. Later I'd phrase this kind of importance as "architectural significance." Our church, Catholic and neo-Gothic, certainly felt significant. For a kid in a small town it seemed pretty darned impressive. A massive carved wooden altar spreading across the entire front encased St. Patrick plus Jesus, Mary, and Joseph. A testament to how many Irish immigrants were working the railroads or tenant farming around our town of Chenoa in 1897 that they could or would build a church that big. God, how high did its ceilings go? Had to be forty feet. This was a lofty height for contemplating the heavens, or why the German-descended Lutheran kids could color and snack on Cheerios in church while we Irish Catholics were left only to elbow our siblings.

Chenoa's sign-proclaimed motto was "Crossroads of Opportunity," since the railroad and, later, Route 24 (Peoria to Indiana), I-55 (Chicago to St. Louis), and Route 66 (Chicago to California) passed through. For us that meant "Easy to Get Going From." We were always flying down the road in the minivan to school or Grandma's or a reunion with different souls than the 1,800 in our own town—Mom and Dad, otherwise mild-mannered, law-abiding farmers' kids, had lead feet, always impatient to get somewhere else. There were few cops and therefore no speed limits on the country roads as far as I could tell. On the highways it was always flat enough to pass, even if Mom met wind resistance and really had to gun it.

The corn and soybean fields were rectangles of copier paper, each one the same exacting levelness, going on eternally in square-mile grids, the geometric perfection of which I've never seen extended so far anywhere else. (And people call Kansas flat—to me, its discernible hills look mountainous compared to Central Illinois.) Up close the fields smelled grassy and sweet, even though the corn here was dedicated for animal feed, not eating off the cob. Here the only thing of interest as we raced past—to me as a kid and to the farmers always and forever—was how high the crops were looking so far.

The seeming emptiness of the landscape made the basics more prominent: the wide sky, the air traveling through and away fast. The writer David Foster Wallace, raised in Central Illinois, would write that with nothing tall between Central Illinois and the Rockies, the winds could "move east like streams into rivers and jets and military fronts that gather like avalanches and roar in reverse down pioneer ox trails toward our own personal unsheltered asses." My future husband would fall behind me, his own personal unsheltered ass panting, during a run in the country outside Chenoa, and call out, "Is this normal?" Did he mean the wind? Sure, it's a light breeze, I'd say, nothing out of the ordinary. "ARE YOU SURE THERE'S NOT A TORNADO COMING?" he'd shout. So later I became conscious of the wind. But neither the most brilliant natives or the most curious visitors ever said a thing about the silos.

Being so tall, the grain elevators every few miles should have stuck out to me even at seven or ten. Maybe because the scale of the prairie dwarfed them, only the towns around the silos impressed me. By then I'd been to Chicago and had learned about suburbs, that my cousins and lots of other kids in the late 1980s were growing up near cities rather than in

small farming towns like ours. Two even tinier towns, each five miles outside Chenoa, existed as settlements around grain elevators. Meadows and Weston, I decided, were Chenoa's suburbs. The better kind. Chicago's suburbs were unknowable and indistinguishable, billboard-tacky and trafficky. Meadows and Weston were cozy, each of their official green Illinois population signs proclaiming 150 residents (not counting the nursing home in Meadows where local farmers eased off their own land and toward the Promised Land). That the grain elevators were important enough to cause even 150 people to build houses around them on the otherwise featureless plain didn't strike me then as notable.

II. AWAY: Buffalo, 2014

When I was growing up, a favorite band of my gentle, farm-raised parents was the Moody Blues. In my twenties I was discomfited to read in *Rolling Stone* that their music was best appreciated by "the kind of people who whisper 'I love you' to a one-night stand." The larger world, it seemed, didn't always appreciate the earnest taste of midwesterners. Almost as startling to learn, almost thirty-five years into life, was that the larger world did in fact admire something we had that we'd never really thought about: The silos jutting up like skyscrapers from flat land were considered modernist achievements. Their admirers likened them to Egypt's pyramids. Like church steeples and temple columns, these new round grain towers reached for the heavens, but without offering homage to any god, just a proud testament to human industry.

Their stark near-ugliness and lack of adornment inspired new wave architects in the early twentieth century. The demanding Swiss-French architect Le Corbusier called them the perfect marriage of form and function. The design that got started in Middle America was soon copied in Europe and all over the world. Gaping at Charles DeMuth's 1927 painting "My Egypt," all reverent cubist lines and angles, at the Whitney Museum of American Art in Manhattan, I finally appreciated the grain elevators the way you do your parents only once you've left home: as remarkable, impressive, poignant.

The modernists celebrated the grain elevators' simplicity of design. They loved their round shape, their freedom from windows or decoration of any kind, and above all their scale. The silos were elephantine in their color and size and even in the long snouts that dumped grain into railcars. Yet these architects and designers witnessed only the birth of the solid concrete form. The silos were built to last centuries, to near-immortality. The modernists would never see their death. Nothing, it seemed, could touch them, not even those notorious tornadoes.

Yet grain moves with the money, my Uncle John assured me. He'd left the family farm in the 1970s for the global grain-transport business, landing in a grand home in suburban Chicago along the way. He understood the ins and outs of elevators and the commodities business better than anyone I knew. "Like water moves to the lowest point, grain moves to the highest price," he explained. "It never fails. Ever." And so many silo complexes, in both the country and cities, were abandoned when grain found more lucrative shipping routes, like south to the Port of New Orleans rather than east through the St. Lawrence Seaway. In Chicago, for instance, only one elevator remains in use. It's managed by Uncle John's son, my cousin Michael (though owned, for the last couple years, by a Chinese company). For the rest, what nature couldn't easily rot would take lots of deliberate money to tear down. So what happened when these everlasting cathedrals to land and farming and productivity were no longer of use for holding grain?

I had to move to Buffalo to understand these were architectural masterworks that artists, poets, and musicians still did want to celebrate, even when they were in an abandoned state. Being in New York State, Buffalo seemed to my midwestern mind like an East Coast city, but a map reveals that after you leave Ohio and nip briefly into Pennsylvania, New York still spreads wide, six or eight hours to drive across. Some city booster early on in my time referred to it as the "Easternmost Midwestern City," and I kept repeating that once I saw how friendly and unsnobbish and open to chit-chat the people were. These were folks who would stop to help dig your stuck car out of the snow even if they were in dress clothes. And there, on

Gray and Gold, 1942. John Rogers Cox (American, 1915-1990). Oil on canvas; framed: 116 x 152 x 12.5 cm (45 11/16 x 59 13/16 x 4 15/16 in.);
unframed: 91.5 x 151.8 cm (36 x 59 3/4 in.). The Cleveland Museum of Art, Mr. and Mrs. William H. Marlatt Fund 1943.60. Courtesy of The Cleveland Museum of Art.

"J.W. Hawes Grain Elevator Museum in Atlanta, Illinois." Photograph by Cynthia Clampitt.

Lake Erie's shore, open to all comers, Buffalo hosted what has to be the world's most impressive collection of grain elevators, all set along the snaking Buffalo River. They'd once served barge traffic off an earlier St. Lawrence Seaway alternative, the Erie Canal.

In one of Buffalo's elevator complexes, Silo City, I inhaled the sweet-and-sour tang that still lingered from barley fermented there in the 1930s. In another I heard a Mohawk group drum, and the reverberations seemed to hallow the place. I lunched with the internationally heralded artist Nick Cave, who was choosing Buffalo for a yearlong residency because of its grain elevators. I paddled the river that twists between the silos with Elevator Alley Kayaks, wrote about them for the *New Yorker*, toasted them with the city's new "Grain Canyon" vodka. A half-dozen were painted bright and shiny to mimic a six-pack of Labatt Blue. A nightly laser light show was projected onto another complex, showering its gray with kaleidoscopes of color.

After three years in Buffalo, work took my husband and me toward New York City, but the grain elevators kept jazzing themselves up more. A complex called RiverWorks added a beer garden dripping baskets of flowers alongside the silos, then a zip line across them. A kitschy thatched-roof tiki boat floated between the different complexes in summer. Surprisingly tanned powerboaters pulled up and docked, ready to party. To be sure, the form-meets-functionality that had made grain elevators so celebrated still made them a devil to

reuse. A would-be hotel in Akron, for instance, had tanked in the past few years—apparently guests didn't love round rooms. (It was converted into college dorms, whose student occupants couldn't be as choosy.) Doubts remained—Silo City's owner still couldn't decide what all to do with his property and mulled trying a boutique hotel. Still, in cities like Buffalo, the most creative minds had successfully imagined some new uses for silos.

III. BACK: Central Illinois, 2018

Even as Buffalo staged its comeback, the grocery store back in my hometown closed. A Dollar General (the chain that *Bloomberg Businessweek* called a "bet on a permanent American underclass") moved in. The rich, loamy Illinois soil is still being farmed, the corn and beans still being trucked to the aging elevators, but there are fewer families living around, much less in a position to appreciate the silos. The green Illinois population signs proclaim fewer residents now in towns like Chenoa, Meadows, and Weston. I went back in spring, just as my uncles and other farmers were getting into the fields to get their crops planted, to see my retiring parents and take stock.

Whether Bloomington-Normal, the 200,000-resident twin college towns that were the big cities nearby, were also slouching downward like the farming towns was unclear. On one hand, the State Farm Insurance national headquarters there kept quietly transferring employees to Dallas. In April another 900 people were expecting relocation orders after the school year ended. On the other hand, once-grungy uptown Normal seemed to be thriving, fresh-scrubbed full of murals and boutiques.

The Upper Limits climbing gym in Bloomington-Normal, fashioned out of an abandoned grain elevator when I was in high school, was unexpectedly busy on a drizzly weekday afternoon. Its ambitious reuse had come to the silent amazement of locals—so silent I never even heard about the place when it was first converted twenty years ago. The walls were now stuck with hundreds of colorful handholds that looked like squashes of chewed-up, crazy-flavored Bubble Yum, and crawling with roped-up young climbers. I smelled slick vinyl mats and fresh sweat.

The flatlanders who tried this strangely round climbing gym seemed to be inspired to go elsewhere—to the rock formations depicted on the walls, out to Colorado for the adrenaline of being an outdoor guide or ski instructor—like the college-age guide who showed us around. As I watched the kids clamber lightly around in their harnesses, the elevators seemed like a springboard out for them. The twelve-year-old whose dad eagerly suited him up would likely take that experience to the Rockies, or maybe California. The couple who converted the complex into a gym don't live in Central Illinois anymore. They, too, have moved to a bigger city.

There was less action to be seen ten or fifteen miles down I-55 in Atlanta, Illinois (population: 1,600) at the J.D. Hawes Elevator Museum. Dating to 1903, it is one of the few old wooden grain elevators remaining in the country. Homer, our elderly guide, wore a cap with the elevator and dozens of stars embroidered on it, in a blue that'd faded a couple decades back. Homer was used to Route 66-loving European tourists—the Germans and Brits who are amazed at the 2,400 miles of open road and the kitschy Americana along it—but seemed thrilled that anyone besides the road-trippers and local agriculture students would want to see the place. He agreed to come out anytime that Sunday afternoon to personally guide Mom and Dad and me around. He'd already been waiting twenty minutes in his pickup when we arrived, and climbed down immediately to tell us how well-built the place was.

In a Southern-country-sounding drawl I could hardly believe originated about thirty-five miles south of Chenoa, Homer dismissed the wooden elevator's descendants as insignificant. "It's just concrete," he said. "You can paint it. These here have a history. Those don't have a history." My mom seemed to agree. Since retiring from teaching, she'd often commented on the beauty of the sky in Central Illinois. "I really notice it all now," she'd say. "You can see forever!" But she'd never had anything to say about the tall round towers silhouetted every night against that sky.

This wooden elevator, though, Mom liked. "It's all so pretty, the lines and angles," she said. My dad was more impressed with the concrete, having returned to Central Illinois decades ago from a perspective-widening few years in the Navy. When I'd come back from Buffalo talking about the new grain elevator uses, he said he'd thought for awhile that the silos were neat. The towers over the fields reminded him of naval-ship superstructures on the ocean.

The few new grain elevators rising up in Central Illinois were now being made not with concrete but galvanized steel. Gaping at the new farmers' co-op elevator complex being built five miles outside Chenoa, I felt that an alien spaceship had landed. The silvery steel was wide but squat, and gleamed with what appeared to be pipes and wires poking out everywhere. This looked like oversized machinery, not the permanent buildings the concrete silos seemed to be. I went out to see it all up close. Its thirtysomething project manager, a straight-shooting University of Illinois College of Agriculture grad named Matt, who'd grown up in another small town, offered to let us to sit in his pickup truck as we talked about it, since it was so gusty out that day. The project's cost was in the tens of millions, Matt told me, but for concrete it would have been even higher.

The steel was designed to last up to seventy years, not the hundred or more that the concrete could endure. But so few people care about continuing to make money beyond their lifetime. Central Illinois and its farmers, so many descended from the Germans and the Irish, are practical more than anything else, Matt told me—that might be his favorite aspect of the people. Their chief concern, although he didn't say it, was evident: How could they and their land be profitable in the here and now? There wasn't much room left for sentimentality about older grain elevators, or questions about design elegance or architectural permanence. Then again, maybe there never had been much local concern with all that.

Looking across the land at towns several miles away, it was plain that the church steeples of towns like Chenoa had long since been outgunned by the temples to industry. Yet not even the grain elevators—neither the tall, commanding concrete ones nor the squatter new steel versions—were dominating the landscape any longer. Wind turbines now stood in formation up to 300 feet high, dozens and dozens blinking their red lights up top in perfect, robotic, slightly unnerving sync. A new part of the midwestern economy was being built not on what we produced, but on the air that—like a good number of the natives—wanted to get going elsewhere fast. In cities they might be architecturally celebrated, but on the Central Illinois prairies, reengineering themselves for a new source of power and might, the old concrete grain elevators stood in starker loneliness than ever.

"Protest at Civic Arena." Men and women, including musicians, protesting in front of Civic Arena with picket signs that read "The Soundness of Our Cause Should Prick Your Conscience," Pittsburgh, Pennsylvania, October 1961. Photo by Charles 'Teenie' Harris/Carnegie Museum of Art/Getty Images.

Under the Big Dome:
The Modernist Nightmare That Buried Little Harlem

DANTE A. CIAMPAGLIA

At 5:30 p.m. on October 21, 1961, a group of black Pittsburghers—kids and adults, blue-collar laborers and starched-collar professionals—congregated under darkening skies outside the Civic Arena to protest discriminatory hiring practices at the city's sleek new auditorium. They carried signs that could easily have been spotted at similar demonstrations occurring across the country: "We Want to Work Too," "Job Opportunities for Us Too!" "Not Later, Now!" They sang "Nearer My God to Thee" as they marched. A couple men brought trumpets, another a large drum. It wasn't the first protest decrying Pittsburgh's bigotry—prior actions targeted segregated public swimming pools in 1949 and Isaly's restaurants' refusal to hire black counter clerks in 1953—and it wouldn't be the last. But this one was different; more raw, more personal.

The Space Age stainless steel marvel of modern engineering where they gathered was built on the ruins of the Lower Hill District, the center of black Pittsburgh known nationally as Little Harlem. The neighborhood had struggled with decrepit housing, virulent disease, and violent crime, but the community was tight-knit and vibrant when, in the early 1950s, the city identified the Lower Hill as ideal for urban renewal and condemned ninety-five acres as a blighted slum. Thousands of residents were displaced and hundreds of businesses shuttered, shredding the fabric of the neighborhood. The massive highway constructed at the base of the arena severed the residents of the Middle and Upper Hill from downtown and any kind of continuity with civic life.

Still, Hill residents were assured of adequate, affordable replacement housing and new job opportunities. And while progress was slow, there was a sense that this time things would be different. Pittsburgh would surely use its eye-catching new auditorium—a UFO-shaped building boasting the world's first retractable dome—as a first step toward reversing the racism that led those who arrived during the Great Migration to dub the city "Up South."

Reality set in at the arena's dedication. "'JIM CROW' HOVERS OVER CIVIC ARENA," howled the *Pittsburgh Courier* in its September 23, 1961, banner headline. More than 5,000 people attended the opening six days earlier, including hundreds of black Pittsburghers who wondered why their community leaders were shunted to the back of the official crowd. Then they noticed the arena staff. "Gosh," the *Courier* reported, "all of the ushers and guides are white! So are the concession employees! In fact, all of the employees seen are white! This can't be! . . . No Negro employees in the New Arena! Impossible!" Black workers were eventually found, as expected, as bathroom attendants, and even then in small numbers. "Whether 'Ole Jim' was there by request, or whether he came uninvited, the aggrieved did not know," the *Courier* wrote. "Being veteran watchers of the 'bird,' they recognized him on sight."

An October 7 follow-up documented the lack of representation: all but five of the arena's eighty-six ushers and all twenty-eight ticket takers were white, as were its six engineers and six electricians; no blacks worked concessions or among the four-person office staff or four-member watchman's crew. "We have been very patient in Pittsburgh on this kind of treatment," local NAACP president Byrd Brown wrote to arena director Edward Freher. "We are determined to get our fair share of employment, [and we] propose to take positive action unless the Auditorium Authority and your office makes some move to equalize the employment picture at this arena."

Protesters organized by the NAACP and Negro-American Labor Council assembled two weeks later. In one photo taken by Charles "Teenie" Harris—along with Gordon Parks, one of the most important chroniclers of twentieth-century black American experience—an older woman in a fine hat and knee-length winter coat looks directly at the camera. She wears a slight smile, perhaps happy to be photographed, as her unflinching gaze bores into you. When you look away you notice her sign: "The Soundness of Our Cause Should Prick Your Conscience."

That cause is fair and equal employment opportunities, but also something bigger: the assertion that communities are more than collections of buildings, and people are more valuable than any single structure. It was a direct repudiation of the modernist principles that guided the city's postwar Renaissance program and promoted the Civic Arena—a community's tombstone—as one of its crowning achievements. Nearly sixty years ago, little attention was

"Lower Hill District Before Demolition." Allegheny Conference on Community Development MSP 285, Detre Library and Archives Division, Senator John Heinz History Center, Pittsburgh, PA.

paid to that message outside the black community. But today—as the calamitous failures of urban planning and civic responsibility that devastated the Lower Hill repeat themselves around the country—the soundness of such nascent anti-gentrification no longer pricks; it stabs.

For nearly a century, as they disgorged the guts of the nation's skyscrapers and bridges, Pittsburgh's iron and steel mills belched enough smoke, soot, and fire to render the city "hell with the lid taken off," as *Atlantic Monthly* writer James Parton famously gasped in 1868. By the end of World War II, not much had changed. The incessant wartime demand for material to build planes, tanks, and weapons kept the mills on full blast, and as the country transitioned to peacetime, Pittsburgh "saw itself older, grimier, more unlovely than ever," as *Fortune* wrote in 1947. Its three rivers were toxic and routinely flooded, air quality was noxious, and parkland was seemingly extinct; there was a growing housing crisis, streets were choked by increasing automobile ownership, and the first flutters of white flight had begun.

The solution presented by mayor David L. Lawrence and the coterie of corporate titans who comprised the Allegheny Conference on Community Development was the Pittsburgh Renaissance, a colossally ambitious program of civic rebirth, environmental rejuvenation, and economic stimulation. A key aim was aggressively targeting blight and replacing dilapidated infrastructure with new, exciting opportunities attractive to outside investment. At the tip of Pittsburgh's Golden Triangle, for instance, two shabby bridges that connected at the Point—where the Monongahela and Allegheny rivers confluenced to form the Ohio—were torn down to create Point State Park. Above the Point, a thicket of old Pittsburgh was demolished for Gateway Center, a plaza consisting of a hotel, apartment complex, and three polished steel cruciform office buildings that realized Le Corbusier's modernist fantasy of towers in a park. The Renaissance eventually attracted a bonanza of mid-century masters—Mies van der Rohe, I.M. Pei, Natalie de Bois and Myron Goldsmith, Max Abramovitz, Philip Johnson—who reshaped Pittsburgh's built environment. Congested, cacophonous zones of timber-and-brick low-rises were cleared for open plazas and superblocks anchored by ordered, efficient metal-and-glass buildings and skyscrapers.

Modernism's clean-lined anticipation of the future formed the backbone of Pittsburgh's architectural rejuvenation, which made it inevitable that the Hill District, which connected nearly 100,000 black Pittsburghers with downtown's eastern edge, would find itself in the crosshairs. For close to fifty years, the benign neglect that begets slums had done its work on the Hill. Many lived in substandard housing, some without access to indoor plumbing; drug use and prostitution were rampant; crime was commonplace. Yet the community thrived. Trailblazing jazz artists such as Billy Strayhorn, Billy Eckstine, Earl Hines,

Erroll Garner, Mary Lou Williams, Art Blakey, and Roy Eldridge honed their skills at the legendary Hill clubs like the Crawford Grill. The Hill-based *Pittsburgh Courier*, one of America's most important black newspapers, led the dramatic and still extant realignment of black voters from a Republican to Democratic bloc. So many celebrities and influential personalities passed through the Hill that the corner of Wylie Avenue and Fullerton Street was dubbed the "Crossroads of the World."

All Lawrence, the ACCD, and Urban Redevelopment Authority of Pittsburgh saw was a slum standing in the way of progress (and potential property tax windfalls). "The Hill District, as we have come to know it, must be destroyed, residents [have] learned," the *Courier* reported on February 25, 1950. The reason, according to URA executive director John Robin, was that "living patterns . . . are neither desirable, acceptable nor endurable." Six years later, the city finally brought in the "headache balls" to clear the Lower Hill for new housing, office space, and hotels. Work also began on the Crosstown Expressway, proposed by Robert Moses in his 1939 Arterial Plan for Pittsburgh, which severed the contiguous link between the Hill and downtown Pittsburgh.

The marquee project, though, was the show-stopping Civic Arena. Designed by architect Dahlen K. Ritchey, it was initially intended as a home for the Civic Light Opera company and drew fawning attention for its unique 415-foot retractable dome.

Constructed of six 300-ton steel leaves that opened into a 260-foot arched cantilever that held two more stationary leaves, the dome was heralded as an engineering marvel and gave Pittsburgh an iconic building to promote its Renaissance success story. "The auditorium will stand as a symbol of an era here," Lawrence said.

The arena was officially added to the URA's Lower Hill plan in 1952 after an earlier site for the auditorium in the East End was met with stern resistance from white residents, and at first the Hill was encouraged to embrace it. "[S]ome 8,000 residents of the sector, crowded into slum and substandard dwellings, will be moved to more wholesome quarters," the *Courier* wrote on January 16, 1954. "The remodeling job will be a revelation for residents of the Lower Hill, who now have sixty-three residents to the acre compared to only five in residential areas like Squirrel Hill." The paper also assured its readership, a year later, there was "no cause for alarm" as the city plotted the gutting of their neighborhood.

But by the time the Civic Arena finally opened in 1961, hope had curdled to enmity. Many Lower Hill residents were still in temporary housing or out of the area altogether, and they were denied jobs in the marvel of modernism. The *Courier*—the voice of the Hill—was forced to relocate its newsroom. The Crossroads of the World was a parking lot. And all for a building that never served its purpose. The stainless steel leaves made for crummy acoustics, immediately

scaring off the CLO and frustrating other organizations. "It is impossible to play here without a shell on stage," conductor Leonard Bernstein fumed in 1963. "The music is wasted. There is no projection. As far as I'm concerned, this is my first and last concert in the Arena." It quickly became a sports venue, with the Pittsburgh Penguins hockey team its anchor tenant, and over time so many cables, speakers, and other equipment were added to the ceiling, it became futile to open the roof.

The Civic Arena's failure of function compounded its insult and catastrophe. The Hill District, as generations knew it, was gone, as were a community's friendships, support systems, culture, and identity. Even though the arena began hiring black employees after the 1961 protest, Lower Hill jobs never fully materialized; neither did quality, affordable housing, which exacerbated the tragedy. The few projects that were built became new ghettos ridden with worse crime, drug use, and civic detachment than existed before redevelopment, and the many Hill residents who sought homes in surrounding neighborhoods were met with hardened bigotry and segregation.

Pittsburgh attempted to cleave off more of the Hill District throughout the 1960s for more development projects, but the community had had enough. "Urban renewal means Negro removal," NAACP president Brown famously said in 1962. Hill and civil rights leaders drew a line at the intersection of Crawford Street and Centre Avenue in the Middle

Opposite: "Civic Arena construction with parked cars and Connelley Trade School on right, Lower Hill District, Pittsburgh, Pennsylvania, c. 1960 - 1961." Photo by Charles 'Teenie' Harris/Carnegie Museum of Art/Getty Images.

Hill—memorialized today as Freedom Corner—where they would not allow any further encroachment. None occurred, but the worst had been done. The Renaissance had driven a stake through the heart of the Hill.

"In hindsight, I suspect no one . . . could have envisioned the frightful effects this particular Urban Renewal effort would visit upon the low-income families who peopled the neighborhood," wrote Rev. James W. Garvey, former pastor of Epiphany Parish, in 2010. "The infrastructure of the whole neighborhood collapsed almost overnight."

❖

For more than forty years, the Civic Arena, renamed Mellon Arena in 1999, attracted white suburbanites to hockey games and rock concerts while the predominately black Hill District residents struggled with deteriorating housing, worsening crime, and municipal apathy. But an unprecedented opportunity emerged in 2007. The Penguins secured a new facility, across Centre Avenue from the Civic Arena, which would leave the old building—described by then-city councilman Jake Wheatley as "the symbol of the beginning of the end of our community and communal process"—vacant as of June 27, 2010. Pittsburgh had a chance to correct an historic injustice.

Many called for the arena's demolition and for the site to be redeveloped in a way that reconnected the Lower Hill to downtown and restored life to the community. But a vocal minority, led by local architect Rob Pfaffmann, demanded the arena be preserved for its historic value to modernism and the Renaissance and reused for the benefit of the city, hockey fans, and architecture lovers. The Allegheny County Sports and Exhibition Authority was unmoved, and in a thirty-second proceeding on September 16, 2010, its seven-member board voted unanimously—as someone shouted "Gestapo!"—to demolish the arena. By the end of 2012, the site was empty. Seven years later, despite some restoration of Wylie Avenue and Fullerton Street, it's still a parking lot.

Like the mid-century plan that preceded it, there has been a flurry of activity around the twenty-eight-acre site. The Penguins control redevelopment rights, and in April 2018 signed a new agreement with the city to develop eleven acres by 2023. The team's $500 million plan includes new housing, office space, and entertainment venues, with the Lower Hill reconnected to downtown via a government-funded cap park over the Crosstown Expressway. Unlike Renaissance planners, though, the Penguins and city leaders have committed to involving Hill residents in the process. In 2008, the team, politicians, and One Hill Neighborhood Coalition, representing 100 community groups, signed a regional-first community benefits agreement that led to investments across the Hill and a promise to prioritize hiring residents in the future. There have been public hearings on the Hill, and the Penguins signed a letter of intent with a minority developer to build some of the proposed housing units.

Still, the process has been bumpy, and the Hill's veteran birders vigilantly watch for a new breed of discrimination: gentrification. The modernist housing projects and superblock ghettos built a half century ago on the ruins of urban minority neighborhoods are themselves being designated blighted, crime-ridden slums and marked for demolition, replaced by sleek glass towers, big box retailers, and restored streets to accommodate white residents fleeing suburbs. In the Hill District, community leaders carry the generational scars of urban renewal and pounce at the slightest hint of exclusion, be it a design competition that didn't solicit proposals from local and minority firms or a dearth of actually affordable housing. And like their forebears, they have no hesitation mobilizing residents to stop unfair treatment before it roosts. Even if this time is different—that maybe the Hill District will experience its own renaissance—too many know what's at stake.

"Tall, gleaming buildings housing transplanted middle-class suburbanites cannot hide the ghettos, slums, and racially segregated schools and churches of the city's economically deprived," *New Pittsburgh Courier* executive editor Carl Morris wrote in 1967. "Aluminum and steel are poor substitutes for human dignity." ✠

Building detail in Detroit, Michigan. Photo by Brian Boyer.

The Geo-ornithology of Detroit

BRYAN BOYER

My shortcut for understanding a city is to spot its geo-ornithology: the population of stone and metal eagles that can be found on buildings around town. These birds tell us how a city sees itself—or wants to, anyways. Look carefully and you'll find them roosting atop columns, occupying the center of pediments, and contributing their decorative splendor to moments of architectural importance. Since the adoption of the Great Seal of the United States featuring a bald eagle in 1782, the big bird has become an adaptable and widely utilized symbol across the country, adorning numerous structures in seemingly every American city. This makes geo-ornithology an accessible hobby, even more so due to the fact that geo-eagles rarely migrate south for winter. Drop me into a random American city and I'll spot you a geo-eagle in twenty minutes or less.

Some hundred years after the bald eagle was officially adopted as a symbol of the country's might, the midwestern city of Detroit was revving the engines of its economy. Walk around downtown and eagles are everywhere, because projections of power are everywhere. Stand on Griswold in front of the Buhl Building, completed in 1925, and among an otherwise Romanesque decorative scheme you will find a solitary geo-eagle crowning a four-story arch that marks the principal entrance. As an office building that was called "the cathedral of finance" in its day, there's bound to be at least one geo-eagle here. This particular bird was likely crafted by Italian-American sculptor Corrado Parducci, who worked on many of downtown Detroit's most famous buildings.

Progress up Griswold one block to the Penobscot Building, completed in 1928, and you will be under the watchful eyes of the twelve geometric brass eagles that adorn the entry. One each, with wings outstretched, is embedded in the brass tracery over the four entry doors, while another eight small geo-eagles take on a quasi-anthropomorphic form and appear to be looking down from a ledge above the doors. The larger decorative thematic of the building is an art deco take on Native American iconography and patterning, which means the geo-eagles here are doing double duty as symbols of twentieth-century American prowess while also giving a nod to the importance of eagles in Native American cultures—a complicated duality to say the least.

The corner of Shelby and West Fort provides a study in how fickle power can be. In 1915 Albert Kahn completed the Detroit Trust Company building with a finely detailed classical facade featuring a run of co-lossal pilasters that terminate in Corinthian capitals. Taking the place of the fleuron at the top of each capital is an affronté geo-eagle with wings inverted (pointing toward the ground). Like the acanthus leaves of the capital, the geo-eagles are executed with a degree of precision so fine that one can still clearly see the eyes of these sentinel birds despite their diminutive size.

Directly across the street are four eagles carved into the limestone facade of the Theodore Levin US Courthouse, designed by Robert O. Derrick and completed in 1934. Where Kahn's geo-eagles are sur-prises hidden amongst the greater decorative scheme of the building, Derrick's are the most figurative aspects of the original facade (which has since had two additional federal seals carved into it). Here the eagles also sit atop pilasters, seemingly in dialogue with their neighbors across the street, but they re-place the capitals altogether instead of adorning them. The bank nestles its markers of power amongst lapidary flora; the federal courthouse makes sure its geo-eagles' talons are unmistakably on display.

Eagles roost near bodies of water; geo-eagles make their home near centers of power. Beyond downtown that often means Post Office buildings. At the corner of Woodward Avenue and Tyler Street, the Highland Park Post Office features perhaps the largest geo-eagle in the city, sculpted by Erwin Springweiler in 1940. This sculpture in the round features a streamlined form with details carved in low relief and looks like something that would fit comfortably next to a vehi-cle designed by Raymond Loewy. Six miles away, at a post office on East Jefferson Avenue, highly graphical linework forms a deconstructed interpretation of the great seal. Thirteen stars, a fasces, an olive branch, and a geo-eagle form a strikingly asymmetrical com-position superimposed on the square gridlines of the facade's stonework. It looks nothing like the other geo-eagles in town, but it's a remarkable and deftly executed specimen.

Step back to consider the entire flock of geo-eagles across a single city like Detroit and you start to see the individuals as variations on a theme. The logic of the geo-eagle population is reminiscent of a certain union of fifty independent states. Each geo-eagle is an opportunity to express the creativity of one partic-ular building and the time in which it was built, and yet the flock as a whole reminds us that there is no singular truth to be found.

The surprisingly diverse array of forms assumed by bald eagles when executed in stone or metal reflects the challenges of translating the vitality of such a dynamic creature into a fixed medium. The bird's organic curves and the strong patterning created by its feathers conspire to make the sentinel eagle a surprisingly intricate form when captured as a decorative object. The sculptor has choices to make. To carve individual feathers at accurate scale and attempt to mimic the patterning of the plumage, like the geo-eagles on Kahn's Detroit Trust Company building; to simplify this busy pattern to some more abstract level, like the Penobscot birds; or to ignore feathers altogether and favor the silhouette, as the anonymous New Deal sculptors did on East Jefferson Avenue? Does one obsess over the curves of wing, head, and iconic beak, or allow the shapes of the bird to be interpreted in a more apparently "architectural" geometric configuration favoring right angles, as did the sculptors responsible for the federal courthouse on Fort Street? Shall the wings be shown rousant, presenting a bold and imposing profile with wings outspread, or is it more appropriate for the bird's wings to be affronté, pointing down toward the earth with unruffled confidence?

The widest variety of interpretations is to be seen in how the feathered tibia is portrayed. Whereas live eagles exhibit a continuity from breast to leg, geo-eagles are generally depicted with a high degree of prominence given to the silhouette of the leg, which makes it look as though the bird is wearing britches. If the sculptor emphasizes the metatarsus, which is the lower portion of an eagle's leg clad in yellow skin, those britches may appear more like capris. Based on

a study of geo-eagles in countless cities documented on Instagram via the hashtag #eaglepants, it appears that identifying the type of pants that the geo-eagle will sport is among the primary considerations one must make while executing such a sculpture. Even the most potent of power symbols is subject to delicate deliberations of decoration.

If ornithology is the pursuit of observing and tracking migratory birds, geo-ornithology is the study of power, how it moves through cities, and the role that architecture plays in this ebb and flow. Spotting the location and the size of the local geo-eagle population tells you where power is or was to be found, while the style and specific artistic choices of geo-eagles mark a moment in time. Compared to two dimensional representations of eagles, the expanded set of choices that go into the composition and manufacture of a geo-eagle means that they resist the flat symbolism of their printed cousins. Even the most shallow of bas reliefs generally have a symbolic depth to them when read in conjunction with the full details of the structure they embellish. It may be an unlikely tool, but the geo-eagle is a tender lens through which to analyze the subject of real or projected power.

Because of the era in which the geo-eagle population peaked nationally, this is a pastime that is particularly rewarding in midwestern capitals such as Detroit. This city grew wildly in an era when decoration was expected and geo-eagles were prevalent. As Detroit's economy trends upwards and construction cranes—a

Building details in Detroit, Michigan. Photos by Brian Boyer

different kind of geo-fowl—are starting to grace the skyline once again, one is left to wonder what markers will identify our time to future generations. When the awkwardly named "Hudson's Site Building," designed by SHoP architects, rises to become the tallest building in the city, what details will onlookers spot to interpret the vision of the world that is implied by this architecture?

Contemporary architecture, like the structures of power that finance and own it, is abstract to the point of carefully arranged ambiguity. These buildings often present complexity without the possibility of contradiction. Will particular curves, faceted geometries, or curtain wall details come to imply a specific power dynamic to future generations, or will that be left to the spherical inky eyes of security cameras, dangled haphazardly off parapets? Traditionalist, richly decorated buildings thankfully do not appear to have any shot at regaining the vanguard in contemporary architecture, but once the geo-eagles have gone for good, what markers will we use to trace the migrations of power? ✠

"Traders World Entrance—Monroe, Ohio." scottamus/Flickr.

Flea Market Urbanism

SAMANTHA SANDERS

If you set out to write a certain kind of story about Monroe, Ohio (population 12,442) you might begin by drawing attention to its city newspaper (online only), *Main Street Monroe*, and its front page that prominently features a church directory and a post about a Dairy Queen coming to town. Maybe you'd mention the article about the initiative from the local Carpenters Union meant to address the "skilled labor shortages [that] continue to plague Ohio contractors" and contextualize it within a larger story—maybe the one about the dearth of trade education, or the one about the unforeseen effects of immigration crackdown.

This would be, after all, a story told during what we'll have no choice but to refer to in coming years as the Trump Years, when newspaper editors from both coasts deservedly caught flak for airdropping reporters into places like Ohio purely for the sound bite potential, before promptly scooping them back up again.

You might note that Monroe, which straddles both sides of Interstate 75 and is nearly equidistant to both Cincinnati and Dayton, sits at the far edge of Butler County, home to author J.D. Vance and the setting for his bestselling *Hillbilly Elegy*, a fact that will likely elicit either a solemn nod or an exaggerated eye roll, depending on the reader's politics.

But I'm from the area, too. And stories preoccupied with the past have never sat right with me, largely because that past was rarely as romantic as whatever present is being unfairly compared to it. The Midwest is as dynamic a place as any other and for as much is made of it being a dying place, its outsiders would be better served by thinking of the place as a massive iterative process; repeating cycles and processes, living with their outcomes, before beginning again, each time maybe moving closer to a kind of perfection. And if that's not hope, I don't know what is.

And for all the dismissive terms that speak to the supposed sameness of the culture, or to the empty blandness of the natural and manmade geography of the place (flyover country, land of big box stores, the cloyingly sweet "heartland"), there remains an impulse, as in all places but especially in those where vast land filled with endless acres of geometrically rigid and inhumanly scaled cash crops threatens to swallow you up. That impulse is to gather together. Main Street is on the ropes, but midwesterners have long had another outlet to meet this basic human need for connection: the flea market.

And while it's true that fleas flank the highways along exurban edges all across the country, there's something uniquely midwestern about the character of the flea—the industriousness of bringing product to market, the weekend excursion ritual of it, the chance to see and be seen in places where that's a relative rarity, the angling for a deal, the validation that your nostalgia for knick-knacks means *something* even if that something remains an undefined feeling.

Any thrifter or flea enthusiast knows the feeling the accompanies a trip. The anxious sensation in the stomach or the impulse to stop by the bathrooms near the entrance so you won't get distracted later. You are, after all, on a mission, and today could be the day you find something great. In the Midwest, the flea is a vernacular expression of longing and hope, nurtured by a common history, spurred by a collective boredom, and all sheltered by a pole barn down by the highway.

Save your entry ticket. There'll be a raffle later.

✻

Long before the outlet malls came to Monroe, before the truck stops went corporate and got cleaner, and before AK Steel took its jobs and left, there was Traders World Market, a massive indoor flea market my parents would take me to most weekends when I was a kid. To give you an idea of the scale, its website describes it (currently) as "16 buildings, 850 inside vendor spaces, 400 outdoor vendor spaces, a combined area of 11 acres, plenty of paved parking and over two miles of store fronts." In my memories, it is even bigger.

As a kid, I'd feel the excitement build on the drive there. It took about twenty minutes, which to my kid brain felt just long enough to qualify as a true outing; a step above a trip to the mall, a few rungs below an amusement park. For a while in the early 2000s, if you'd taken the same route, you'd have passed the megachurch that erected a sixty-two-foot statue of Jesus along the eastern edge of I-75. Officially titled "King of Kings," it was more colloquially known as "Touchdown Jesus" for its outstretched arms raised heavenward, until a lightning strike and resulting fire arrived in 2010.

Still, there's plenty to look at. The land surrounding Traders World is orderly; rows of soybean and corn, the area's two largest crops. The methodicalness of it is obvious, even at ground level doing seventy. The environment here is something to be disciplined because so much depends on it.

Visitors approaching the massive complex must drive first through the front gate, underneath two massive statues of horses rearing up on their hind legs. A couple bucks paid to the parking lot attendant earns you access to a massive sea of concrete where you can leave your car behind, making careful note of the number of the building you slip into.

Walking into one of those buildings is like walking into a photo relief of the world outside. Inside is dark, cavernous, and the air conditioning feels crisp and merciful in the summertime. And there are people, a critical mass of them, everywhere. And they're walking. I grew up riding my bike to the entrance of our subdivision and back, tethered by my mom's warnings to not go farther. It was a thrilling but limited kind of freedom. I was separated from any places I might want to walk or bike to on my own by miles of sidewalk-less streets where cars were the only thing you'd expect to see on the road. It made sense, since you weren't getting anywhere without one.

And the majority of America is car dependent, so to be a kid, navigating the weekend crowds of people at the flea was an unfamiliar but exciting feeling. Inside, the rows of stalls promised potentiality around every corner. And even though most people put out the same things at their booth every week—bins of tube socks, boxes of farm tomatoes, moldering issues of *Life*

Magazine—I still felt a thrill at what I might find.

Outside, the vendors were day renters, usually selling produce or seemingly random assortments of everyday items you might find at garage sales: old magazines, collectible plates, that one olive green Pyrex casserole dish with the white daisy pattern that seemed like it followed me everywhere as a kid. Inside, the vendors were there for the long haul. The majority of the booths—the leather Harley gear, the sneaker place, the food stalls—stayed in place all week, only to open for a few hours each weekend. The whole place was built as a series of long wings coming off a central hub, where dozens of picnic-style tables were set up around the few roller-skating-rink-grade food options. In the center of it all, a man in lederhosen played accordion to polka backing tracks with pre-recorded backup vocals so lifelike that when he sang "I don't want her / You can have her / She's too fat for me / HEY! She's too fat for me" it sounded like a dozen men proclaiming it while you sat and ate your roller grill hot dog.

Shopping at a flea was a markedly different feeling than shopping at, say, a mall, that other defining feature of the countryside and the era. A mall felt purposeful; you were there to buy things. A visit to the flea felt more freeform. You were there as much to move through the space and experience the surroundings as you were to pick through the merchandise. And in an era before big box bookstores or teenagers hanging out at Starbucks, *the flea was a true third place.* You didn't have to buy. You could just *be.*

It might initially seem odd to consider the flea market from an architectural perspective. After all, most fleas are the kind of depressing, pre-fab and post-frame construction you usually see in downmarket self-storage facilities. But if vernacular architecture can be said to respond to the needs of its environment and be made with what's at hand, I can't think of a kind of building that speaks more to the part of the Midwest where I grew up than the sturdy-if-unsightly pole buildings that house many of the fleas I know. These pre-fab buildings are relatively easy to build, economical and the architectural equivalent of meat and potatoes, all utility and short on garnish. While at a distance, they may be nearly indistinguishable from the big box stores and mall husks that flank the highways, they function in a very different way.

In these places, it's important to consider that architecture is as much about the physical manifestation of our ideals as it is about the materials used. We didn't have a Main Street where I grew up. Fewer and fewer small towns do now, as big boxes supplant and core out a wider and wider range of small business storefronts, so we made a new Main Street, albeit in the form of a flea, with paid parking and air conditioning. And like a Main Street, the fleas function as a space to experience some sort of civic awareness and community as a place to buy something.

It's no surprise that in an era of online shopping and the heavily curated feeds of Instagram influencers, that the shopping mall, with its cookie-cutter stores and limited selection, is quickly becoming a relic. It's true that flea markets often have footprints as large if not larger than those of the typical mall, and fleas are rarely planted in the same kind of sought-after land most commercial real estate is after. Further, fleas' limited hours and distance from cities often require a dedicated consumer—presenting what a retail wonk might call a "barrier to purchase."

Yet given all that, the mood on the National Flea Market Association website is bullish if not downright combative; 2.25 million vendors, it trumpets, over $30 billion in sales annually, more than 150 million customers each year. And the number of fleas? More than 1,100.

We've reached a point in American retail history where—if not now, then soon—flea markets will outnumber malls. Given everything we know, this shouldn't make sense within the context of where retail is headed. But it does within the context of where America is headed.

Traders World was founded by a couple named Jay and Helen Frick about thirty years ago (the website is a bit confusing on the official date and requests for interviews were not answered). And while that only takes us back to the late 1980s, you'd never guess that from the way the Fricks (or whoever authored the website's History page) talk about it. The Fricks "grew up in the unique era of Americana [sic]," the introductory paragraph explains, handily if accidentally leapfrogging the concept of America-as-a-country in favor of landing right in my sweet spot: Americana-as-culture.

The Traders World site goes on to explain that this was a time "when lives were transitioning from agricultural farm living to industrialized urban living. It was a time that spanned from the depths of the Great Depression to the booming years that followed World War II—a time in American history that some refer to as 'the greatest generation.'" I'm calling this out not to dunk on the sentimentality of a couple who built a place that brought me so much joy, but to note that by mythologizing their past through the flea's marketing and decor, the Fricks are following the blueprint of so many fleas that have found success by commoditizing our collective nostalgia.

Traders World was thick with bric-a-brac. Long before I ever set foot in a Cracker Barrel, I knew what it was like to sit in a dark, wood-paneled room eating fried food underneath a rusty scythe, or a repro tin sign advertising spark plugs. Often, the only way I could remember how to find my way back to the entrance where I came in was to find the particular folksy woodcut hanging from the ceiling I could last recall ("AT QUIZ PA AINT NO WHIZ BUT HE KNOWS HOW TO KEEP MA HIZ.").

The website also explains that Helen's earliest memories "included plowing the fields with horses, planting the crops by hand—sometimes one seed at a time; and sleigh bells on a team of horses gliding effortlessly through the snow on a winter's night." I suspect I'm not alone in being drawn to fleas because they evoke a world I never knew, but have been told was more authentic, more tangible, better than my own.

But to take that view might not be giving the flea its full credit. The past is compelling, but the present is, too. In fact, flea markets are an awfully good indicator of how our culture and economy are changing—and being changed.

As Rob Sieban, CEO of United Flea Markets, explained recently, "The value proposition [of flea markets] is evolving." For him, that means opportunity. Where we might see nostalgia, a private equity firm might look at flea markets, often family-run operations, and see motivated sellers (perhaps a second or third generation not as eager to run a flea as their parents may have been), comparatively affordable real estate, and reliable income from vendor space that might be an easier rental than a traditional mall's lease.

Which is to say: Today's third places are becoming increasingly commodified. From POPS, or Publicly Owned Private Spaces (think of the blandly inviting plazas outside corporate buildings), where your presence is tolerated as a zoning-mandated means to an end, to Edison-bulbed coworking spaces whose spare Scandinavian aesthetic can now be seen from Stockholm to St. Louis and everywhere in between, we've begun to passively accept that our presence must generate revenue for someone. And while flea markets may never (fortunately) be top-of-mind to most private equity groups hoping to make a buck, there is something to be said for the ways in which flea market entrepreneurship offers a real leg up for some vendors who will never be invited to sell their wares at a pop-up celebrating a new boutique hotel opening.

And there's plenty of evidence fleas are becoming important parts of local economies, serving as de facto business incubators in places as yet untouched by the entrepreneurship-as-spirituality crowd. Not every product makes sense to sell in an online Etsy store, but there's a decent chance at a flea that you might get a passer-by to impulse-buy some laser cut floor mats for their Silverado.

Fleas are often an ideal place for would-be restaurateurs who aren't yet food truck-ready to test their concept. When there are some pretty significant steps between you and a brick and mortar location, fleas are a low-stakes place to dream unwieldy, impractical dreams. Or even very practical ones that mainstream culture may be blind to. The last few times I've been to Trader's World, I was heartened to see that it had grown into not just a place where the local Hispanic population

was beginning to visit, they were also selling. Fleas that recreate the *mercados de pulgas* of Latin America have long been a fixture of life in parts of the country with large Hispanic populations, but as the Midwest's Hispanic population grows, stores inside these fleas (particularly in very rural areas or those where immigration is relatively recent) can serve as both lifelines to culture and as a parallel economy in places where goods from home might be hard to come by.

Whether a given item for sale at a flea is a treasure is highly subjective, and maybe my can't-miss booth is one your eyes might quickly scan past. But I'll always appreciate the egalitarianism of landing a vendor's spot at the fleas I remember as a kid. It's true that urban fleas, while long a fixture in some cities, have started to pop up all over. But their curated sameness depresses me. I hesitate to write about how there's always a beard oil guy because in a few years, I wonder if I'll even remember what this was. But he's there, along with the handmade soap lady and someone selling bird art suitable for framing. I wonder what we're saying with our current hyper-specific cultural bric-a-brac. Which of it will be picked over, suddenly hip again, at future fleas? Which of it will be some ten-year-old's inescapable olive green Pyrex twenty years from now?

I don't live in Ohio anymore. I'm no longer a regular at Trader's World. But fleas will always serve as a tether to home for me, no matter where I am. And for many people—especially those with perhaps more drive than creditworthiness and more ideas than square feet, fleas are much more than just symbolic, they're a livelihood. For people who might feel alone during the week, they're culture. And for people who just want to spend time in a place that's not work or home, they're a quirky kind of public sphere. And as the culture changes, the population shifts, and the economy fluctuates, fleas will adapt. In that way, they'll be a bellwether of the Midwest. One foot in the past, one in the future, but always with ample parking, just off I-75, past Touchdown Jesus. ✠

SECTION 2

PEOPLE

Opposite: Lillian Leenhouts at a celebration for the river (early 1970s). Collection of Robin Leenhouts.

Above and opposite: "Quasqueton, Iowa—10/17/2015: Lowell and Agnes Walter Residence. Architect Frank Lloyd Wright." Jim Packett/Shutterstock.com.

Making Nature Present:
Frank Lloyd Wright's Magazine House in Iowa

DANIEL NAEGELE

In 1945, as the war in Europe came to an end, popular press journals throughout America featured designs for houses to be built rapidly and inexpensively for returning soldiers and their future families. Frank Lloyd Wright, at the time seventy-eight years old, understood this need as an opportunity to populate the nation with his novel design for what he called "the little American house." Wright believed the domestic environment should be "organic" and "natural" and that each house, no matter how small, should be custom-fitted to its site. But the great demand for houses suggested they not be custom-fitted to a unique site, but that they should be closely packed on flat, monotonous parcels of land with no natural amenities, and that they be built quickly in the easiest way possible. What to do?

✤

The Ladies' Home Journal, "The Magazine Women Believe In," anticipated the postwar building boom. Beginning in January 1944, the *Journal* published "a dozen new [. . .] designs by the country's outstanding architects—houses that point the way to better, less expensive living after the war." The series concluded in June 1945 with Frank Lloyd Wright's design for a moderately sized, single-level, three-bedroom house. The *Journal* described Wright as "the world's most distinguished architect" and noted that this 1945 design was a "continuation of a series of houses he designed for this magazine in the early 1900s." Illustrated with a plan drawing and several photographs of a model, the Wright design was titled Opus 497 and billed as a "crystal house for town or country."[14]

Wright might well have been "the world's most distinguished architect" in 1945, but his fame rested not on generic, affordable house designs for anonymous clients and unknown sites but, more often than not, on expensive, site-specific houses designed for the wealthy, including himself. His best-known work was Fallingwater, a $150,000 vacation house built over a waterfall for the Pittsburgh merchant prince Edgar Kauffmann Sr. and featured in the January 17, 1938, issue of *Life* magazine. At seventy-eight, however, Wright was very interested in designing a house for the middle-class family, a house that could "point the way to better, less expensive living," a house that would "have far-reaching effects on future living for

all of us," as the *Ladies' Home Journal* claimed. And though it was not where his fame resided, from time to time for more than forty-five years, he had designed speculative houses for anonymous clients and anonymous sites. Some of these houses had been published in popular press journals including *Life* and *House and Home*, and as early as 1900 (and then again in 1901 and 1907) Wright's designs had appeared in the *Ladies' Home Journal*. Most famously and influentially, his Usonian homes, begun in the 1930s, promised affordable-yet-bespoke design from the master, which often achieved the second value at the expense of the first.

For Wright, the house-of-moderate-cost problem was not only one of *how* to build inexpensively, but also one of *what* to build. He believed that a house could teach people how to live—and his notion of "how to live" was far from conventional. His own life and residences in Wisconsin and Arizona were essays in bespoke design endlessly responsive to their sites, which Wright could consistently mine for endless material and motif variation. For each of his many clients, for nearly half a century, he had made proposals for houses that declared their singular authorship loud and upfront. Throughout, there was a sense of polemical zeal, for not just what people should live in, but for *how* they should live. "Every house is a missionary," he once remarked. "I don't build a house without predicting the end to the present social order."[15]

In the summer of 1945, it was entirely reasonable to think that a different way of life, a new social order, might be desirable in the US. The long, seemingly endless war was over. The economy was recovering from a Depression that had begun some fifteen years earlier. And an optimism of possibility, of dream-building, prevailed.

✳

Many were intrigued by Opus 497, but only one person built it. In January 1945, at the age of forty-six, Lowell Walter[16], a Des Moines road contractor who had recently become wealthy when he patented something like blacktop, and who knew of Fallingwater from the January 17, 1938 issue of *Life*, wrote a letter addressed to "Frank Lloyd Wright's Architectural Company."[17] In it, he asked Wright if he would "possibly be interested in drawing plans" for an all-season house for himself and his wife. The house was to be located in remote northeast Iowa near Walter's hometown, Quasqueton, less than seventy miles from Wright's home in Spring Green, Wisconsin. The site was 3,500 acres of farmland. Walter noted in his letter that the house should be about 1,800 square feet, with an additional two-car garage, perhaps a basement, and should open to the south and the west with extensive views of the nearby Wapsipinicon River. "Regarding costs," he wrote, "I would like something quite nice, but of course, not extravagant." Walter imagined that $10,000–$15,000 would be sufficient, and with the letter he included a snapshot of the site and single-line plan drawings that he himself, had made. Nine days after Walter

mailed the letter, Wright telegrammed a twenty-two-word reply: "My dear Mr. Walter: We will design a dwelling for you. Send further details. There will be no basement nor any attic."[18]

In the months that followed, the busy architect did little to advance Walter's project. Impatient, Walter increased to $20,000 the intended cost and purchased idyllic hillside acreage that joined his farmland to the Wapsipinicon River. In early summer, Walter and his wife Agnes saw Wright's Opus 497 in the June 1945 *Ladies' Home Journal*. Finding the design both fitting and not unlike his own schematic, Walter asked Wright to build it in Quasqueton and Wright agreed.

Construction on the house did not begin until July 1948. Seventeen months into construction, in December 1949, it seemed to Lowell Walter that the house might never be finished. By then, the cost had escalated to nearly seven times what Walter had set out to pay, in part because he had added extensively to the initial program, but also because finding a residential contractor to build a Wright house in the small, remote town was extremely difficult, more so because Wright insisted the house be built in "fireproof, vermin proof" concrete and few residential contractors knew how to build in that medium. The exasperated Walter wrote Wright a long letter expressing his concerns about the protracted house-building process and the ever-escalating costs.[19] Wright's reply was sympathetic, thoughtful, and brief: "We were brave men to try to set up the last work in heaven way off on the midwestern prairie—miles from anywhere?"[20]

The house was completed in August 1950 and is available to tour today during the warmer months. At Wright's request, America's premier architectural photographer, Ezra Stoller, photographed the house, and color photographs appeared in both professional and popular press literature throughout the country. The house quickly became nationally renowned. It cost approximately $150,000, a price that included a boathouse, entry gate, fire pit, extensive landscaping, Wright-designed furniture, and Wright's fees (10% of the cost of construction). Walter named the house Cedar Rock and on the first and second Sundays in July 1950, shortly before construction was completed, the house and grounds were opened to busloads of curious Iowans (4,178 in all) and featured in the state's most prominent newspapers.[21] In his opening day speech, Walter compared his house to Wright's Fallingwater, Thomas Jefferson's Monticello, and George Washington's Mount Vernon.

The beauty and elegance of the Lowell Walter estate are overwhelming. Clearly, though, it was not Fallingwater, Monticello, nor Mount Vernon; nor was it an affordable house for the middle-class and its origins as a magazine house for mass consumption, were seldom mentioned. Indeed, only five years after its completion, it was lauded not for its affordability or for its resolution to the issue of "how we should live." Instead, it was celebrated for its ideal fit with the special site on which it was built when

John DeKoven Hill, Wright's apprentice who had supervised the construction of the house, featured it in the November 1955 issue of *House Beautiful* as a prime example of Wright's belief that "The Character of the Site is the Beginning of Architecture." Wright fervently believed that the successful marriage of site to house was essential, yet as originally conceived the house had not been designed with Walter's Quasqueton site in mind. Rather, it was conceived as an ideal house—not designed for any specific site, but cleverly construed to adapt to many diverse sites. To this end it was composed of parts easily modified or displaced so that it might readily be adapted to a variety of unique sites. This was not for practical matters only. Adaptation—"holding," "cradling"—enlarged the presence and importance of "nature."

"I put a capital 'N' on Nature," Wright once declared, "and call *that* my church."

How did Wright do it? How did he take a standard Wright design and modify it so subtly yet so fittingly that its stock origins are forgotten and it is praised as the near-perfect paradigm for site-specific building? The answer is not obvious.

The Walter house, the single built manifestation of Opus 497, was not a two-story, compact box with a basement as was typical of houses at the time, but rather long and low and stretched to maximize its interface with the exterior. Wright compared its floor plan to the shape of a tadpole. The tail of the tadpole contained two bedrooms and two baths accessed by a long corridor of closets and open shelving that Wright called a "Gallery." The head of the tadpole was a large, square room at a forty-five-degree angle to the tail. Wright labeled it the "Garden Room" and designed its furniture for informal living, dining, and recreation.

Important elements of Opus 497 were made malleable and could be pushed and pulled, opened up and closed down, shaped not ideally but as need be. Wright used a concrete slab roof with seventeen tons of steel reinforcing, for instance, allowing for the possibility of pushing the roof back and forth without the need to consider structural beam directions. Thus, the roof could be extended on one side or shifted from this side to that as a means of modifying light and controlling solar heat without affecting other aspects of the construction. The kitchen gave the house a pivot point. It joined the private to the public realms, the tail to the head of the tadpole. Unlike the bedrooms, gallery corridor, and Garden Room, it was not a preconceived entity but could assume any shape necessary to accommodate the angle between the two. This joint—mostly kitchen, but also mechanical closet and entrance 'throat'—worked in both plan and section, allowing the massing to vary with the land. In plan, it could open or close like a jackknife. In section, it could rise up or step down or project out. Because in plan and section the design accommodated the land, there was no need to level the site. Wright valued the site's

uniqueness and designed a house to reinforce it, giving presence to both simultaneously.

This weave extends to the interior as well. "Land" in the Walter house is not just "out there," it is also "in here." The Garden Room is half of the house and in the middle of the room its floor opens directly to the earth. It has no interior walls. Instead, it has "plants, growing in earth panels at floor level, [that] form a flower-and-foliage partition." Its ceiling is low and flowing, with a sense of centrality established where it rises in the middle of the room to form a clerestory punctuated by nine skylights. The skylights provide light for the plants, which grow out of the floor, across the ceiling, and into skylight cavities. The ceiling/roof has no obvious means of support and stretches across the room uninterrupted, ultimately extending visually through the glass walls out into the yard where it dissolves into upturned eaves. In this way, Wright united inside and outside while reinforcing the openness of the Garden Room, the essence of the house. This focal point is a landscaped pavilion as much as it's the room of a house, and it demonstrates Wright moonlighting as a landscape architect, orienting space around living matter as much as brick and mortar.

The beauty and seclusion of Walter's wondrous site allowed for this openness. But the Walter house is only *one* realization of the *Ladies' Home Journal* house. The *Journal* design was intended for both "town and country." But how to open the inside to the outside in a denser, suburban setting without compromising privacy? Wright created privacy with nature. Outside of the glass walls, in a radius defining a yard, he placed a second partition of vegetal material, thus providing the three open sides of the Garden Room with a high wall of greenery, what the *Journal* described as "a surrounding view . . . the circular planting of flowering shrubs and trees."

❀

"I don't build a house without predicting the end to the present social order." Opus 497 was a critique of the suburban dwelling, of the way we Americans had come to live. It entered the public realm—quite importantly—directly through the popular press. Couched as a kind of competition in which the winner would be the house design most built, the *Ladies' Home Journal's* eighteen-month probe into postwar house possibilities was not a competition that Frank Lloyd Wright could have expected to win. Yet his entry, without predicting the end of the social order, made apparent what the order neglected to consider. "Land"—including the sky, the sun, the stars and the moon; views, breezes, smells, and the immediate built environment—was of great importance to Wright. The houses that he built were *of* the land, not objects dominating it. A house, he said, should grace its site, not disgrace it. Instead of taking up land, his buildings made the land visible, valuing and bringing forth the unique qualities of the site. And this—site, weave, atmosphere—is

exactly what the other entries in the *Ladies' Home Journal* competition neglected to address.

The Lowell Walter house is of great importance in Wright's œuvre, but not so much as a unique house. Unquestionably wonderful and a rare recipient of the Wright-initialed red tile of approval, the Walter house is most important as the sole, built manifestation of a highly theoretical project: an essay in would-be affordable elegance. As such it is a kind of permanent exhibition. It shows how we Americans might live. ✠

"Peoples' Savings and Loan Association in Sidney, Ohio." Photo by Milenko Budimir.

Louis Sullivan in Central Ohio

MILENKO BUDIMIR

Louis Sullivan, America's most famous architect at the turn of the twentieth century, is well known as one of the early originators of the modern skyscraper. Among his designs are a number of iconic buildings that signaled a new era in American high rises, including the Wainwright Building in St. Louis and the Prudential Building (formerly the Guaranty Building) in Buffalo. But less known about is how later in his career he transitioned away from skyscrapers to much smaller, more modest buildings. In the early 1900s, Sullivan was commissioned to design a number of bank buildings throughout the Midwest, including Minnesota, Iowa, Wisconsin, and Ohio. Sullivan designed eight such bank buildings from about 1908 to 1919, two of them in the central Ohio towns of Newark and Sydney.[22]

Critics at the time denigrated Sullivan's shift away from building pioneering skyscrapers to getting commissions for small, inconsequential bank buildings across the Midwest. They viewed it as a period of decline, the work of a towering genius executed in the fading light of his once great career. Later historians have tended to disagree, seeing the bank building commissions as the full realization of Sullivan's dictum that "form follows function." The bank buildings were a different sort of challenge; to apply that philosophy to a type of building he had never designed before, and which had a history of being built in the neoclassical style, which Sulivan derided as being completely out of place in the modern world.

In the early decades of the twentieth century, Ohio was no stranger to modern architecture and design. The thriving state already could boast a long history of impressive projects. The most significant at the time was the Gothic Victorian bridge over the Ohio River at Cincinnati designed by a young German immigrant named John Roebling, who would go on a few years later to design one of the most iconic bridges in the world: the Brooklyn Bridge. The other significant modern building was the Wyandotte Building in Columbus, designed by Burnham and Root in 1897-98.

Newark, the seat of Licking County, smack in the middle of Ohio, got a Sullivan building for a few reasons, one of which involved an ugly act of violence. In the early 1900s, Newark had a reputation as a rowdy saloon town, complete with a culture of lawlessness, brawls, and violence that temperance activists saw as inextricably linked with alcohol. Things got so bad that in 1910, a nineteen-year old "dry agent" named Carl Etherington was dragged out of his jail cell, taken to the center of town and lynched.[23]

As a result, a number of Newark's most influential people got together and decided something had to be done to clean up the town and its tarnished reputation. They tapped into the City Beautiful movement, which flourished into the early 1900s. This was an architectural and urban planning philosophy that emphasized the beautification of civic spaces that would lead, so the belief went, to an improvement in the moral and civic virtue of citizens.

Emmet Melvin Baugher, a Newark banker, commissioned Sullivan to design and build a new structure to house the Home Building Association Company. In a March 1912 issue of *Bankers Magazine,* Baugher read about a bank in Cedar Rapids, Iowa, that Sullivan had designed. Baugher was impressed and decided that Sullivan was the architect that could help to change Newark's image. But Baugher was also motivated by notoriety and wanted it for himself and his Newark bank, hence why he sought and hired Sullivan for the job. At this point in his career, Sullivan needed work

desperately, as his commissions had dried up, partly due to a revival of the classical styles that Sullivan had mocked as being sad copies of old forms that were out of place in the new, modern world.[24]

Sullivan's desire was to produce something different, something new in American architecture; something "in a style never before seen." It was an attempt to follow Emerson and Whitman, an embodiment of the spirit of newness in American culture. What Emerson had achieved in literature and the essay, what Whitman had done in poetry, Sullivan, a pupil of this same spirit, sought to embody in architecture. The Newark Bank Building does just that.

Stroll through downtown Newark and it looks like any small Ohio town center. You'll see low, sturdy buildings of brick and stone in the Italianate and Gothic styles popular in the late nineteenth century. Houses sport turrets and stunning verandas, with dashes of ornamentation, sometimes veering into over-the-top territory. But step into the center of Newark and catch sight of Sullivan's bank building, and immediately there is the sense that this is something new—something alien, even.

Just off the square from the Licking County Courthouse, built in the classic nineteenth-century Second Empire style, Sullivan's bank building announces that we're not in the nineteenth century anymore, though the Beaux Arts influence is clearly visible in the building's stark ornamentation. Sullivan infused the facade with elements of nature, as seen on the decorative terra-cotta exterior, including a stunning griffin, its two front paws, claws visible, clutching a shield with a trademark Sullivan medallion on the front. Other parts of the facade feature explosions of flowers bursting forth from a long, slender stem seemingly growing out of the concrete sidewalk.

The two-story building with a basement occupies the northwest corner of the square, with only two sides visible. The south facade is a sturdy rectangle taking up the space of two storefronts while the narrow east facade abuts a typical red brick nineteenth-century building.

Early on, Sullivan had studied at the Ecole des Beaux Arts in Paris and incorporated elements of the school's aesthetic philosophy into his early building designs. For the Newark bank building Sullivan called for the use of greenish-grey terra-cotta for the exterior, the only one of his bank buildings to do so. Sullivan felt it appropriate for Newark because of the predominance of industry in the town, which included several famous glass works and a B&O railroad works. This was in contrast to the other bank buildings he designed which were built using red bricks to harmoniously align with what were primarily agricultural economies.[25]

The Home Building Association Company's Sullivan-designed bank building opened in 1915 and housed the bank for nearly three decades. Shortly before World War II it became a butcher shop, then an ice cream parlor amidst a few bouts of vacancy. In between it was listed on the National Register of Historic Places. In August 2015, the city marked the hundredth anniversary of the building's dedication. It's currently under restoration and is set to become the home for Explore Licking County, a convention and visitors bureau.[26]

One hundred or so miles west of Newark, it's equally easy to spot the Louis Sullivan-designed bank building at the center of the town of Sidney, the seat of Shelby County. It is situated much in the same way as the Newark building is, near the town square and opposite yet another late-nineteenth-century Second Empire style courthouse rising above the modest brick buildings surrounding it.

The Sidney building is more in the style of Sullivan's other bank buildings, dubbed "jewel boxes," with the exterior made of handsome red brick and a line of terra-cotta ornamentation atop the second story.

Walking around the exterior, one notices instantly that it is in much better shape than the Newark building. In fact, remarkably, the building still houses its original business, the People's Federal Savings and Loan Company (the "Federal" being added some years after the opening in 1918.) A typical day finds customers coming and going, bank tellers and employees going about the day's work in neat oak-panel-lined offices while tourists and busybodies (like me) roam inside and along the sidewalks, gawking and snapping pictures.

Lafayette M. Studevant, secretary of People's Bank for more than fifty years, was the prime mover in getting Sullivan to design the new bank building. The People's Savings and Loan Company was established by Studevant in 1886. He helped in financing many of the businesses and industries that sprang up in Sidney and its surroundings during the late nineteenth century. Studevant was also appointed a national bank examiner by President Grover Cleveland.[27]

Studevant and other bank executives knew of the Newark bank building that Sullivan had designed and took a driving trip to Newark to have a look. After seeing the uniqueness of Sullivan's style and the impact the new building had on the town, they decided to contact Sullivan and commission him to design a unique new bank building for Sidney. The People's Bank at the time was housed in a twenty-five-year old building, a typical sturdy stone structure characteristic for the time. It was eventually torn down to make way for Sullivan's new design.

The bank became an Ohio Historical Landmark in 1965 and a National Landmark in February 1978. One look at the building and it's easy to see why. It is generally recognized, along with the other series of bank commissions, as an architectural gem, and although small in scale, exquisite in detail. Under the entrance arch and just above the two front doors a blue mosaic with two-foot-tall white tiles reads "THRIFT"—and to this day people will wander inside asking if it is a thrift store.

When I visited Sidney in the spring of 2018, bank officials were gearing up to celebrate the building's centennial, having been dedicated on May 31, 1918. And just the day before I visited some bank employees found a framed triptych of pencil drawings and sketches of the building in the basement storage area. As it turns out, the drawings were done by Sullivan himself, with his initials in the bottom corner of the drawings.

While it's true that the last decade or so of Sullivan's life was far less productive than his earlier period, the bank buildings are nonetheless outstanding examples of Sullivan's vision of what architecture could be in the new American century. That these exquisite examples of modern design still stand across a swath of middle America is a testament to the foresight of their architect and the enduring design values of beauty, function, craftsmanship, and pride. They may not be as tall or as well-known as Sullivan's skyscrapers, but their power to motivate as well as their sheer beauty, are every bit as real. ✠

"The Home Building Association Bank in Newark, Ohio." Photo by Milenko Budimir.

"Redeemer Lutheran Church." Photo by Caitlin Veteto.

The Flamboyant Futurism of Bruce Goff

ALLISON C. MEIER

While the elegant steel and glass angles of Mies van der Rohe's Farnsworth House were being erected alongside Illinois's Fox River, a far more startling architectural statement was rising just a short drive away in Aurora. Locals nicknamed it the "bird cage," others the "tomato" or the "jockey cap." With its bright orange-red steel arches swooping over walls of coal and aquamarine glass cullet, and a central point that rose with curves similar to a stupa, its intersecting domes appeared like a settlement on some alien planet.

Architect Bruce Goff designed this 1947-49 house for Ruth and Albert Ford. Its spherical forms contain an interior dome adorned with a herringbone pattern in cypress boards, with a hearth and kitchen at its heart. Different levels rise inside, with an open area acting as a sort of indoor patio, whereas bedrooms are walled for privacy. Many of the materials were repurposed, including war surplus bomber windows and the cage-like structure made from painted Quonset hut steel—mass-produced during World War II for pop-up military buildings. Stained rope decorates the walls; marbles are embedded in the mortar for a glittery flare. The natural light, the utility, were all specifically envisioned for Goff's clients' needs, and were meant to create a sense of unified space rather than the rigid angles which dominated the other homes in the areas. And if those neighbors sneered or shook their heads at this buoyant, boldly hued home, the owners did not care. A sign out front declared: "We don't like your house, either.—THE FORDS."

Goff, in his lectures for the architecture studio he taught at the University of Oklahoma—as related in Arn Henderson's 2017 book *Bruce Goff: Architecture of Discipline in Freedom*—compared the "orchestration" of building materials to that of music. He played instrumental recordings for his students like Claude Debussy's *La Mer* (1905) and Igor Stravinsky's *The Rite of Spring* (1913) and noted that music's rhythms were "becoming much more complex and free" as opposed to the "rigor mortis" in architecture. "We have an opportunity, a challenge, when architecture is freed from being static. We can not only have free forms but free rhythms, which is one of the next big steps in architecture."

I grew up in a town where Goff's bombastic designs, which are both futuristic and approachable through their humble materials, dot streets lined with early twentieth-century oil industrialist mansions and subdivisions of uniform suburbia. Bartlesville, Oklahoma, was a hub for oil money from the early 1900s through the twentieth century. My family's home clad in yellow siding was on a downtown stretch where you could walk from the 1909 neoclassical home of Frank Phillips, the first of the state's big oil men, to the 1956 Price Tower. Designed by Frank Lloyd Wright and detailed with embossed copper, its cantilevered concrete floor slabs are positioned around a tap root support, fitting as it was built as the headquarters for Harold C. Price's pipeline construction company. Wright had initially designed it in 1929 as part of a group of apartment buildings for New York City. Amidst the Great Depression, the project never took off. Instead his "Tree that Escaped the Crowded Forest," as he called the tower in reference to its trunk-and-branches structure and

distinctness from Manhattan skyscrapers, became a grove of one out West.

After teaching at the University of Oklahoma, Goff set up an office in the Price Tower from 1956 to 1963. Largely self-taught, Goff took some individualistic cues from his mentor Wright, including his alchemy of materials with influences ranging from Gustav Klimt to Japanese pagodas. And like Wright, here among the rolling hills of northeastern Oklahoma, he found clients for public projects and private homes who felt his dynamic style matched the economic possibilities of the area. As a kid I played in Sooner Park near his fifty-foot 1963 Play Tower, its cylindrical steel body capped with a sphere inspired by mathematical principles such as the Möbius strip. The top orb was anointed with a spritely antenna that made it look like a rocket ship that had rusted in place, especially because by the 1990s it had fallen into disrepair. Its spiral stairway—intended, in Goff's words, for kids to "jump up and down (to make noise!) and run up and down, safely enclosed in a steel fencing cylinder"—was closed, and its once dynamic color scheme of red, yellow, and green had faded. I went to Sunday school in his 1959 Redeemer Lutheran Church Education Building, sitting folded at a perpendicular angle in its diamond windows, and imagining that the towering metal shafts at the entrance were arrows shot by some gigantic archer. The most spectacular Goff building in town was the 1956 Shin'en Kan, built for Joe Price (son of Harold) as a home and private museum for his Japanese art. I remember taking off my shoes to tour its plush rooms with their deep shag carpets, goose feather ceilings, and simple but transporting details like mobiles of colorful cellophane strips and cheap ashtrays on the windows as a sort of dime-store stained glass. I loved the hidden doors the best, which opened from unexpected places into kaleidoscopic rooms where light played on the flamboyant structure.

I didn't know how unique, and iconoclastic, Goff's architecture was until I moved away from it, and how divisively architects either love it for the inventive shapes and materials, or dismiss it as style over substance. In all ways, it was an eccentric disregard of the glass and steel minimalism embraced by postwar modernism. And its anticipation of a futuristic, organic path for design never arrived, meaning Goff's buildings are still oddities, and those eclectic materials can make preservation a challenge.

Shin'en Kan burned to its foundation in 1996, its arson never solved. Another of his imaginative homes in Oklahoma—the 1955 Bavinger House that had a corkscrew of floors lofted on cables, the exterior blue cullet and stone spiral appearing to rise out of the red earth—was reported destroyed in 2016 by its owner. The neglected Play Tower seemed doomed for demolition when, in 2008, someone rammed it with a backhoe, severing a support cable. Yet with community fundraising, it was restored, brightly painted once again, and reinstalled in 2014. And when I visited the 1951 Hopewell Baptist Church in Edmond,

Oklahoma, in 2011—let through its locked doors by the pastor who was enthusiastic about a fellow Goff architecture fan—its shingles were deteriorating and the floor had caved in. However it now has a foundation working on its restoration and return of access to the community, slowly restoring its teepee-like architecture of salvaged oil field pipes to its former splendor. While some of Goff's work is gone forever, his appreciation for a new way of modern living, where right angles were optional and pie tins could be lighting fixtures, may finally be getting the mainstream attention it has for so long lacked.

Goff mostly worked on the Great Plains, with a handful of commissions in California, including the expressive Pavilion for Japanese Art at the Los Angeles County Museum of Art (LACMA), crowned with protrusions that look like tusks of a colossal creature. The coasts had some of the major modernist statements of postwar architecture, in the New York skyscrapers and the Case Study Houses of Los Angeles, yet things got a bit stranger in the Midwest. Along with the poetic experimentation of Goff, a futurism in architecture was fueled by postwar economic optimism and the subsequent building boom.

Los Angeles might be where Googie, that term for the Space Age exaggeration in boomerang swoops and sloping roofs, got its name (coined from a 1949 West Hollywood coffee shop by John Lautner), but the Midwest was where money was flowing from many technological industries, and with it a surprising

"Sooner Park Play Tower." Photo by Caitlin Veteto.

embrace of architectural exuberance. Although Goff's 1964 octagonal Nicol House in Kansas City, which incorporated Murano glass ashtrays for a celestial pop, is a far aesthetic cry from the sci-fi kitsch of the (now demolished) UFO-shaped 1966 Gas n' Go by Ray Keyes in Ashtabula, Ohio, they shared a confidence about a future when those "boxes with little holes," as Goff described so much of architecture in a 1951 *Life* magazine, would be as old-fashioned as velocipedes and hoop skirts.

The heyday of Midwest futurism was after World War II and into the 1960s and early 1970s. While the 1950s set the stage for design experimentation, the 1960s really brought out the beauty, and sometimes abominations, of Space Age style. Adding to the undulating curves and sculptural concrete were rocket-ship style appendages and futuristic shapes, tail fins, and UFOs. (The opening of Oklahoma City's 1960s "Bank of the Future" had women dressed as aliens dancing on its series of flying saucer towers.) The early twentieth century was all about the machine, as expressed in artistic styles such as Precisionism that had painters including Charles Sheeler and Charles Demuth meticulously rendering factory scenes with no human workers in sight. The creation and dropping of the atomic bomb revealed the terrible power this progress could produce, and raised anxiety about the potential of technology, particularly its ability to completely eradicate an old way of life. If humans could invent obliterating, godlike power, how could they possibly go on living as before? In the October 1954 issue of *Popular Mechanics*, Paul Laszlo envisioned "Atomville," the town of 2004, with streets in concentric circles, and underground homes that connected to outdoor lawns and pools. Beautiful as the future metropolis was rendered, the living areas still appeared more like bomb shelters than homes.

The innovations of war also led to peacetime experimentation in design. Materials including plastic, acrylics, aluminum, and plywood, all developed during the war, supported biomorphic forms in Eames chairs and the seductive tail fins of the 1959 Cadillac Eldorado. Meanwhile military prefabrication techniques, such as the Quonset materials utilized by Goff, enabled more rapid construction, perfect to respond to an atmosphere of optimism about design. Even Styrofoam got its architectural moment. The material was introduced as electrical insulation during World War II, and then promoted for home use following the war's end. A technique called "Spiral Generation," patented by Dow Chemical Company, was used to quickly form dome structures around Michigan, like the 1966 Robert E. and Barbara Schwartz House in Midland and the 1964 Park Place dome in Traverse City (demolished in 2017). Smoothly soaring like machine-made igloos, they look not unlike the alien crafts in *The Day The Earth Stood Still* (1951).

Material shortages in the war years also inspired space frames and geodesic domes in steel and timber. And the expansion of corporate and cultural complexes realized these innovations at large scales. In Russell Township, Ohio, the 1958 headquarters of the American Society for Metals kept their latticework geodesic dome open to the air, constructed with 65,000 parts after a design by John Terrence Kelly and Thomas C. Howard. In St. Louis, architects Murphy and Mackey adapted Buckminster Fuller's geodesic dome principles to the 1960 Climatron, a conservatory of Plexiglass and aluminum, its support-free interior allowing for more light and volume for an over half-acre tropical rainforest garden. A few years later in St. Louis, the 1963 James S. McDonnell Planetarium by Gyo Obata (who would later work on the National Air and Space Museum) was built with a thinly poured concrete shell in a hyperboloid shape, a flying saucer from which to learn about the stars and perhaps dream of traveling to them.

Even mid-century midwestern churches, where you'd think a conservative streak would keep things traditional, had a new futuristic flair. The sculptural possibilities of concrete allowed for gravity-defying forms that reached to the sky while offering cave and tent-like spaces for congregation, recalling primitive meeting places. In Norton Shores, Michigan, Marcel Breuer and Herbert Beckhard's 1967 Saint Francis de Sales Church has a sculptural trapezoidal plan with a smooth plain of concrete simply adorned with a cross, which appears impenetrable from the outside. Within, the hyperbolic paraboloid sidewalls swoop towards a skylight, creating a modernist grotto in concrete. Eero Saarinen's hexagonal plan for North

Christian Church in Indiana reaches to the sky with its cast-in-place concrete; its sanctuary has the atmosphere of a sacred cave, drawing the eye upwards as if on a mental journey to heaven.

This push towards the future fizzled in the 1970s, with inflation and perhaps the conclusion of the Apollo missions to the moon in 1972 causing a waning enthusiasm for UFO buildings and frivolous appendages on architecture and cars. The geodesic domes, the concrete domes, and the roadside diners with their ray gun flourishes were surrounded by more boxy architecture, and by strip malls. Not old enough to be "historic," and having specialized, and often weather-prone, materials, their adaptive reuse for new tenants is often considered more trouble than it's worth. Across the Midwest these buildings that anticipated a future that never was now stand out starkly in comparison to modern needs and taste. In my home state, two futuristic projects are in limbo as they await their fate. The 1956 "Church of Tomorrow," aka the First Christian Church, in Oklahoma City, designed by R. Duane Conner and Fred Pojezny as a mammoth white dome of thin-shelled concrete (nicknamed the "egg church"), is on the market, awaiting a new owner who will determine how much of its mid-century structure to preserve. Nearby the geodesic Gold Dome, built in 1956 as the Citizens State Bank, is empty after revitalization plans fell through. Even Wright's Price Tower, his sole realized skyscraper, spent several years closed and for sale in the 1980s during the oil crisis, until it was opened as an arts center and now a hotel. But grander plans for its museum extension designed by Zaha Hadid have not been realized.

Goff died in 1982 in Tyler, Texas. In his *New York Times* obituary, his former apprentice, architect William E. Murphy, stated that Goff "did not think anybody was an ordinary person," and thus he never designed an ordinary home. His organic architecture wasn't growing from theory or academia, it was responding directly to client needs with a radical reevaluation of what a home could be. With no immediate family around, his ashes were kept by his patron Joe Price, and never buried. Finally another apprentice, Grant Gustafson, rallied for a proper memorial. With the support of Price, a plot was acquired in Chicago's Graceland Cemetery, and a marker was unveiled in 2000, designed by Gustafson. (Although it didn't include the epitaph that, according to Henry H. Kuehn's 2017 *Architects' Gravesites*, he wanted: "I had more influence than an alley cat.") He was interred a stone's throw from the simple dark granite grave of Mies van der Rohe.

In 2011, I was visiting a friend in Chicago and went walking in the cemetery. At the time, I didn't know Goff was buried there. But in the grass, I saw a glimmer I would recognize anywhere. Set in a triangular cast bronze marker was a piece of blue glass cullet salvaged from the ruins of Shin'en Kan, glinting just like it did in the Oklahoma sun. ✠

"Bruce Goff's Grave in Graceland Cemetery, Chicago." Photo by Allison C. Meier.

"Wright College." Photo by Zach Mortice.

Bertrand Goldberg's Temple to Futures Past

ZACH MORTICE

In October of 2013, Luis Collado and Jose Luis de la Fuente visited Wilbur Wright College, one of the City Colleges of Chicago's seven campuses, located in the city's far northwest side bungalow belt. Founders of the architecture firm STL Architects, who often work on education projects, they were interested in an RFQ the school issued for a potential renovation and were stopping by to investigate. The duo knew little for certain about Wright College, but they knew what to expect. Many of the city colleges are ultra-rational modernist boxes, deployed either with an exacting, ultra-rationalist sense of proportion, or as lazy replications of this aspiration that ended up as austere shoeboxes.

But that's not what they found. "The moment we stepped on campus, we looked at each other, and we said, 'This is *somebody's*,'" says de la Fuente. What they saw was a community college designed and situated to be an entire world of its own. Slanted from the relentless Chicago street grid, Wright College is a series of four buildings connected by elevated airlock tube hallways that plug into a stainless steel 130-foot pyramid. Collado and de la Fuente approached the building through a landscaped courtyard laid between two concrete bulkheads of a building, with round-edged pre-cast panels and small porthole-style windows that would be at home on a space station, with the connector tunnels hovering overhead. In the distance, the steel pyramid leaned away into the horizon.

As they got closer, they reached for their phones and started Googling. Who designed this? Then it all fell into place; the fearless use of concrete, the building-as-city superstructure, and the gee-whiz retro sci-fi aesthetics.

"Shit, man. Is this Goldberg?" said Collado.

That's Bertrand Goldberg. Goldberg was the last of the great Chicago modernists, educated within the city's Miesian tradition. He evolved it into fantastical new visions of city life—like his twinned Marina City mixed-use apartment towers—that were both commercially successful and daringly experimental.

"We had no idea," said de la Fuente. Both natives of Spain, they'd been practicing architecture in Chicago for nearly twenty years but had never come across this strange coda to Goldberg's career. In the months and years ahead, STL would be asked to reinterpret Wright College, Bertrand Goldberg's last major work; the end of a career that hasn't yet earned its rightful place in the pantheon of designers who made the contemporary city.

With its *Alphaville*-style concrete block propagation and embrace of Archigram megacities, Wright College seems like a quintessential product of the 1960s, when god-emperor architects dared to dream of new worlds and let the people in their wake decide if it was utopia or dystopia. But it's not. Wright College is just shy of thirty years old, completed in 1992. That was when architecture was deep into the most awkward, repetitive, and commercially lucrative era of postmodernism, when Michael Graves enlisted the Seven Dwarfs as columns to prop up the roof of a neo-parthenon Disney compound.

Wright College is an airlock to another world; the past's vision of the future, completed long after that

vision had faded. Its most salient feature is how unstuck in time it seems. "You don't know where to place it. It's kind of like mature 1960s, done in the '80s and early '90s," says Geoffrey Goldberg, Bertrand Goldberg's son, who worked on the project extensively as a young architect.

Part of this unstuck-ness results from the technology Bertrand Goldberg was chasing at the time. The college has a mid-century, wide-eyed technological optimism, arrayed toward what the ubiquity of the personal computer could do in a higher education setting. Goldberg knew he was designing for a moving target during the mid-1980s, a transitional phase between room-sized computers explicable only to a select order of white-button-down-collared-and-horn-rimmed-glasses techno-monks that surveyed miles of magnetic tape, and the ephemeral, wireless omnipresence of today. In between are the desktop computers that Wright College's signature feature, its steel pyramid, is designed around. And this oddball's disjunction with time and aesthetics offers lessons on how evolutions of information technology are changing perceptions of education and public space.

❧

Unlike Mies, Frank Lloyd Wright, and Daniel Burnham, Bertrand Goldberg was a Chicago original, born and raised in the city, in Hyde Park. He studied at the Cambridge School of Landscape Architecture

"Wright College." Photo by Zach Mortice.

"Marina City—Marina City, two 65-story corncob shaped buildings, was designed by Bertrand Goldberg in 1959 and is located along the Chicago River."
Lauren Manning/Flickr.

(later absorbed into Harvard), and at the Bauhaus and Illinois Institute of Technology. He worked briefly for Mies, who was a strong early influence, and completed a series of single-family homes in the minimalist Miesian vein.

Goldberg's early career was marked by quirky one-offs; rapidly deployable architecture for perilous needs (a mobile penicillin lab and a delousing unit) and trivial desires (an ice cream stand that could be erected and collapsed via single mast.) He worked with the modular architecture specialists Keck and Keck, and you can see elements of this in his work, though Goldberg's buildings maintain a much more cellular, organic sense of replication.

A precursor to Wright College was Goldberg's SUNY Stony Brook Health Sciences Center, a medical school and teaching hospital. Consisting of three towers placed on a rectilinear mat connected via skyways, it similarly offers a grounded campus center point, with distinct, superstructure masses emerging from it. At his firm's peak in the 1970s, he employed more than a hundred people, with satellite offices in Boston and Palo Alto. Goldberg died in 1997.

He was a true believer in urbanism that never wavered during the depths of the urban crisis that gripped cities in the middle of the twentieth century. To combat government-subsidized flight to the suburbs, he proposed the "new town in town," high-rise su-perstructure buildings within established urban areas that could provide all amenities and activities easily at hand. The sense of hermetic self-containment here could be credibly accused of being anti-urban, but Goldberg applied this model to the entire socioeco-nomic spectrum, from low-income apartments at the Hilliard Homes, to his luxury Astor Tower, and mid-dle-income Marina City, which perfected the mixed-use apartment tower in an unmistakably iconic form. In these, the walls between rooms look like the walls of a plant cell; protozoic spirals and squiggles abound in his built and unbuilt work. It's often a sublime meeting place between uncompromising and asym-metrical concrete Brutalism and the delicate order of the natural world.

One of the few books written about Goldberg, *Bertrand Goldberg: Architecture of Invention* (published to accompany a 2011 Art Institute of Chicago retro-spective), unfurls a lineage of influences on him and emanating from him. There's the Bauhaus, Corbusier, Mies, Archigram, the Japanese Metabolists, Bruce Goff, Eero Saarinen, and Chicago's own Jeanne Gang. (The resemblance of her Aqua Tower, perhaps the best American mixed-use apartment high-rise of its generation, to the biomorphic corncob towers at Marina City is unmistakable.)

Many of these influences are impossible to ignore at Wright College. The main entrance to the steel pyr-amid which houses its library confronts visitors with thick concrete ribs and the semblance of a sternum hoisting up the building's second floor; an inhabitable cyborg beast that's Stanley Kubrick by way of Gaudi, or maybe even H. R. Giger with the right sort of lighting. At the Art Institute of Chicago's architecture and design archives, a cut-away drawing of the school renders it as a splayed-open space ark. At first glance, it's an imposing, even pharaonic, temple to the now-prosaic subject of Goldberg's curiosity: the personal desktop computer.

Wright College seems to be the result of grand visionary premonition, but Goldberg was never a willful napkin sketcher, and the school was the result of months of technocratic, sociological research. Goldberg had been fascinated with how computers could be integrated with architecture since the 1960s, and Wright College was an opportunity to design for them at a critical juncture; the early stages of a broad consumer market. And the desktop computer's immobility hints at the architectural solution Goldberg was after.

And as outdated as this approach is now, Goldberg's tenure as a futurist on architecture and technology featured few embarrassing misfires. For his River City apartments, he envisioned a "two-way television" videoconferencing system. Goldberg told the Art Institute of Chicago's architects' oral history archive that, "We look forward to a time when the teachers may be permitted to originate their own educational software, much as they would write a book," predating Silicon Valley's insistence that learning to code is the highest

form of self-expression known to humankind. Faculty saw computers as rivals, and Goldberg wanted to break down that division. Most presciently, Goldberg pushed against spending extra money to install additional fiber optic and coaxial cable infrastructure at the school. "My father fought long and hard, saying 'The future is in the air. It's not in burying money in walls,'" says Geoffrey Goldberg. "He was correct in the long term, but at that time . . ."

Bertrand Goldberg called the computer a "lonely device" in need of collaborative and social context. "It's meant for personal education, but we still have the need, it seems to me, to allow for group education, with the use of the computer," he said.

His firm began working on Wright College in 1986, around the time Geoffrey Goldberg had returned to Chicago from the East Coast, after finishing graduate school at the Harvard Graduate School of Design, and a stint working for I. M. Pei in New York. The entire office worked on the school's design for three years from 1987 to 1990.

Given the City College's stock of strict modernist boxes, the Chicago Public Buildings Commission told Goldberg, "We don't want a round building." And despite his past portfolio, he complied. In this way, it's something of a return to form, toward Goldberg's early-career Mies-influenced houses. Spread across more than twenty acres and canted from Chicago's grid, Goldberg's plan is given rectilinear edges. "I think it's rather fascinating for a very creative architect known for his forms [to work] within a constraint which is contrary, and yet still manage to do an inventive building out of that," says Geoffrey Goldberg.

The campus' centerpiece pyramid—called the Learning Resource Center (LRC)—is the main expression of Goldberg's geometric compromise and grand ambition. In addition to the library, it contains faculty offices, and computer labs arranged in a variety of plans to encourage socialization alongside computer-aided learning. The LRC is connected on its second and third level to two classroom buildings clad in repetitive pre-cast concrete panels via the airlock tunnels. Completely opaque and pleasingly scale-less from the inside, their muted up-lighting reflects off of fine-grained tile and a military-green ceiling. They're every bit as otherworldly as the library pyramid. A fourth building not connected via tunnels contains an auditorium, gym, and swimming pool. At ground level, all four buildings are connected by the Campus Center, a small circulation hub that shows off the different materiality of the LRC and concrete blocks through glass walls.

Pedagogically, "all of the learning activities were tied back into the learning center," says Geoffrey Goldberg. The LRC is the "cheese in the mousetrap."

Computers and spaces for them were sprinkled throughout the LRC in large groupings and small, not limited to any specific area or program. This sense of dispersion is aided by the Piranesian complexity of the library. An alternating pattern of elevated platforms at the center of the pyramid and perimeter catwalks at its edge brings students to its fourth-floor atrium reading room. From the ground looking up, it's a crystalline web of stairs, rendered in burly concrete.

And within these layered concrete shelves of library stacks and reading desks there's a humanist sense of intimate scale. Much of Goldberg's planning work (especially at Wright College) tended to focus on "very small-scale units of human interaction; six, eight, ten, twelve people," says Geoffrey Goldberg. "He's interested in smaller clusters of people. There's a kind of individualization that runs through the work. It's from the small pieces up. It's not a top-down kind of thing. There's a strange feeling in this facility that there's an attention paid to the individual." That is, strange for its apparent era. In the 1960s, when Wright's ideological frame was set, architects heedlessly clear-cut miles of Brazilian wilderness to build the new, perfectly abstract, capital of Brasilia, and encircled the most vulnerable parts of each American city center in a ring of freeways. It wasn't a great time for listening to the little people.

"You can find small spaces tucked here and there in the learning center," says Geoffrey Goldberg. "You tend to think it's going to be a large, grand space, but in fact it doesn't feel that way. You find places for people to be in."

There are the small faculty offices, six to a corridor, that end at tall, narrow window strips that staff have decorated with plants and seating; lush terrariums amid the grey concrete. There are study nooks placed under the space tube skyways, and all manner of quiet corners at the pyramid's canted edges. The idiosyncrasy of the space encourages you to keep exploring, to find your secret place in Goldberg's machine.

The LRC's approachability also seems strange because it exists within a steel temple fetishistically dedicated to a piece of technology that's lost its modernity-defining salience. But spend some time there, and you'll learn that it's about as un-pharaonic as you can get for a pyramid. Its low roof angle slopes away from you quickly, and the top floor reading room atrium is modest in proportion. The entire campus is set within a lushly forested Alfred Caldwell landscape, and in perspective, the LRC rarely rises over the treetops as you look up. It stubbornly resists monumental photography. You have to scramble on top of a small ridge along Montrose Avenue to get a full profile; there's no "postcard shot" says Geoffrey Goldberg. "It's almost shy." In the early stages of its design, any time more strident versions of the LRC would arise in the office, Bertrand would push them aside. Its pyramid peak was originally flat, though it's not anymore, and students used to scale its 130 feet to stand on top of it. It's warmer and more welcoming than it seems to have any right to be, made ever more so because of its blatantly outdated aesthetics and forms. It's just too much of a misfit to ever be threatening.

❦

Collado, of STL, says Wright College is not Bertrand Goldberg's best work. But that doesn't mean much when his best work is Marina City, the building that perfected the mixed-use apartment tower in an era where faith in the city was at an all-time low. Wright College does have very real weaknesses. There is functionally no primary front door, which blurs and diffuses its dramatic entry sequence. It's not easy to navigate, and its relentless, micromanaging sense of control weeds out any aura of spontaneity.

And though the campus is like nowhere else, within this strange realm, Goldberg's enforced uniformity and granular control over every element means it's hard to locate oneself exactly in space. After a tour of the building, facilities manager and chief engineer Mike Dompke, who has worked at the building nearly since its opening, remembers perusing Wright College's photography club photos of the school and not recognizing what he saw. "I see them, and [I say], 'Where is that?' I think they went somewhere else," he says. "No, they snapped the picture right on campus."

Collado and de la Fuente repeated a similar exercise for their research on the school. They took photos of campus and asked students where each was taken. "Overwhelmingly, people did not know where it was," Collado says.

From its custom-designed window fixtures, hamster tube skywalks, and the axial courtyards that place students in a bowling alley of mid-century modernist concrete, it's a fantastical, fully-formed world, but not one open to interpretation. "This obsession with control is [Goldberg's] worst enemy," says Collado.

There are fewer and fewer places for spontaneous, social interaction as one scales up from the small groups the LRC accommodates well. There are places for people, but the formality of the library setting means it's most attuned to hushed whispers across a desk, not boisterous pin-ups across a hall. (Architecture studios are taught at Wright College.) And this sense of intimacy is at odds with contemporary ideas on learning space. "[Wright College] deserves some credit for being a case study on the evolution of how our society approaches education," says Collado.

If the operative metaphor at Wright College is campus-as-city, then Collado and de la Fuente detect a lack of a public realm at the school, the campus equivalent of parks, plazas, and sidewalks, to be made ubiquitous and introduced in more fine-grained patterns. This isn't how the previous generation of designers thought of education facilities or any sort of space. From the strict segregation of greenfield residential suburbs from the retail and commercial centers that served them, to Goldberg's hyper-rational machine for education at Wright College, work, play, and anything in between didn't mix. "The celebration of community and learning are two separate things in the 1960s and '70s," says Collado.

What Wright College needs, Collado and de la Fuente say, is more "social infrastructure." That is, "the spaces in-between that don't necessarily have a program," says de la Fuente. In the context of education, this means the "celebration of community as a learning experience," says Collado. Today, "places of socialization become places of learning."

The idea of free-floating places of collaboration that exist between work and leisure (yet are united by the omnipresence of media screens) has been widely successful, and an entire class of people are entering the workforce that will likely spent their entire careers—and more—in them. This is exemplified by the co-working space with "huddle rooms," "phone booths," a craft beer stocked bar, and an endless hunger for spatial arrangements that prize the mythical "spontaneous interaction" that will break open the world of smart toenail clipper app testing. This shared material and spatial sensibility has been exported to hospitality design, residential design, cultural institutions, and of course, education. The university library's terraced roof deck, the apartment tower with three separate amenity floors catering to work-at-home entrepreneurs who need a space to bring clients in for meetings, the museum learning lab with interactive exhibits synched with what's on the walls, and any space with brightly colored loungey furniture where you'd feel equally comfortable emailing your boss or watching YouTube videos are all contemporary expressions of what STL calls "social infrastructure."

This new paradigm has evolved alongside and because of the Internet, which allows its untethered access to information. And because of this option, when you plop down a bunch of desktops today, the subtle message is that this is not actually a place to socialize. Positioning the LRC as a knowledge hub was a good idea, say Collado and de la Fuente, but now the value is in the network, not in the hardware. So STL Architects' plans for Wright College are to provide the built context for this social network.

To address this need and solve an overall space crunch at the school—with 18,000 students, the City College's largest—STL spent year and a half producing five volumes of research, much as Goldberg did in his day. Their plan installs a two-level glass canopy over the axial courtyard between the LRC and the science classroom building. At the ground floor and in a catwalk level above, this atrium spine is lined with retail and institutional uses: coffee shop, bookstore, food pantry, student center, etc. The top level extends a single story above the classroom buildings, never challenging the primacy of the LRC, and the new link connects all four buildings in a central hub that allows students to enter each one without walking through a roundabout circular path at ground level. Glass encases Wright College's distinctive pre-cast concrete and stainless steel in a vitrine panopticon,

allowing a new level of visual access and intimacy. And the canopy telescopes beyond the perimeter of the buildings, creating a covered quasi-public plaza, where community programming, like a farmer's market, could take root. "It's a city college. It's not Princeton," says Collado. "It's a place where you want the community to come in and experience it." This revision gives the school a front entrance focal point, encourages a more interactive and porous relationship with surrounding neighbors, and offers up servings of lightly programmed social space.

It's a conventionally contemporary approach to education and public space. But Collado and de la Fuente say they do feel a responsibility to maintain the school's fundamental out-of-time-ness. And since there is currently no money or mandate to build this reenvisioning, Wright College will likely remain unmoored from its age for the foreseeable future.

❧

Though the college's strident mid-century forms have entranced the design community, this sort of Brutalism never gained the widespread trust of the broader public. Even in Chicago, Goldberg's work hasn't always been respected. In 2013, Northwestern University demolished his concrete quatrefoil Prentice Women's Hospital, in favor of a new medical center. STL realizes that any whiff of obsolescence wafting toward buildings with stigmatized or odd aesthetics can quickly be leveraged into demolition permits. Adapting the building, counterintuitively, becomes a strategy for preservation.

Bertrand Goldberg's work hasn't received the attention it deserves because much of it requires a key to get into; his portfolio is thin on major public cultural institutions. Additionally, he seldom taught, and his steadfast commitment to Chicago (which transfixes Chicagoans) kept him outside of the New York-centric design media axis. Similarly, even though it's as public as nearly any Goldberg building, Wright College is overlooked in part because of its remoteness; far from the cluster of architecture at Chicago's center that has largely defined the contemporary metropolis the world over. It was already something of a nostalgia piece when it was new, and its utopian zeal for an era it was never actually present for feels a bit forced, aging it further.

And there's a similar utopian impulse to view its lack of under-programmed hangout space favorably, because when these sorts of places exist today, they're most often stuffed with commercial uses, becoming inherently exclusionary. We're often sold consumerism in the place of populism or community, by buildings that insist (with market-tested forecasting for shopping and cuisine) that they're on our side because they offer the kind of snacks we enjoy.

But Wright College, in all of its inflexibility, insistence on control, and reverence for a very specific era of technology, has never pandered, and never tried to be all things to all people. "It doesn't pretend to be something else," says Geoffrey Goldberg. "It's a mature architect who knows what he's doing late in his career. He was just doing his thing. It's not like we had long conceptual discussions about this stuff. He carried it in his head and worked it out." And the college's clarity of purpose came part and parcel with its outdated aesthetics. If all architecture is inherently political, then a polemic like Wright College has more integrity than a sales pitch.

As a loose, conceptual plan on a computer screen, STL's scheme is appropriate and responsible. It respects Goldberg's intent, provides new spaces that recognize how students learn today, and provides the suite of amenities they expect to find. But it's hard to shake the suspicion that Wright College would lose something we know how to replicate less and less if it's forced to conform, for the first time in its history, to its own era. ✹

Photo from David Haid Archive.

David Haid's Archive

JOE FRANK

The Haid house comes with an archive. When we bought the house in 2012, my wife and I inherited blueprints and a couple of framed awards from architecture societies that now hang along the basement stairs. There's also a binder stuffed with newspaper and magazine articles about the house, brochures from Evanston, Illinois house walks, and black and white photos that we presume were taken by architect David Haid, who designed and built the house in 1968 and lived here until he died in 1993. The binder includes pictures of Haid's notable commercial projects, placing our house squarely in its mid-century context and showing how it fits into Haid's oeuvre. The one-story brick and glass-walled structure is the spitting image, in miniature, of a bank building a couple of miles north at Central Street and Greenbay Road, and the house has elements in common with Dyett High School on the South Side of Chicago, both designed by Haid. It provides a reminder of Haid's original Lincoln Oasis, an elevated rest stop spanning Illinois's Tri-State Tollway, which has been modified (or bastardized) beyond recognition. And of course, it has a lot in common with the Ferris Bueller "house" that Haid designed in 1973. The glass-walled auto pavilion that sets the scene for the climatic Ferrari crash in *Ferris Bueller's Day Off* bears a strong resemblance to our house, if you replace two glass walls with beige brick and take away the setting on the side of a wooded ravine about fifteen miles north in Highland Park.

All of this buildup leads to a house remarkable in its simplicity. Picture a rectangle. The short ends are thirty feet long, about eleven feet high and face east and west. They are entirely glass, framed in black-painted steel. The long sides are hundred-foot expanses of brick. On the north side, a glass inset is the front door. Asking, "Who is it?" as you walk up to answer the entirely glass door is a (bad) family joke that never gets old. On the south side, a square bite taken out of the rectangle with two glass walls makes room for a bur oak that was big when the house was built and now towers over the house.

Haid built the house with three square bedrooms along the back for his daughters. Wisely, those bedrooms and their bathrooms can be sealed off from the rest of the house by closing two huge oak doors. A narrow kitchen runs the width of the house leading to an open dining room, living room, and "library," that takes up a quarter of the entire structure. Remarkably, the photos in the archive reveal that at one point, the dining room could be separated from the main room by a curtain suspended from the ceiling, but that curtain disappeared before we came along, and the undated pictures don't reveal whether it was a brief experiment, an original fixture, or otherwise.

Other changes are easier to chart. We bought the house from a couple who bought it from Haid's estate and lived there for about twenty years. They told us that the floating bookshelves in the library, which set a perfect mid-century tone in the binder pictures, had already been replaced with built-in shelving and cabinets by the time they moved in. But they also told us that Haid's daughters would occasionally stop by to visit their old house and insist that the built-ins had always been there.

The second owners made the biggest change by removing a wall between two of the back bedrooms to create a family room of sorts, where, from all appearances, they spent most of their time. The main room served as an icy museum of steel, glass, brick and terrazzo, full of white furniture and boldly colored folk art. We restored the bedroom wall before

we moved in, so our kids could each have their own space, but we have not been strict preservationists. In fact, the archival ghosts of the curtain and the floating bookshelves were liberating because they showed the house as a living organism and gave us license to modify, respectfully, what could rightly be treated as a museum piece.

A lover of mid-century architecture could easily make the case against change. Haid, while only known to those willing to take a dive deep into the architecture of the 1960s and '70s or the most devoted of Ferris Bueller fans, was on the fringe of greatness. For many years, he was a lieutenant to modernist giant Ludwig Mies van der Rohe. Whether he was the *chief* lieutenant depends on whom you ask, but there's no debating that it is Haid standing with Mies in a picture that appears in the eminent modernist's biography. They met when Haid, an apprentice cabinetmaker, came from Winnipeg to study architecture under Mies at the Illinois Institute of Technology in 1951 and ended up working together for about a decade before Haid struck out on his own. That legacy, living in the mid-century house of an architect who was at the epicenter of Mies's sharp-edged modernism, makes even the smallest alteration worthy of real consideration.

To install crown molding or wainscoting would have been a sin, but to pretend that the house was too precious to modify seemed foolish. Still, almost everything we did tried to honor the mid-century aesthetic. A house built in 1968 doesn't accommodate the role of television in modern life, but we didn't just hang a flat screen on the wall. We installed a full wall of cabinets and new floating shelves that accommodated a screen, but otherwise stayed true to mid-century form, even matching the rift sawn white oak used on the original doors and cabinets throughout the house.

Elsewhere we may have gone astray. A purist might be nauseated by the chandelier we hung over the dining room table, disrupting the clean lines of the main room, where every other light fixture is recessed. Picture a three-tiered cake hanging upside down from the ceiling. The sides of the cake are long ball chains that sway gently as air circulates. The chandelier is beautiful and makes a statement, but you have to ask yourself what Haid would make of it.

Just as the chandelier stands out from the rest of the period details, the Haid house stands out in our neighborhood. Our compact house is surrounded on all sides by massive old houses that predate it by fifty or sixty years. Seven-bedroom houses are not unheard of on our street and every one but ours is two or three stories tall. The Haid house sits in the shadow of a massive stone and wood Victorian. Haid bought that house and subdivided the lot to make room for his statement piece. He granted himself an easement so that the front walk could curve across the property line around another bur oak that he didn't want to remove. Another easement lets us use the driveway of the old house to get to our garage.

I can't say that our house fits into the neighborhood. Newer houses were built to reflect their surroundings, while ours is an obvious, but quiet rejection. The Haid house all but disappears between much larger houses and is hidden behind naturalistic landscaping that creates beautiful views through the window walls and also provides a little privacy.

The funny thing is that even though we think of our house as invisible, we have slowly come to realize just how many of our neighbors know it is there. We know this because the Haid house produces a steady stream of spontaneous purchase offers from people who all fit the same profile. They move into the neighborhood as their families start to grow and they live happily in their giant houses for ten or fifteen years until the kids go off to college. Eventually, they get tired of knocking around in a house with rooms they may not go into for months at a time. Time and again, they show up at our house and leave a note in the mailbox or just knock on the door ("Who is it?"). They don't want to leave the neighborhood with its beautiful trees and houses, a few blocks from Northwestern University and Lake Michigan and a short ride to downtown Chicago, but their houses have become too big for them, which doesn't leave many options unless they are ready to move into a condominium and start sharing walls again. So far, we've never even entertained the notion of selling (or even asking "how much?"), and the offers have only heightened our appreciation for what we have.

Still, we know we won't stay forever and we do think about what we will add to the archive when we leave. I know for sure that we will leave behind the pen and ink drawing of the house that illustrated a brochure when the Haid house was included on the Evanston History Center House Walk (for the second time). My wife hates the picture and I don't blame her. It is pretty clear when you compare it to the artist's drawings of the more traditional houses on the walk that she either hated trying to illustrate glass or found no inspiration in our house whatsoever. For our house, she placed the outside brick wall of the master bedroom courtyard in the foreground and used a perspective that makes the house look like little more than a brick cube, surrounded by unruly landscaping with a few windows peeking out on the side. It's fair to say that she could not have chosen a less becoming angle, providing no reference to the beautiful oak trees and walls of windows that define our house.

Beyond the illustration that we will gladly leave behind, we will try to find something that expresses our sense of the space as we lived in it on its fiftieth birthday in 2018. That may just be a picture of our family sprawled on sofas reading or watching TV in the main room, presented like the old black and white photos in the archive. What such an image shows that escapes most people is that the Haid house isn't a cold space or a "dentist's office" (overheard from a visitor when our house was part of the Evanston History Center's annual housewalk). The house, with its one central room, brings our family together simply because there is no place else to go, unlike the big Victorians and Tudors, where each person in the family can have their own wing. You could call the house cold because it has sharp angles and hard surfaces, but this formal austerity brings our family together for better or worse. This is even true when my wife and I sit in the backyard and the kids are in their glass-walled bedrooms, which function as teenager terrariums until, inevitably, the curtains are drawn.

And maybe we'll add a Ferris Bueller memory to the archive because right now there isn't one. I'm sure we could find an old VHS tape on eBay for a few bucks. That addition would make sense because when we give the tour or tell people about our house, the third or fourth sentence is always about the kinship of our house and the setting of the Ferrari scene. And the relationship makes perfect sense when you think about the movie. Other than *Ferris Bueller's Day Off*, the John Hughes movies are character driven, moving between generic houses and plush high schools that could be in Scarsdale, New York, or Bethesda, Maryland, or any prosperous suburb. But *Ferris Bueller* is Hughes's love letter to Chicago, moving along Lake Shore Drive between Wrigley Field and the Art Institute of Chicago and a parade on Dearborn Street. (Unlike *The Blues Brothers*, it shamefully ignores the South Side.) Each scene in the movie conveys a strong sense of place and you don't have to stretch too far to find some connection between the scenes in front of Mies's Daley Plaza and Federal Plaza post office and the mayhem back at the Haid auto pavilion. Those

Mies buildings and the auto pavilion and our Haid house are integral to Chicago's distinct architectural heritage so lovingly showcased in the movie. The city embraces modernism not in distinct outposts but by weaving it directly into the fabric of magnificent older buildings erected since the fire of 1871, creating a vibrant architectural archive that will always find room for new additions. ✖

"Leenhouts Home in Milwaukee". Collection of Robin Leenhouts.

Lillian Leenhouts's Milwaukee Eco-Socialism

MONICA OBNISKI

In an attempt to amplify the work of women, the January 1973 issue of *Ms.* magazine recognized Milwaukee architect Lillian Leenhouts (1911-1990) as a "Found Woman," alongside other women of creativity and achievement who deserved attention, but, ostensibly, were completely obscure to all until the magazine swooped in to document them. Of course, Leenhouts had been active in Milwaukee, practicing architecture along with community activism for nearly thirty years. In the article, Leenhouts was identified as an architect who fights for environmental causes through a social lens, but if anything, that was underselling her commitment to designing environments that were as equitable as they were resourceful. Lillian and her husband Willis were interested in principles of sustainability, which they understood largely as it's understood now: efficiency of materials; using local resources; maximizing and minimizing heat and light from the sun when appropriate. But Lillian was also a fervent socialist, and nearly everything about her architectural practice extended from that way of seeing the world.

Early in their career, as the male in the enterprise, her husband Willis legitimized the architectural firm in the wider world of the mid-twentieth century, but, according to their daughter Robin Leenhouts, Lillian was the "real force in the partnership."[28] (It was Lillian who lectured about sustainable and energy efficient buildings at national conferences during the 1980s, and drew plans to patent solar ovens and louvered windows.) The duo were considered equals when they were inducted as a couple as Fellows of the American Institute of Architects for outstanding contributions to the field of architecture. Regrettably, women in architecture are still underrecognized and underrepresented, and sexism is sometimes quiet and other times overt. For example, in an article in one of Milwaukee's local papers titled "Architecture: A Practical Part-Time Career," the author outlines Lillian's work as an architect and a mother. The notion that either profession is part-time is laughable, considering both are all-consuming enterprises, which Lillian well understood. As Robin recalled years later, Lillian was very interested in ideas of work-life balance, as she and several female professional friends discussed writing a book about how to be a wife-mother-career woman. We all would have benefited from this modern-day domestic science manual, assembled at a time when women were given far fewer accommodations for family life and positions of leadership.

Reflecting upon Lillian's practice—specifically on its relationship between ecology and architecture—her dedication to environmental concerns and passive solar architecture was fundamentally related to her socialism. With an influx of German immigrants who participated in the 1848 revolutions, Milwaukee was a fertile place for organized labor and the development of socialism in America during the late nineteenth century. In fact, during the twentieth century, Milwaukee had three socialist mayors, the last of which, Frank Zeidler, made progressive causes, such as human rights and social justice, central to urban life. Lillian's socialism also meant that she engaged deeply in civic concerns in Milwaukee. As a socialist—and thus a forerunner to today's resurgent left—she desired to lessen the burden on the environment through building practices that did not privilege fossil fuels, and she understood the

power of working with government to enact positive change for the masses. In contemporary parlance, we might consider Leenhouts as an eco-socialist architect. For example, she believed that the city was not harnessing the capabilities of the Milwaukee River, so she jumped into action by forming the Architect's River Committee (after being an integral member of the Mayor's Beautification Committee). In her words, Leenhouts helped the city take the Milwaukee River "back from Commerce" and redeveloped it "for the people." Had she stayed by the sidelines when chain stores had started to move in, today's waterfront residences and the RiverWalk district, for example, would not be part of Milwaukee's charm. She also advocated for urban planners to consider retaining historic structures, as opposed to tearing them down—which was rampant in 1970s Rust Belt America. The concerns that occupied Leenhouts's architectural practice are still relevant today, as climate scientists warn us about the deleterious effects of fossil fuels on our planet.

As an extension of her socialist beliefs, Lillian believed that the built environment directly affected the condition of people living in a city. She was a part of several citizens' groups and founded the Architects Concerned Committee in 1969.[29] Architects Concerned in WAICO (the Walnut Area Improvement Council) was composed of twelve architects alongside landscape architects, lawyers, an editor, architectural students, professors, and urban planners to total twenty-eight people who volunteered their services to a neighborhood self-help group located on the city's largely

African-American north side. The city was going to clear this area of "urban blight," but Leenhouts and her group stepped in to provide assistance for this urban re-development project.[30] At her urging, the city stopped demolition of large residential swaths of the neighbor-hood, and established an ordinance to clean up vacant lots. Leenhouts secured half a million dollars in grant money to purchase new land for housing, and spent time at the WAICO community house coordinating book donations and adult literacy classes, and enlist-ing the help of University of Wisconsin-Milwaukee architecture students. As her daughter remembered, Lillian "really wanted people to have better houses to live in."[31] The many years of work in service of this project demonstrates her deep, abiding commitment to and compassion for underserved communities. As recalled by daughter Robin, Lillian believed, "if you lived in a good house . . . that's going to make your life better" and "that your environment, and that the way that [your] house relates to other houses in the neigh-borhood" with green spaces for communal activities will make for safer neighborhoods.[32] In a city that is one of the most segregated in America, in a state that incarcerates African-Americans at a much higher per-centage than the US average, the work that Leenhouts and the council implemented would be welcome to-day as a way to guide Milwaukee's built environment toward solving systemic issues of inequality.[33]

While Lillian was a student at the Layton School of Art (Milwaukee's progressive art school from 1920 to 1974), with formidable women Charlotte Partridge and Miriam Frank at the helm, there was an exhibi-tion about Frank Lloyd Wright that stirred the future architect. After graduating from the University of Michigan's Architecture School in 1936, Lillian com-pleted a series of draftsman jobs during World War II until she and Willis moved back to Milwaukee and began working for the office of Harry William Bogner, in which housing was the major concern. Lillian was the first registered female architect in Wisconsin when she began working in 1942. When the couple started their own firm in 1945, one initial project they worked on (presumably, to spark interest in the burgeoning practice) was "Masterpiece House no. 6" for the magazine *Popular Home*. They received hundreds of letters from across the United States from people who wanted to buy a set of the drawings for this speculative house.[34] This plan for *Popular Home* allowed the pair to experiment with some early ideas about domestic architecture, which would inform the design of their own home completed in 1949.[35]

The Leenhouts bought a vacant lot in Riverwest, a di-verse, working-class neighborhood in Milwaukee, and planned their house around the existing trees, which they worked to save. On the property, the Leenhouts pre-served fifty-four trees, about which Lillian sagely noted in an article some years later: "Have you ever heard it takes 40 trees to balance the pollution of one car?"[36]

When designing their own home, the Leenhouts incorporated many characteristics of postwar do-mestic architecture—freely planned interiors to encourage a less formal lifestyle, usable outdoor spaces such as terraces and porches, and the disappearing wall—a sliding glass wall or picture window to allow in light—all of which made the house look like a prototypical mid-century modern dwelling. The Leenhouts's home was an experimental space where the architects tested traditions to evaluate outcomes: "Roman heated floors, Japanese garden courts, early American natural wood balance one car's exhaust fumes with vagrant growth on small lot back from traffic."[37] Through the rhetoric (which sometimes soared above what they were actually able to achieve), the architects attempted to persuade others to embrace aspects of solar homes. Throughout their career, the Leenhouts completed private residences alongside schools, churches, apartments for the elderly, and urban design projects. Planned to take advantage of nature and the sun, the majority of their architectural practice were Milwaukee-area single family residences, which featured functional built-ins and storage space, garden solariums and sliding doors, and flooring with radiant heating. Each house's rich natural materials added an aura of warmth and intimacy to their mid-century modern flat roofs and open floor plans.

Their location in the Midwest ensured that the legacy of Prairie School architecture was palpable. Following Wright, who similarly believed that a house should grow out of the ground and maintain a symbiotic relationship to its context, the Leenhouts viewed nature as an intrinsic element of architecture. (For many years there was a tree in the middle of their carport.) Frank Lloyd Wright also believed in promoting glass as a new resource in building: as an aid to air, cleanliness, and light; and as a way to extend vistas and build architecture into nature. While discussing the various plants on their property, Lillian noted, "glass can let nature do our decorating for us and it will never be in bad taste."[8] The Leenhouts liked to use deciduous trees in the landscaping of their homes, using their leaves to block the summer sun.

Through their solar homes, the Leenhouts were one of a number of small but influential architects that began to make consistently harnessing the sun's energy for warmth and light both a practical and contemporary reality. A solar home, through its utilization of glass walls and picture windows, visually engaged with outdoor vistas (vital for post-World War II suburbanizing communities) and achieved the ideal of fluid indoor/outdoor living. The Leenhouts built their 1949 solar house, characterized by its use of wide expanses of glass, radiant floor heating, open plans, experimentation with new materials, and prudent site orientation. Which is to say, these solar houses mirrored the rise of modern architecture of the period, which was often delivered with far less eco-consciousness by practitioners (unlike the Leenhouts's) convinced of the total lack of consequences of endlessly cheap fossil fuels.[39] Houses were oriented to face south, to catch some of the most consistent light. Landscaping was also integral, not simply to enhance the view, but also to provide screening for privacy and to offer shade in the summer. Double-paned windows were used to reduce heat loss. The sun's energy was additionally controlled via roof overhangs. Solar houses were also recommended for cold climates, provided that good heating, insulation, and weather-stripping would be used in conjunction with solar heating.[40]

The emergence of solar homes in the 1940s developed alongside postwar domestic architecture, most notably characterized by large plate glass windows. As a building typology, solar houses were proposed in the pages of shelter magazines in order to appeal to everyday Americans. For example, *House Beautiful* and Chicago architect George Fred Keck, in conjunction with Green's Ready-Built Homes, designed a system of glass wall panels at multiple price levels, demonstrating the attractiveness and ease of the material to a broad middle-class audience.[41] Lillian knew the work of Keck, one of the first architects to focus on solar house heating beginning in the 1930s. She was impressed and inspired by Keck's House of Tomorrow at the Century of Progress, Chicago's World's Fair of 1933. Like Frank Lloyd Wright, Keck was interested in regional concerns, but he also experimented with new technologies. The House of Tomorrow embraced passive solar energy, as large windows allowed in the sun, and heat was stored in a concrete slab at the base of the building. Unfortunately, primitive glass insulation technology meant that the house was extremely hot in the summer. Still, the experience of viewing the House

of Tomorrow while a student forever changed Lillian. Years later, she discussed the power of Keck's entry in the Chicago World's Fair as the "conscious rebirth of passive solar heating and cooling."[42] Today there are an intense series of requirements and codifications for a building to be considered a high-performance Passive House (as outlined by the German Passive House Institute), and with only a fraction of today's climate and building science research, the Leenhouts's obliquely followed some of these principles simply because they seemed practical.[43]

Leenhouts's greatest contribution to architecture in Milwaukee was a focus on nature and the ecological impact of buildings—all of which were inextricably linked to her position as a socialist. Lillian Leenhouts should be remembered for her dedication to passive solar architecture alongside her commitment to improving people's lives—a devotion to nature and humanity that becomes more and more critical the further in time we move from her powerful example. ✠

"Packard and Yost Train Station Terminal." Photo by Amanda Page.

The Packard Presence in Columbus, Ohio

AMANDA PAGE

I was living in Columbus for the third time when I first heard of Frank Packard, a prolific, turn of the century architect. During my first two stints in the city, I had noticed the buildings that seemed to have character, but I didn't dive any deeper. I appreciated them, but I didn't seek out their stories. At that point, Columbus did not yet feel like my home. I was just passing through. I didn't have the time to really get to know it.

When I decided to return the third time, after several moves back and forth across the country, I knew that I wanted to live in a particular neighborhood. Specifically, I wanted to live in the one with all the ravines.

I grew up around hills, and Columbus's flatness had a remarkable effect on my mood. The first two times I lived there, I felt like the landscape: vast and empty. Sure, there were tall buildings downtown that provided some height in the distance, but skyscrapers aren't covered in trees, and unless you are a parkour enthusiast, they're not kind to climb. When I drove the outer belt, I felt consumed with a sadness I could not place. After I returned to the hills of southern Ohio, I wondered if the Columbus sadness might have been a type of flatness madness; if I had been sick for the sight of hills.

When I came back to Columbus I knew I needed to stand on the ground and be surrounded by natural elements much taller than me.

I moved into an apartment within walking distance of a ravine, and I promptly contacted an organization called "Friends of the Ravines." I saw their newsletter at the local grocery store, and knew in that moment that I wanted to befriend the ravines, too.

I was welcomed into the fold and the other friends quickly made use of my wordy nature. I was tasked with writing articles for the newsletter that connected us in the first place. They asked that I start with an article about a school that was built on the lip of Glen Echo Ravine. The school was designed by one Frank Packard, who, I was told, had designed lots of buildings in the capital city.

My curiosity was piqued, because Columbus is not a city renowned for its architectural achievements. We're known for college football, or artisanal ice cream, or maybe as a test market. The state government lives here. Much of the city looks like it was built overnight, and many apartment complexes and condominiums are literally constructed from the same blueprints. To say the city is devoid of architectural distinction is an understatement. An accurate one. Developers like to build mixed-use buildings along the High Street corridor, which runs north and south through the entire center of the city. Every now and then, as you drive up or down High, you might spot an older building that survived the demolition and development onslaught. Chances are, the building that caught your eye was designed by Packard.

Frank Packard was born in Delaware, Ohio, in 1866, and took a few architecture courses at the Ohio State University. He transferred to the Massachusetts Institute of Technology, where he studied Beaux Arts architecture, and finished his degree. He returned to Ohio and settled in Columbus, where he became known in the Arts and Crafts movement as a champion of using the natural elements of the surrounding

area of a building in the structure itself. He designed houses from stone by nearby quarries. At the end of his career, his architectural firm designed approximately 230 buildings, many of them in Columbus alone. He was prolific and he seemingly suffered through no scandals. He didn't seem to hunger for fame. He simply seemed to do his job.

Which makes him seem remarkably midwestern.

My article about Frank Packard pushed me into the preservation movement in town. I was inspired to do every walking tour provided by a local organization that produced art walks throughout various neighborhoods. I attended a Columbus Public Schools community meeting to speak up for a building designed by a Packard mentee. The system decided to go ahead and tear it down, because the system in town often makes that same decision. Each time another demolition began, I thought of Packard. His work was all over the city, and the city seemed determined to wipe it out.

Without Packard's buildings, though, I didn't know the city. Those buildings had been standing long before I arrived, and several were standing when I did finally get there. I may not have known much about them, but I noticed them. They were an important part of my memory of the city, and what is a city if not a place that exists in the minds of the people who live there?

I traveled around in the United Kingdom in 2017. I needed things to do in Scotland, and I didn't want to do the usual pub crawls or tourist fare. I wanted to do things that sounded like things I would do. I signed up for a class on "narratives of place" at the Scottish Storytelling Center, planned a van excursion to the Isle of Skye, and bought a ticket to a walking tour around Glasgow that focused on the work of Charles Rennie Macintosh, the man behind the Glasgow Style.

I took the train from Edinburgh. I'd be in Glasgow only as long as the tour, and then I'd commute back to my bedroom in New Town, where I'd sleep away the chill I was developing in Scotland in June. I was not prepared for the hills of Glasgow, and I was out of breath as I arrived, finally, at the Glasgow School of Art. I stood in the gift shop, chatting with other Americans who were gathering for the tour, proud of myself that I got on the train and didn't scrap my plan and stay in the other city. In my brief walk through Glasgow, I already had a sense of just how different it was from Edinburgh. I knew that a walking tour would be a mere snapshot, but it still felt like an important point on my self-designed itinerary. Our guide, an architecture student at the Glasgow School of Art, introduced herself and as we stood in a circle around her as she explained that that we'd be seeing Mackintosh buildings, as well as buildings designed by his contemporaries, which were contemporary at the turn of the century, when the Glasgow Style came into existence.

The Glasgow Style was immediately recognizable by its font. The free map we'd been given for the tour had the Glasgow School of Art logo on the front, and the font was distinct. A popular television program at that time was even using it for its title credits. I felt as if I had a head start in what I'd learn during the day, but I would be woefully corrected once we made our way around the city.

The tour included gems of Scottish architecture, designed by men whose work came long before Mackintosh. Our guide pointed out work Mackintosh had contributed to, as well as work done while he was a junior in his field. We heard tales of his wife, Margaret, and even gathered in front of the Glasgow Society of Lady Artists, which was established in 1882. We learned about tea room culture and Mackintosh's role in designing the places where artists would come together. I was fascinated. I felt like I really got to know the man, and I'd been in his city for less than an hour.

I'd lived in Columbus for a total of eleven years at that point, and I could not tell you the name of Frank Packard's wife.

We wound our way around the city, and our guide led us to a small museum of Mackintosh designs. We were told to explore, and we would meet back on the street in half an hour. Tour participants scattered throughout the building, free to learn on their own for a bit.

While I was wandering about, I happened upon a display that included photos of the architect's home. Right in the center was a framed quote that said, "Yes, dear, this is the architect's own house, and if it had been in our country he would have been Frank Lloyd Wright." The quote was attributed to, "AMERICAN WOMAN IN THE MACKINTOSH HOUSE, TALKING TO HER DAUGHTER, 1992."

Yes, the attribution was in all caps.

The quote stopped me in my tracks. My first thought was, "Of course, that's the only architect we know or celebrate in the states." My second thought was, "Why?"

Frank Lloyd Wright designed some amazing buildings, certainly. Many use enterprising incorporations of natural elements, such as a stream running beneath the structure. He lived a big life, one that included scandal, and for some reason, I remembered that he sought fame. He cared deeply about his reputation. He left one wife and his mistress was murdered and his home and studio were destroyed in a fire. I stood there in the center of Mackintosh lore, and thought about how in the States, we worshipped the architect with the flashiest life.

We didn't spend much time thinking about the architects of the buildings we used everyday. We made

architecture exotic, something we travel to see. Or at least, I did. I knew there were local tours that pointed out significant buildings, often Packard's, in Columbus. I'd been on them. But, those tours did not make me think much more about the man responsible for designing the landmarks of the city I called home.

❦

I came back from Scotland with an idea.

I had vague knowledge of different pieces of a puzzle, and I wanted to put them together. I knew that the art school in downtown Columbus had a "Packard Library." I knew that there were four or five buildings designed by Packard in a corridor in walking distance from said library. I knew that it was not difficult to walk around downtown Columbus, and that there were several routes I could connect in my mind that passed several Packard buildings.

I had coffee with a friend who works in historic preservation.

I mentioned the Mackintosh tour. I mentioned how easy it would be to walk around downtown Columbus and point out the work of Frank Packard. I mentioned how important the small Mackintosh museum was to the Glasgow tour.

My friend mentioned a state agency that awarded

planning grants for projects like cultural heritage tours. I nodded. I said, "Good to know."

From there, I went home and started to make inquiries.

I emailed a contact at the art school and asked, "Hey, do you know if the Packard Library is named after Frank Packard?"

She didn't, but she forwarded my message to an archivist there saying, "She should be able to help you."

And she did.

It turned out that the archivist had recently been tasked with creating a display about the life and work of Frank Packard for the entryway of the Packard Library, which absolutely was named for the architect, who donated money to the art school that was just getting off the ground at the turn of the century. Columbus College of Art and Design was born from the minds of a small group of women who started an art school at the brand new museum. Packard contributed to the efforts to start an art school. He did not design the school, but he had a hand in it. Packard had more of an impact on the city than just designing the buildings that populated the landscape.

I began to design a tour of Packard's architecture that incorporated the bits of his story that I knew. I wanted to walk a path that extended beyond the buildings and their facades and revealed a legacy that had yet to be properly celebrated. I held the Mackintosh tour up as a measure of such.

Reader, I applied for the grant. I was awarded the money to assemble a team of humanities professionals, myself included, and design "Packard's Columbus Walking Tour," which highlighted his work, as well as the work of his peers. It would include time at the Packard Library, where participants could take in the display about the man whose presence made an indelible impact on the city of Columbus.

In a room in the Columbus Metropolitan Library, the small team gathered. Joined by the Packard Library archivist, two employees of the local landmarks association, and a woman from the state historic preservation office (who was writing a book about Packard), we deliberated the best route, duration, and distance for a tour. We confirmed the existence of restrooms along the route. A ticket price was set. In a little over an hour, we created the equivalent of the Mackintosh tour, but for our own Frank Packard.

The tour begins and ends at Columbus College of Art and Design, with the display at the Packard Library. Although Packard's work is sprinkled throughout the city, in its suburbs and along its ravines, the concentration of his work downtown, in a one and a half mile walk, says a lot about his presence in the capital city.

"Franklin County Memorial Hall." Photo by Amanda Page.

"Seneca Hotel." Photo by Amanda Page.

"Atlas Building." Photo by Amanda Page.

You can barely walk a block without seeing a structure that he touched in some way. In the first minutes of the tour, for example, you encounter the Seneca Hotel.

I once worked next door to the Seneca Hotel. It was a rat-infested structure that my boss called "an eyesore." I thought it could be magnificent. A developer must have thought the same. In 2008, the hotel was converted to luxury apartments, and an architecture firm keeps an office on the first floor. On the tour, you walk past it at the beginning and you walk past it at the end. It is a true landmark, and on the Packard's Columbus Walking Tour, it is a beacon. It assures you that your journey is almost complete.

The hotel is on the opposite side of the street, though. The first Packard-designed building that you come to on the north side of Broad Street is Columbus Memorial Hall. It was built to honor veterans, and to be a venue for big bands—one that rivaled Madison Square Garden. I remember it mostly as COSI, the Center of Science and Industry. It was a popular destination for elementary schools looking for field trips, and it was filled with space capsules and hair-raising static electricity machines. The center eventually moved across the river, and Columbus Memorial Hall removed the shiny black glass facade and reverted back to its more traditional Packard look, along with its focus on veterans affairs. The county's Veterans Services Commission moved in to exist among several other county offices.

The Empire Building sits at the corner of Broad and Fourth. When the building was constructed, it was named the Yuster Building, but eventually became the Empire Building, and like many of the buildings in Packard's Columbus, it was eventually listed on the National Register of Historic Places. The white stone used to erect the building is reminiscent of that used for Columbus Memorial Hall, and contrasts with the brick on display in many of the Packard structures in downtown Columbus.

Next to the Empire Building, and moving west along Broad, the Athletic Club is exactly what the name suggests: an athletic and social club. Founded in 1913, it has been host to several notable folks who've come through the city. It stands now as a beacon of economic class, its blue awning reaching toward the street, ready to cover the members as they walk from curb to door. The Athletic Club eventually earned a plaque from the National Register of Historic Places as well.

Continuing west, you'll reach the corner of Broad and Front streets, where you can consider the Scioto Mile, which is a 175-acre park along the Scioto River. Packard developed a plan in 1908 that utilized the river and the riverfront. The city eventually did incorporate some of his plan into the new and improved waterfront, although it is hard to tell exactly what parts without studying the plan online before you enjoy it in person. In the distance, beyond the river and further down Broad Street, you can see the Packard and Yost designed Toledo and Ohio Railroad

Depot that was made to mimic the Macklin Hotel that once stood beside it. Both structures included pagoda-like pieces of architecture, and the former train station still stands out as a remarkable landmark in the landscape of the city.

The next leg of the tour includes a walk up a slight incline, back to High Street, where you head north to the Atlas Building on East Long Street. Built to be a savings and trust, it's undergone two major renovations. The first floor window long featured an ad for "New York City Style Living," in the building's apartments.

Turn east toward Fourth Street, where you'll turn right to walk past the Columbus Athenaeum, which was constructed as a meeting place for Masonic lodges in 1899. The building has acquired several additions through the years, but the Packard flair is unmistakable. It is the last Packard building you pass as you head back to Broad Street, and a bastion for weddings and teacher conventions. If you've driven on Fourth Street with any regularity, you've slowed down to watch gussied-up guests spill out of the building and light up the street.

The final stretch along the south side of Broad takes you past the Columbus Club, a formidable mansion that became an exclusive club in 1886. Many an Ohio governor has been honored there. The house is spectacular, and passerbys can assume it still stands as a playground and gathering place for monied locals.

As you pass the Columbus Club, you get closer to the Seneca Apartments, and you know your tour through Packard's Columbus is coming to an end.

The entire tour has a radius of less than three miles, and yet, it introduces you to only a small selection of buildings in the Packard legacy in downtown Columbus. Walk further along Broad and you'll pass two churches and a mansion made from Packard plans. But, because they're not inside the easy loop identified by the experts on the planning team, they must be encountered on their own. You can drive past them. You can drive all around Columbus to see Packard's work. But for this particular journey, a walk makes the most sense. You can stand beneath the buildings and understand their scale. You can absorb the history of the structures. You can listen for their ghosts.

The tour will be led first by the foremost expert on Packard and his work, Barb Powers from the state historic preservation office. She will train other guides who will continue to produce the tour. The hope is that the audience grows beyond the already curious. The hope is that it creates interest, possibly even of art students who pass the buildings almost every day. The hope is that the tour fosters connection between those who live in the city, and the man who helped design it.

❧

I no longer live near the ravines.

At least, not near the ones where Packard has a presence. I've moved north, closer to a different ravine, one that separates my neighborhood from a small Usonian one. I walk my dogs near the houses inspired by Frank Lloyd Wright, and I think about the American woman who understood his fame, his impact, his legacy. She stood in the house of a famous Scottish architect and thought of the most famous one in her own country. I've found that not many people in the city know of the Usonian neighborhood's existence. If they do know, they've never been through it. Fewer know the name "Frank Packard." If they do know, they rarely know his work by sight. It took a trip across the Atlantic Ocean for me to care more about making his name known. It took a two-hour architectural tour in Glasgow for me to understand what it's like to know the story behind the buildings you pass every day.

I no longer live near the ravines, but I still tell the stories of the Packard buildings along them. I walk my city and ask that others do the same. There was a man who designed the buildings of our lives. There is a presence here. The name is Packard. ❖

"Earl Young and fireplace in Weathervane Restaurant." Photo courtesy of the Charlevoix Historical Society.

Stories in the Stones:
Earl Young's Boulder Buildings

JONATHAN RINCK

Most people affectionately refer to them as "Hobbit Homes," nestled, as they are, on streets with charming names like Thistle Downs. But the earliest was erected nearly two decades before Tolkien introduced Hobbiton to the world in 1937. These quaint, stony curiosities have their origins in the Paleolithic-era Wisconsin Glaciation dating from 100,000 to 11,000 BCE, give or take several millennia. This glacier carved the western coast of Michigan and left in its wake a coastline strewn with massive boulders, many of which found their way into the stone-built houses and commercial structures that populate the gently undulating coastal hills of Charlevoix, Michigan, a small resort-town cozily situated on an isthmus between Lake Michigan and Round Lake.

These beguiling stone structures were the imaginative creations of Earl Young (1889-1975), a realtor never certified as an architect. Organic, curvaceous, and defiantly bucking architecture's slavish infatuation with the rectilinear, they've received media attention in sources like HGTV's *Extreme Homes* and *Martha Stewart Living*. It's easy to understand their mass appeal; who *wouldn't* want to live in a quaint stone home capped with a thatched roof, furnished with a flamboyant fireplace, and positioned with a commanding view of Lake Michigan's blazing sunsets? As a realtor, Earl Young had a vested interest in luring potential clients to this part of northern Michigan. Nevertheless, Young's architectural philosophy seems to possess real depth, and even rhymes uncannily with the artistic intent of America's twentieth-century starchitect Frank Lloyd Wright. Though Young's homes seem almost to have popped out of a children's book of fairytales, they amount to *serious* fun.

The stone homes for which Earl Young would become famous were the product of an enduring love Young had for the city he called home for nearly his entire life. Born thirty miles south in Mancelona,

Michigan, in 1889, Young and his family came to Charlevoix in 1900. The small resort town had been an attractive tourist destination since the late 1800s thanks to both its proximity to so much water and its distance from so much urbanization. With his Kodak camera, a teenaged Young showed off his latent artistic potential in the rugged beauty of the region.

In 1914, Young studied at the University of Michigan's School of Architecture, but dropped out after a year, disenchanted with what he perceived as the stifling classicism of the school. Returning to Charlevoix, he married his high-school sweetheart, Irene Harsha, in 1915 and set up shop, first as a photographer, then as an insurance agent, and finally as a realtor, a job which supplied Young with an incentive to help Charlevoix live up to its deservedly self-imposed nickname, Charlevoix the Beautiful. To this end, Young once even joined an association of local business owners who purchased waterfront land on Round Lake specifically so it would remain undeveloped—during the Great Depression, no less—preserving for visitors the commanding view of the lake and marina still enjoyed today.

Although Young laid the stones of his first home in 1918, he had been collecting boulders from the Lake Michigan shoreline for years. All his life, Young traveled Lake Michigan's coast in search of particularly interesting rocks and boulders, carting them off and burying personal favorites in the woods for later use. Never writing down their measurements, Young simply remembered their dimensions, and—sometimes decades later—would exhume them for use in various building projects. This system, such as it was, was mostly foolproof, though in one instance, an 18,260 pound boulder which had lain buried for twenty-six years proved to be too large to fit in its intended spot inside one of Young's commercial ventures. "It must have grown eleven inches after all those years in the ground," Young quipped to his exasperated workmen; he stuck to the story for the rest of his life. Doing all he could to help beautify the town and make it more appealing to tourists, Young even deposited favorite boulders in strategic locations in Charlevoix's city parks, without permission. His well-intentioned efforts were tolerated by the locals, if not always appreciated. But, tellingly, none were removed after his death.

These stony deposits from the Wisconsin glacier became the substance of Young's architectural endeavors. Supplementing his university studies by learning from local stonemasons, Young claimed he taught himself how to build because he couldn't get any contractors to agree to his own wildly eccentric plans. His first creation was his own home on 304 Park Avenue, built between 1918 and 1921. This Arts and Crafts style home emphasized natural elements in place of the factory-made, its outer walls fashioned entirely from Charlevoix boulders, which emphatically anchored the home in every sense to its location. The home's roof sported deep overhanging eaves, and its recessed entrance gracefully blurred the

"House called Abide, 1938." Photo courtesy of the Charlevoix Historical Society.

"Weathervane 1954." Photo courtesy of the Charlevoix Historical Society.

distinction between interior and exterior space. The home has been radically altered since its construction (the pitch of the roof significantly increased, and its original wooden shingles replaced with thatch), but its original form established the vocabulary that defined all Young's subsequent architecture.

Visitors who venture a mile southwest of the city center to the shoreline resort village of Boulder Park, the largest concentration of Young-built homes in the town, will see Young's architecture at its most articulate. At thirty-five years old, Young purchased this undeveloped swath of land in 1923 and divided it into eighty-five asymmetrical lots. Prices began at $100 each, and in a memorable attempt at business acumen, Young enticed early buyers with the prospect of winning a new Ford Coupe. While most of these homes weren't built by Young himself, those that were reveal Young's robust love of nature through their evocation of organic forms, leading critics and tourists alike to remark that they seemed to have sprung up from the ground.

Young took the contours of the landscape into account when designing a home, as seen in his undulating roofs that echoed the serenely sloping lots upon which they were built. "I start with the roofs and shove the homes under them," Young once said. The cascading roof of his especially Hobbit-like "Half-house," for example, possesses subtle crests and valleys in respectful mimicry of its immediate surroundings.

In Boulder Park, Young liberated himself from the tyranny of the right angle, preferring instead more organic forms. He even abandoned rectangular windows, as most dramatically demonstrated in the pair of circular, anthropomorphic "eyes" in his appropriately named "Owl House." Even his working process was organic . . . and exasperating. He never worked from blueprint; the plans for his works only ever fully realized in his imagination. Much to the consternation of the stonemasons, Young—and only Young— knew where each boulder ought to be placed, and he kept a watchful eye over the building process.

The Mushroom House, Young's most iconic home, was inspired by the low, rounded form of the Michigan button mushroom. Its walls were up to three feet thick in some places, and its owners have never been able to definitively assess its precise square footage because of its curvaceous walls. One's gut reaction is to call it otherworldly, but that would be exactly wrong; the home looks so emphatically worldly and natural that one can easily imagine that it slowly sprouted from the ground, or perhaps somehow always existed as part of the terrain. Even his shingling became spontaneous: when Young discovered the professionally trained roof-layers were methodically laying each stone shingle carefully and flush, he, visibly flustered, began throwing slate shingles haphazardly onto the grass, exclaiming "*This is how I want you to lay them!*" Within easy walking distance from downtown Charlevoix (unlike his

Boulder Park homes), the Mushroom House became for many Young's definitive work, and visitors and locals alike affectionately refer to all Young's homes as "Mushroom Homes," regardless of their inspiration. Curious passersbys frequently peered into this storybook home's inviting windows at night to catch a glimpse of its interior, so one owner found it necessary to plant a friendly barrier of shrubs and flowers around the house as a subtle deterrent.

The interiors of Earl Young's mushroom homes were every bit as nature-inspired as their exteriors, not least because of their rustic stone walls. In 1948, when he designed a home for the owner of 79 Gas Corporation, Young stood on a grassy spot that would eventually become the living room, and said, "From this spot, I want you to see one third grass, one third sky, and one third water." The finished home boasted a living room window that showed those elements in exactly those proportions, visually bringing nature into the home. Young sometimes created nature-inspired furniture for his homes, like the rustic wooden table he fashioned for Boulder Manor. But the focal points in each of his structures, whether domestic or commercial, were their sometimes exaggeratedly large fireplaces, which, far more than simply being utilitarian, allowed Young to create unrestrained, expressionistic sculptures in stone.

His wildly original fireplaces integrated nature into his homes by the ton. The diagonally striated stone of his Mushroom House fireplace consumed an entire wall, and is as ambitious as a mural in its scale. (Little surprise that it was once featured on an episode of HGTV's *Extreme Homes*.) The stones of another radiate outward, as if imitating rays of light, or perhaps a spider's web. But his most monumental fireplaces are to be found in his two commercial ventures: The Weathervane Restaurant and the Weathervane Terrace Inn. In 1954, Earl Young completed construction on the Weathervane Restaurant, nestled along the bank of the town's Pine River. Like his homes, the building was constructed entirely of boulders, one of which was so large that it had to be split just to be moved. The visual fulcrum of its interior was a nine-ton boulder which capped the fireplace in its main dining room. Discovered (and promptly buried in the woods) by Young nearly three decades previously, the boulder looked—with some imagination—like Michigan's lower peninsula, replete with veins delineating its highway system with startling accuracy. And the imposing fireplace in the breakfast room of the Weathervane Inn—constructed with just a few staggeringly large, tactfully positioned boulders—seems more befitting of the Nordic Vahalla than of a Michigan resort hotel. But his most visually complex fireplace is to be found in the lobby of the inn, which, using stones much like mosaic tiles, ruggedly depicts a bird's eye view of the Pine River emptying out into Lake Michigan as seagulls fly overhead.

It might be tempting to write off Young's stone buildings as kitschy architectural bait to lure tourists—and potential clients—into the town, and Young certainly had a financial interest in making Charlevoix attractive. But the way he articulated his love for Charlevoix stone (and their sheer weight and burdensomeness) suggests a philosophical depth and obsession that perhaps makes these structures something more than just novelties. For Young, each stone was a piece of Charlevoix's history made tangible, and their histories left him wonderstruck. "Stones have their own personalities. People say I'm crazy when I say so, but they really do," Earl Young passionately asserted to an interviewer in 1973, and one can detect a sense of wonder in his tone when he continued, "I found a stone that weighed 160 tons. It was formed 350 million years ago at the bottom of a warm sea and was carried here 10,000 years ago by glaciers." To better understand these stones, Young would send samples of his stones to geologists to learn their respective histories. No surprise that when Young began writing a history of Charlevoix (only its first two brief chapters ever published, in serial form, in the *Charlevoix Courier*, the local newspaper) his opening chapter began with a poetic and affectionate account of the Wisconsin glacier which scooped out Round Lake and left the area strewn with boulders:

The advance and retreat of the last glacial age of 10,000 years ago became a tool which tore away great quantities of material, great cliffs of stone, and shoved ahead to gouge out future landscapes. And in this way, Michigan was formed with its north and south ridges and valleys, with its varied-sized lakes and streams, leaving our own immediate area uniquely different from any place else—situated not back on a deep bay away from the blue waters of Lake Michigan and not in an unprotected place, but with the indentation of the big lake shoreline broken only by a winding stream [Pine River], widening to a jewel-like, land-locked, deep water right up to the shoreline harbor of Round Lake.

Young's homes were a tangible expression of his affection for the land, in an era when prefabricated Sears Roebuck homes could be purchased from a catalog and assembled anywhere in the United States. His homes, counterculturally, asserted the importance of local materials and local histories.

Furthermore, though Young ardently denied the influence of any other architects, it's difficult not to detect the uncanny parallels between Young's work and that of America's most celebrated twentieth-century master builder: Frank Lloyd Wright. Wright—who also stalwartly denied being influenced by anyone—championed an architecture that celebrated local materials. His beloved Fallingwater applied only stone local to the land for which it was commissioned. Wishing to seamlessly integrate his homes into the Midwest's predominately flat landscape, Wright developed the Prairie Style, a type of home that emphasized its horizontality to match the region's terrain. Wright believed in the integrity of total design, going so far as to design the furniture that furnished his

interiors. Each of his homes was custom-built specifically for the needs of each individual client, as the Meyer May house in Grand Rapids, for which everything inside—from the height of the doors to the placement of the windows—was designed specifically for May's height at just over five feet. Wright believed that the fireplace, a space that united the family, should be the center of the home. The sum total of these attributes was a finely-crafted architecture that eschewed America's infatuation with the mass-produced and the prefabricated—"cardboard houses," as Wright sneeringly described in *The Future of Architecture.*

The parallels between Young and Wright are striking. Although Young wasn't as uncompromising as Wright regarding custom-made furnishings, Young would sometimes inventively find ways to craft unique furniture from local material. The cocktail lounge of the Weathervane boasted a table crafted from an 800-year-old redwood tree, and the upstairs bar was created from a two-ton plank salvaged from a schooner that had grounded near the town's shoreline. The fireplace mantle in Young's office in the lower level of the Weathervane was salvaged from a piling from Round Lake. (Young's office remains much the same today, and the mantle occasionally still sprouts with lichen, just as it did when Young was still alive, quite literally integrating living nature into the structure's interior). Like Wright, Young custom designed each home specifically for the needs of each individual client, once going so far as to live with a client in

Chicago for a week to better understand his lifestyle. And all of Young's structures were generally built from local boulders, though one notable exception, a meteorite ornamenting the Weathervane, may have its origins from the Kuiper Belt well beyond the orbit of Pluto. While an Earl Young home certainly wouldn't ever be mistaken for a Frank Lloyd Wright, the former characterized by an irrepressible architectural vocabulary of undulating stone, both architects worked toward similar ends: an architecture that respected the land.

Today, Earl Young's beloved "Mushroom Houses" have become a tourist attraction in their own right. The Charlevoix Historical Center now offers walking tours of Young's architecture, and several of his homes (including Young's original 304 Park Avenue home) can even be rented nightly. Travelers on a budget can still enjoy a meal at the Weathervane and tour Young's downstairs office. And Young's two Charlevoix hotels still welcome guests. So in the end, perhaps it doesn't matter whether Earl Young's architecture amounted to a frontal assault against America's conventionally mass-produced "cardboard houses," or whether they were simply whimsical play that just happened to resonate—however accidentally—with the architectural philosophy of Frank Lloyd Wright. Both men applied differing architectural vocabularies, but the ends of their intentions were essentially the same: the creation of custom-made, handcrafted architecture that respected nature.

In one revealing instance, Earl Young was offered the potentially lucrative prospect of designing and selling blueprints for homes that could be produced elsewhere across Michigan. Young would have none of it. His homes, he insisted, were inseparable from the terrain for which they were designed, and simply couldn't be mass-produced. They were designed both for—and from—Charlevoix's land, and to transport them elsewhere would be to ignore the stories within the stones. ✠

Wilson Hall at Fermilab. Energy.gov.

The Architecture of Fermilab:
Building a Quirky Science Lab in the Middle of an Illinois Cornfield

MATTHEW R. FRANCIS

I didn't come to the prosaically named Silicon Detector building for its roof. I was there to look at some cutting-edge telescope technology, soon to be implemented at one of the world's leading observatories. But here I was looking up at the interior of a funky squashed geodesic dome, constructed of triangles in muted reds, blues, and golds, like an electron micrograph of a virus built of stained glass by Buckminster Fuller.

The Silicon Detector (or SiDet) building itself is a squat concrete structure with sloping sides and a trapezoidal profile, a distinctly 1970s structure. The geometrical dome originally was intended to be a patriotic red, white, and blue, but time has faded it into autumnal colors.[44] The geometrical panels are made

out of recycled beer and pop cans with their ends cut off, arranged between two sheets of colored plastic reinforced with glass. Light shines through the cans, but not so brightly as to create a glare.

The SiDet building is all the more striking for what and where it is: it's a physics lab devoted to the fabrication of next-generation detectors for experiments and telescopes. More specifically, SiDet was originally part of a facility meant to study neutrinos: very fast-moving, low-mass particles that are notoriously hard to detect.[45] Similarly, the facility itself is hidden from the general public's view behind a security perimeter on the grounds of the Fermi National Accelerator Laboratory, more commonly known as Fermilab. Named for Enrico Fermi, the physicist who—among many other accomplishments—led the first successful nuclear chain reaction experiment, Fermilab was designed to be the United States' flagship particle physics facility, created to probe the fundamental particles of nature and the forces that govern them.

Since I'm a science writer specializing in physics and astronomy, my interest in Fermilab science is self-explanatory. However, it was Fermilab's architecture rather than its science that caught my eye on this visit: sparks of humanity among the faceless institutional cement cubes. Like the beer can roof, these buildings are pleasing when their more fanciful elements work well, and frustrating to occupants when they don't. The search for subatomic particles is far removed from daily experience, but here, it's intimate and familiar, literally made from any household's refuse. The flourishes like SiDet's roof were relics of the era when particle physics was in full flower, pushing to discover new particles and test more exotic theories, and the architecture reflected that spirit. Like the physics experiments they housed, some of the fancy buildings were wild successes, while others were interesting failures. Bravery isn't universally successful in any venture—scientific or architectural—but buildings that survived to the modern era were remade to fix their flaws, like a repeated experiment that benefits from prior failures.

Fermilab, located in Batavia at the western outskirts of the Chicago megalopolis, is a 6,800-acre complex with dozens of buildings. Some of those, like a few barns, are relics of the days when Batavia was a rural community. Today, Chicago's exurbs have grown to envelop the region.

If you aren't one of the physicists who work at Fermilab, you need to have special permission to get past the security gate to see SiDet. Like a sensitive teenager's artwork, painted only to be seen by perhaps one or two friends, the building is both flamboyant and secret.

Fermilab has a number of these semi-hidden architectural gems: spirals, scalloped roofs, and other geometrical features appear throughout the facility. Even the power lines running into the complex were designed to look like the Greek letter pi (π).[46]

Mixed in with these architectural monuments to the heady heyday of 1970s particle physics are the hideous utilitarian sheds and trailers housing many of the research scientists, and the unimpressive boxy metal structures containing some of the major experiments. Portions of the extensive Fermilab grounds are as close to wilderness as you can achieve in suburbia. Though surrounded by all the trappings of modern urban sprawl, Fermilab is home to a small herd of bison, along with coyotes, herons, and other wildlife—a true nature preserve, worth visiting for that reason alone.

The lab's many quirks reflect both its history and the vision of its first director, Robert R. Wilson (1914-2000), who served from 1967 to 1978.[47] Though he was a physicist with a remarkable scientific pedigree, Wilson also studied sculpture at the Accademia di Belle Arti in Italy. He was born in Wyoming in a town literally named Frontier, and kept up his Western affectations even as he moved from place to place. The herd of bison was his idea, and he was known for riding around Fermilab on horseback.

In keeping with his interest in art, Wilson either designed or directly influenced the architecture of many of Fermilab's buildings, including SiDet. He particularly wanted the lab's headquarters to be a significant and attractive structure. Architect Alan H. Rider worked for the architectural firm Daniel, Mann, Johnson and Mendenhall, which was part of the consortium of architects, contractors, and engineers that built most of Fermilab's buildings.[48] (Among his many projects, Rider helped design the John F. Kennedy Memorial at Arlington National Cemetery).

In 1976, Rider wrote a perspective on the headquarters building, which would later be renamed for Wilson:

> In recognition of the intellectual intensity at which the physicists work, it was considered important that their physical surroundings be attractive and comfortable, while avoiding any feeling of regimentation. At the same time, the physicists were to be encouraged to meet and interact with each other and with the other lab personnel as a means of promoting the cross fertilization of their ideas . . .[49]

At fifteen stories and 200 feet in height, Wilson Hall is by far the tallest structure around, and undoubtedly Fermilab's most famous building. Its shape reportedly was inspired by the Gothic cathedral in Beauvais, France, though to someone of my generation, its sweeping curves create a profile strongly reminiscent of the Atari logo.[50]

The building has an inner courtyard extending nearly the height of the building, with glass from base to ceiling on either end creating a space filled with light. Many offices look onto the atrium; none of the windowless and airless workspaces typical of academia. The courtyard level, which visitors enter via doors at the top of a broad set of stairs, contains a garden of ficus plants. Balconies overhung with ivy look over the open cafeteria space at the far end, which is a common gathering place in accordance with Wilson's original vision. Overall, Wilson Hall's atrium is one of the most attractive spaces in science, like a museum atrium dedicated to particle physics.

Not all of Wilson's ideas were so successful or well-received by Fermilab staff. He was under a lot of pressure from the United States Atomic Energy Commission to finish a world-class national laboratory in seven years, with a budget of $240 million.

(That's roughly $1.8 billion in 2018 dollars, which isn't a lot of money for a construction project consisting of dozens of buildings.) For that reason, Wilson had his builders recycle as much material as they could, up to reusing whole farm buildings. He also took personal responsibility for which corners to cut, or more precisely: which floors to lay.

To be specific, Wilson reasoned that a lab didn't truly require cement floors, when the Illinois turf would do (and save money at the same time). As a result, this multimillion dollar state-of-the-art physics laboratory originally had many buildings with dirt floors. The Meson Lab, one of the larger structures, had a roof made out of steel culvert plates that leaked onto the dirt floor in the rain. Fermilab physicists ended up battling water and mud in addition to the typical experimental snafus. As Wilson wrote years later with Fermilab historian Adrienne Kolb:

> The building itself, originating from my fevered brain, was a triumph of architecture (well, in my opinion), but it was something of a catastrophe from a practical point of view. I am ashamed to report that the users therein regarded it more as an Inferno than the Paradise I hoped it to be.[51]

"I still find it difficult to understand why those users all stopped speaking to me," he joked, but his light tone masked a defensiveness: he thought he was doing the best he could under difficult financial circumstances. (It's also easier to laugh about it when you're not the one trying to protect delicate equipment during a midwestern thunderstorm.)

SiDet building was also originally floorless. "The geodesic roof of that metal structure leaked badly during rainstorms and the floors were dirt," wrote Paul Halpern in his book *Collider*, "so team members often needed to wade through muddy puddles to get to their equipment."[52]

The Fermilab sheds, unofficially known as the "proton pits," were even more notorious among scientists.[53] These were simple metal huts without any toilets or other amenities. These were designed to be movable to various places along the kilometer-long tunnels along which the protons traveled, but in practice were inadequate shelter for the experiments they housed. Wilson noted that, despite those problems, physicists first detected a new fundamental particle in the proton pits: the bottom quark, also known as "beauty." That "beauty" was discovered in a place of mud and mayhem is somehow apt.

By the time I visited Fermilab in 2012, the dirt-floored buildings were gone or modernized.[54] For instance, the SiDet building bore no trace of its original dirt-floored state, and the funky geodesic roof was sealed so it no longer leaked. The original centerpiece of the building was a huge particle detector known as a bubble chamber. This was a huge metal construct designed to track particles produced from a source over a kilometer away. To save money, the builders reduced the size of the building, making it slightly too small for the bubble chamber. Wilson fixed the problem by designing a cutout in one wall, with an odd-shaped structure to accommodate the detector's dimensions. Physicists using the building called it "Wilson's nose." (Unfortunately, the "nose" is gone and as far as I can tell, no pictures of it are online.)

Fermilab held a drive to collect enough cans to make the roof, and even constructed a special machine to cut the tops and bottoms off the cans. Though the drink can roof was partly a cost-saving measure, Wilson took ecology and recycling seriously, and was willing to spend money on it. He kept much of the grounds open as a nature preserve, recycled materials wherever he could as a deliberate reduction of waste, and turned scrap into art. The "Broken Symmetry" sculpture standing at the gates was made of the leftover material from a surplus battleship used to build a particle detector.

Like all science—like all architecture—politics looms large over Fermilab. Even the facility's location in Illinois was likely one of President Lyndon Johnson's deals, in this case as a favor to Illinois Governor Otto Kerner Jr.

Robert Wilson and his deputy director Edwin Goldwasser worked for open housing policies in the community around Fermilab, and made overtures to Martin Luther King, Jr., who faced some of the worst violence of his career in Chicago. Wilson implemented an equal opportunity program for Fermilab staff even before federally-mandated affirmative action. (As you might expect, the research physicists were then as now largely white and male.) The herd of bison was an homage to Wilson's Wyoming origins, but he also hired a Native American caretaker to manage the animals.

Wilson resigned from his directorship in protest over lack of funding in 1978. Not long after, Fermilab opened its biggest experiment: the Tevatron, which turned up more fundamental particles, including the first tantalizing hints of the Higgs boson. I visited Fermilab shortly after the Tevatron's closure (again from budget cuts), which felt like an end of an era: the big science version of Rust Belt uncertainty. The facility has lingering traces of Wilson's stamp, largely from the buildings themselves. From the Archimedes spiral of the water pump building, to the sculptures, to the surprising roofs on concrete-block structures, touches of art make Fermilab something other than just another faceless science facility.

In a famous piece of testimony before the Senate in 1969, Wilson said:

> Are we good painters, good sculptors, great poets? I mean all the things that we really venerate and honor in our country and are patriotic about. In that sense, this new knowledge has all to do with honor and country but it has nothing to do directly with defending our country, except to make it worth defending.

Looking past the Cold War phrasing necessary for congressional appropriations, it seems fitting to recognize that basic science—like architecture, like art—is inseparable from humanity and culture. The architecture of Fermilab as expressed by Wilson is as much a statement of values as it is about function, with its accompanying successes and failures almost a metaphor for the scientific process. Sometimes science needs a geometrical roof made from recycled beer cans. ⊠

Darst-Webbe Public Housing, 1971. Courtesy of the Missouri Historical Society, St. Louis.

"The Projects": Lost Public Housing Towers of the Midwest

MICHAEL R. ALLEN

When I was thirteen years old, I was standing next to a public housing tower at the Darst-Webbe Apartments in St. Louis, photographing the abandoned City Hospital, when a rock struck next to me on the sidewalk. A teenaged boy shouted at me from a mesh-enclosed gallery between two brick-clad slab sections that were part of a Y-shaped tower. This was one of seven towers that composed the project, designed by Hellmuth, Obata and Kassabaum and completed in 1960.

I looked up at the stark, unadorned buff brick walls, the small window openings, the open vertical galleries with stained and multiple-times-painted metal mesh guards. I'd never really recognized modernist architecture before, but these buildings began to dawn on me as something alien to the vernacular city. Later, I would read the words of architectural historians like Vincent Scully, who castigated such buildings as part of American urban renewal's "bureaucratized and brutalized phase." Most writers were even less generous. The towers were "the projects," shameful and failed architecture eviscerated from the canon of American modernism.

Yet at the time I first noticed the towers, around 1994, people were fighting fiercely to save Darst-Webbe—architectural merit be damned. Its towers would be gone within just seven years, replaced by a different kind of housing project. The sturdy brick towers, which vibrantly proclaimed both an architectural modernism and a staunch service to residents, disappeared as the federal HOPE VI (Housing Opportunities for Everyone) program claimed Darst-Webbe and many more high-rise public housing projects nationwide. HOPE VI did not require one-for-one truly public unit replacement, and residents went to federal court—unsuccessfully—to retain the 1,225 units of public housing at Darst-Webbe.

Darst-Webbe was gone by 1999, and today its superblocks have been carved into a semblance of traditional urbanism, although with strange jogs, dead ends, and park mall sections to its streets. The streets are lined with

a jumbled assemblage of buildings with strange clip-on details, obviously veneer brick cladding, and ominously fenced side and rear yards. The landscape is lushly planted, but with a homogenous palette of plants straight out of a garden catalog. Few people are out front of buildings, and none of the buildings or lawns give any clues who lives here. Strangely, the old Darst-Webbe landscape, with its stark and unplanted lawns and open parking lots—the work of landscape architect and Washington University professor Emmet Layton—seemed more evocative of residents' identities.

By the time of Darst-Webbe's demise, HOPE VI had already decided the fate of St. Louis's other high-rise public housing developments—with other midwestern cities like Chicago in the works for clearance and replacement as well. These modernist towers once defined the centers of cities, forcefully aligned with the urban renewal freeway system. No one could approach the inner-city areas of St. Louis or Chicago without confronting clusters of nearly identical towers that gave architectural modernism its staunchest—and most controversial—presence in the urban landscape. Today, only a handful of outliers remain in the Midwest, including Ralph Rapson's Riverside Plaza (1973) in Minneapolis, whose six buildings forcefully impact many views of the city. Yet Rapson's artful details, including colored panels, soften the tower forms. Old towers like Darst-Webbe were value-engineered down to basics—down to the most elemental interpretation of architect Adolf Loos's axiom that "ornament is crime."

Top: Pruit-Igoe. USGS. Bottom: Cabrini-Green Housing Project in Chicago. Chicago Bridges Recording Project. Library of Congress, Historic American Engineering Record archive of photos. HAER ILL, 16-CHIG, 148-1.

These towers, of course, had symbolized the ills of architecture and public policy since the Department of Housing and Urban Development (HUD) had initiated the demolition of the massive St. Louis project of Pruitt-Igoe, with three towers brought down in 1972 and the remaining thirty leveled in 1976. Pruitt-Igoe, riddled with crime, broken pipes, and trash-strewn corridors, came to symbolize the failure of new architecture to remedy the ancient ill of urban poverty. The spree of high-rise demolitions that followed would only confirm the fact, not rebuke it.

Yet Pruitt-Igoe had been an endemic part of the St. Louis skyline, and rightly so. Its sleek, modern brick high-rises often take a beating for embodying Le Corbusier's ideal of the *ville radieuse*, while in fact they were a compromise between architectural idealism and bureaucratic pragmatism. The 1949 United States Housing Act funded Pruitt-Igoe as part of a wave of similar urban public housing projects. The federal government had never directly funded housing project construction, but instead had provided financing that had to be remunerated. The 1949 housing act defined a robust federal involvement in housing poor and working people—a provision that accompanied a resounding inflation of mortgage guarantees for new homes segregated racially to whites and spatially to suburbs.

The Public Housing Administration (PHA) favored standardized high-rise building types—a radical, massive version of Corbusier's tower in the park—for their capacity to rehouse large numbers of people, and their supposed cost efficiencies. But there was nothing utopian about American public housing modernism. It represented efficiency and a break with the image of the historic slum, and architects ended up dictated by rather than dictating to federal and local bureaucrats.

Pruitt-Igoe's lead architect, Minoru Yamasaki, at first fought any plan for modular high-rise buildings, urging instead a cluster of mixed-rise structures. But when the precursor to HUD forced Yamasaki to embrace two standardized eleven-story building types, the architect delved into modernist and vernacular traditions to sculpt an environment of thirty-three buildings with many overlooked features.

The towers at Pruitt-Igoe, completed by 1956, had south-facing, open, windowed galleries that admitted lots of light, Their skip-stop elevators attempted to encourage social interaction by limiting easy walks from elevator to apartment doors—some people had to walk stairs and meet neighbors along the way. The landscape below featured playgrounds and eventually a public library, community center, and gym. By the 1960s, the St. Louis Housing Authority had a very detailed and strong landscape plan prepared in part by Harland Bartholomew Associates, which was never fully implemented. Still, Pruitt-Igoe had through intent and execution benefitted from clear and deliberate attention to the design challenges the project posed. Similar ideas worked in other parts of the world, such as Brazil and Yugoslavia, making the indictment of modernist design as the fundamental flaw a glaring occurrence of American lack of self-awareness.

Along with Pruitt-Igoe, the most extreme examples of the new public housing project design were Chicago's Robert Taylor Homes and Cabrini-Green. The Taylor Homes consisted of a regimented landscape of twenty-eight sixteen-story double-loaded corridor towers—adjacent to the eight-tower Stateway Gardens project—that made Pruitt-Igoe seem almost plutocratic by comparison. Designed by Shaw, Metz and Associates, the towers encompassed 4,415 units, making the Taylor Homes the largest single project funded by the 1949 United States Housing Act. The lines of these towers for years ran for more than two miles along the Dan Ryan Expressway, south of the city's downtown core. While the Taylor Homes died in infamy, their forms actually balanced expansive urban views with a counterpart providing poor people with the same luxurious scene—just as Pruitt-Igoe was called the "poor man's penthouse" in early years.

Larger than the Taylor Homes, and even more notorious, was Chicago's sprawling Near North Side complex of Cabrini-Green. The project actually evolved in ten stages from 1942 to 1962, and was a collection of adjacent projects rather than one single project. The Frances Cabrini row houses were fifty-four low-slung, two-story buildings; a later extension added fifteen redbrick low- and mid-rise buildings. The William Green high-rise towers, designed by Pace Associates, consisted of fifteen-story double-loaded slabs with redbrick cladding set into an exposed white concrete grid. These towers, known as "the whites," became potent national symbols of public housing, perhaps even more than Pruitt-Igoe's towers. A more favorable view was disseminated by Norman Lear's Cabrini-based sitcom *Good Times* (1974-79), the only US network television show set at a public housing project.

Yet Cabrini-Green already possessed a divided symbolism by the time of *Good Times*. Architecture critic Lee Bey writes that daily life at Cabrini-Green by the 1980s often produced "sudden and unspeakable cruelty and violence." The deterioration of conditions led Mayor Jane Byrne to move into the project for twenty-five days in 1981, although her embrace of the project did not alleviate its problems significantly. Toward the end of its days, Cabrini-Green was known notoriously for the chilling tale of Girl X, a nine-year-old girl raped, beaten, and left to die in one of the tower stairwells. Modernism began to seem culpable, with its alien-built forms mirroring a social alienation of life within.

Mostly the public narrative of life at Cabrini-Green, the Taylor Homes, Pruitt-Igoe, and other public housing projects perpetuated the same narrative about the slums they replaced. The synchronic conclusion of politicians, reporters, sociologists, and architects was predictable, because it was the same as the one reached about the old slums: the physical environment of the slums needed to be eradicated. Rarely did the narrative account for the paucity of resources given to residents for their own success, or the fact that federal housing money could only fund tower construction, not critical maintenance. The perception of the towers' ugliness allowed for a substitute target to replace the fundamental super-structure of human poverty.

The achievements of the towers in delivering fireproof dwellings with central heat and plumbing, the features like beautiful upper-floor views and open play areas, the durability of the buildings that made them ripe for rehabilitation—all were immolated on the pyre of blame. Under the administrations of presidents George H. W. Bush and Bill Clinton, the seed of antagonism toward towers germinated into HOPE VI. Along the way, though, the federal commitment toward direct provision of housing withered, and lagged into a guarantee of a semi-privatized program that reduced housing units and introduced private profits.

It seems too obvious to note that the HOPE VI regime has replaced a series of pungent, durable architectural forms with timid buildings designed to last less than fifty years. In the breach between these modes of providing public housing lies an attendant diminu-tion of resources for public housing, rather than any meaningful reform. Thus midwestern cities are left with a more palatable era of public housing ahead of an impending crisis—when the brick veneer-clad platform frames of the replacement housing start to fall apart with even less available federal money for repair and replacement.

As awful as life at the towers may have been, and as disreputable—if not sinister—their forms became, they represented a real investment in the lives of poor people. They provided a rupture from traditional urban forms, allowing cities space to resolve whether more responsive architecture with modern amenities could make a difference in the lives of working peo-ple. Of course, the towers failed to solve problems of wealth, education, and happiness, but not nec-essarily by design. Architects like Minoru Yamasaki involved in public housing design ultimately had too little power in shaping their forms and details, not too much. Yamasaki even privately predicted Pruitt-Igoe's failings after losing battles with PHA for a plan with fewer towers, which he thought needed balance to produce a livable human environment.

Walking past the chain stores where Cabrini-Green once stood or the plasticine streets south of downtown St. Louis where rocks were cast from high-rises by errant teens, one can envision the inability of architec-ture to work magic without any concomitant change in public policies related to health, education, and welfare. One also sees that the American psychosis of race still stands in the way of meaningful change. The towers were easy scapegoats for a society unwilling to give its resources directly to human needs, but always willing to build monuments to its own virtue.

"Site of Cabrini-Green House Project today." Photo by Gabriel X. Michael.

Someday, perhaps, when the replacement housing fails, urban governments will confront the roots of poverty that Pruitt-Igoe neither confronted nor exacerbated. When that day arrives, however, the federal government that forced cities to build giant boxes, then to demolish and replace them, will likely evade any further assistance on a large scale. Already, under HUD Secretary Ben Carson, HUD is shutting down rather than repairing buildings with maintenance problems. Neither the Republican nor the Democratic party champions public housing any longer, as both parties rely on market liberalism to resolve housing shortages.

The missing towers in Chicago and St. Louis evoke the "Pruitt-Igoe myth" that urban designer Katherine Bristol identified years ago, but raise it some. The most dangerous myth about public housing is that it no longer is the public's responsibility—that architecture, once blamed for social ills, now has become neglected altogether in our discourse, because now we simply blame government intervention. The right stands by a libertarian bootstrap version of the myth, while the liberal left has its own anarchic construct that holds the systemic racism of the federal government (still not vanquished) as reason to not trust any future perfection. Both sides of the ruling ideology seem aligned in a quest against any future public housing.

Architecture, if exonerated, could resume the quest for new forms that might house people without destroying urban fabric. A new era of public housing ought to be in force, especially as precarity rocks the US labor market. Instead we cower behind policies that took the lapses of modernism as cover for gutting public housing and terminating any further possible architectural experiments. The Midwest deserves to reverse both, so that it can once again make visible and daring forms of care for everyone. As daggers of hyper-capitalist luxury housing rise in Chicago, Minneapolis, St. Louis, and elsewhere, replacing the order of care for the poorest with the exaggerated presence of the wealthiest, the moment calls out loudly. ✖

PLACES

Christ Church Lutheran, Minneapolis. Copyright Peter J. Sieger.

Finding the Sacred in the Secrets of Christ Church Lutheran, Minneapolis

SOPHIE DURBIN

If the Midwest is the big family that birthed Modern architecture in the United States, Minnesota is the quiet middle child. The subtlety of Minnesota design surprised me when I arrived to visit for the first time on a spring break trip. I grew up in the Chicago and Detroit metro areas, which may well be the matriarchs of the Midwest modern clan; my teen years in Chicago in particular so accustomed me to the extremes of modern architecture that I was surprised when I visited cities without it. When I attended college in Appleton, Wisconsin, the architectural footprint was less oriented toward opulent austerity. However, Wisconsin architecture still came with a pedigree as the "Frank Lloyd Wright Trail" signs along the highway ushered all who passed them toward Taliesin, Wright's estate in Spring Green. Upon moving to Minneapolis permanently after college, I was stumped. There were a few Wright houses scattered

throughout the Twin Cities of Minneapolis and St. Paul, but of the quiet lakeside ranch variety; an apartment complex near the Minneapolis Institute of Art was curiously named "BAUHAUS," but for truly foreboding, imposing treasures you had to travel northwest to Collegeville to glimpse Marcel Breuer's campus buildings. I mistakenly thought Minneapolis lacked historically significant modern landmarks of its own. But when I stumbled upon Eliel Saarinen's 1948 Christ Church Lutheran, my eyes were opened to a Minnesota Modern[55] that echoed Minnesota Nice in its preference for subtext and an expectation that viewers read between the lines. Or, as Saarinen would say, "what is secret is also sacred" in both Minnesota's architecture and its culture.[56]

My first trip to Christ Church Lutheran took place on Good Friday, 2016. I had acquired a temporarily disfiguring infection on my face; instead of looking forward to my day off, I felt like a lonesome, conspicuous monster. As I cried into my migas and coffee at Modern Times Cafe, my boyfriend Eli asked where he could take me to feel better. I said I'd like to visit Christ Church Lutheran. Eli, who was raised in Milwaukee by a health food restaurant owner and radio DJ (and as of this writing has never attended a church service), was skeptical but accommodating. My interest in visiting was based off of little besides a vague knowledge of Finnish-American architect Eliel Saarinen as the designer and president of the Cranbrook Academy of Art, which I frequented on youth field trips in Michigan. I was also intrigued that the building featured a 1962 Education Wing addition designed by Saarinen's son Eero. Plus, growing up attending both Lutheran and Episcopal churches, Good Friday meant solemn services and the promise of the Easter Bunny. Perhaps I could take my mind off of my face and climb back into these childhood comforts in a house of God.

We arrived at the intersection of Thirty-second Street and Thirty-fourth Avenue—about four miles southeast of downtown Minneapolis and a little over a mile west of the Mississippi River—and parked in front of the church, a slick brick rectangle sitting square in the fourth quadrant of South Minneapolis's grid system. We proceeded to roam the grounds and explore what we could without going inside, given that no public tours would be offered that day and we had little interest in attending a Good Friday service. It was unseasonably sunny and snowless for late March and the church looked imposingly blonde and severe compared to the leafless trees and the modest single-family homes surrounding it. But the church's severity melted away fast. A rich multi-colored brick pattern stood out against the bare-leaved trees and still-frozen, dull green ground; a courtyard joined the 1948 church building with the 1962 Education Wing, complete with a fountain. Each wall, ever so slightly nonparallel, corrected itself into a straight line as you moved from one end to the other. Aside from a few sculpted panels of biblical scenes, three crosses of Calvary on the south wall and a slender aluminum cross affixed to the tower, we found no religious ornament. When our feet were numb from the bitter cold, we were itching to go inside and see how intact the original interiors might be. My childhood churches, which had been Episcopal or Lutheran, generally fell on the Gothic spectrum. Aside from a few piano recitals and bar mitzvahs, I was up to this point unfamiliar with the ins and outs of most sacred buildings from the twentieth century. Once it was time to take me home to nurse my face wound, Eli and I had reached the following elegant conclusion: you know those drab modernist churches you see *everywhere* across the Midwest but at first glance cannot imagine how they'd be spiritually inspiring? *This* must be the prototype.

It turned out we were partially right. In 1942 Saarinen designed his first modern church, First Christian Church, in Columbus, Indiana. Christ Church Lutheran followed in 1948. Smaller and more streamlined, Christ Church Lutheran echoed First Christian Church's dramatic lines and towering church tower on an intimate scale. It began as a cheaper alternative to the original congregation's desire for a Gothic Revival church design.[57] Saarinen, the son of a Lutheran pastor, combined foundational modern and Lutheran ideals to create a space where the building materials, lines and even the acoustics worked together to stimulate the discovery of the divine. His modernism mirrored the aesthetics of Martin Luther, who saw the spiritual potential in beauty beyond literal, narrative biblical images. It was not only a testament to the effectiveness of modernism in a church setting but also the first great example of this in a Minnesota sacred space.

Nearly three years after our first visit, Eli and I attended the official monthly tour offered by the Friends of Christ Church Lutheran, a group dedicated to the church's promotion and preservation. At the time, I was wading through the elder Saarinen's "The Search for Form in Art and Architecture," a deceptively dense meditation on everything from Saarinen's childhood to his thoughts on the role nature should play in artistic innovation. In his closing thought, Saarinen ponders the secret and the sacred. If something is hidden, and someone deems that thing important enough to search for it, that thing is sacred to that individual.[58] I joined the tour looking for secrets and was gradually rewarded.

"First Christian Church, designed by Eliel Saarinen, Columbus, Indiana."
Carol M. Highsmith/Buyenlarge/Getty Images.

Starting with the exterior, we learned that the brick pattern had been carefully selected for its spiritual significance. Our guide explained that the sculpted panels along the east wall were carved by Saarinen's fellow Cranbrookian William McVey and depicted "Faith, Hope and Charity, and the Education of Children."[59] She pointed out an inconspicuous window along the south wall. "This window will be very important later in the tour," she said as she shepherded us into the church.

As my eyes adjusted to the darkness inside, I was first struck by how *plain* everything was. Aside from a small icon of Christ temporarily propped on an easel near the altar and the cross itself, there were no figurative images to be found. Then I noticed that the silver cross above the altar was illuminated by a soft, hazy natural light. The light came through the window our guide had pointed out, hidden to congregants. I imagined the cross's shadow growing deeper in accordance with the time of day, offset to the right until a fully formed twin hovered alongside the silver one. This gave the church's signature tagline, "Welcome to the Light," a pleasant double meaning. While our group walked haltingly down the aisle I noticed a rippling pattern undulating in the dark brick leading up to the ceiling on the north wall. The tour guide, gesturing to the choir loft, explained that the ripples enhanced the acoustics throughout the hall; that I could perfectly hear her quiet voice from fifteen pews away proved her point. Above the choir loft, the ceiling performed another sound-absorbing trick by slanting from left to

right. There was no need for images. Martin Luther believed that the inner secrets of God are first revealed through outward, material signs.[60] The Christ of Christ Church Lutheran showed himself to us every time we experienced one of these material signs: the soft light at the altar, the shadow of the cross, the soft waves in the brick and the perfect distribution of sound.

The tour progressed into the Education Wing. I marveled at how the Christ Church Lutheran congregation and the Friends of Christ Church Lutheran remained dedicated, after seventy years, to the church's upkeep. The Education Wing was astonishingly stocked with original details. In the quaintly titled Luther Lounge, we sank into immaculately preserved couches and Papasan chairs, fixtures in the room since the 1960s. Next to a Sunday school classroom in the main hallway, a room dedicated to church archives made use of utilitarian mid-century chairs, some complete with ashtrays affixed to their spines. A gymnasium, also located on the lower level, boasted original wood paneling on one wall and was nearly as acoustically immaculate as the nave of the church. Despite the painstaking lengths to which the congregation went to maintain the church's original innovations, the air was welcoming and warm inside. Dinners and community events were held regularly in the gymnasium; in the Education Wing, parishioners chatted over fresh coffee and pastries. Children chased each other through the recently revamped fountain centered in the courtyard between the two buildings. The air was not of a stuffy historical artifact forcefully frozen in time but a respectfully preserved living tradition.

There was another, more obvious aspect of Christ Church Lutheran that I recognized to be uniquely Minnesotan: its Lutheran-ness. The *Star Tribune* newspaper reported in July 2017 that one in four Minnesotans is Lutheran and that Minnesota is home to more Lutherans than any other state.[61] Minnesotans of all walks of life, from grandchildren of Swedish immigrants living in Minnetonka to Hmong families in St. Paul, are likely to return to a Lutheran church for a baptism or Christmas service. It is a fact of growingly secular life that the Lutheran church loses members each year. Regardless of this trend, Lutheran culture reigns supreme in Minnesota. Friday fish fries, as common among Upper midwestern Lutherans as with Catholics, run year-round. As the *Star Tribune* article put it—the Lutheran church in Minnesota has an "image as a Scandinavian bastion best known for hot dish, Jell-O and Ole and Lena." While Christ Church Lutheran's congregation is more likely to invite visitors for coffee than hot dish, its gymnasium dinners and general friendliness are prime examples of Minnesota Lutheran hospitality. The church design itself, too, is essentially Lutheran. The nave's pure acoustics would have delighted Martin Luther, who praised music as a "gift of God and not of man" that "drives away the devil."[62] The silver cross above the altar, the singular focus during any service, also meets the Lutheran preference for simple decoration that brings the worshiper back to Christ. Saarinen's design created a perfect vessel for Lutherans looking to access God through the outward physical experiences Luther spoke of hundreds of years prior.

At the end of the church tour, I found myself daydreaming about joining the congregation, cooking spaghetti dinners in the downstairs kitchen and tasting coffee and cupcakes in the Education Wing lobby after services. This, of course, did not happen. I still appreciate the core compassionate lessons and spiritual mysteries at the heart of Christianity. But after years of being forced to rise early on Sundays and a reckoning with the church's violent history, I simply don't feel drawn toward organized worship as an adult. I guard my empty weekend mornings fiercely. Still, if I were to join a church I would pick this one. There is no place I have visited that is more in tune with the subtleties that drew me to Minnesota, the quiet middle child of Midwest Modern. In a city with a Chain of Lakes rather than a Great Lake, near a point in the Mississippi River that you can swim across without fearing for your life, Christ Church Lutheran doesn't attempt to lure visitors in. It waits patiently and rewards those who do with the quiet revelation of its secrets. ✠

"Indiana beach at dusk." briethe/flickr.

Estranged Twin Cities:
Gary and Magnitogorsk

ERIC LAWLER

On the border of Europe and Asia, just east of the south side of the Ural Mountains, lies a Russian mining town called Magnitogorsk. In 1928, Joseph Stalin inaugurated the first five-year plan to move the USSR into the industrialized world stage and required a central location to concentrate its industrial transformation. If the USSR was to adopt Stalin's policy of Socialism in One Country, Magnitogorsk would be a scaled-down version of Socialism in One City, a prototype for what the socialist future could be for the elevation of humanity.

The year of that inauguration, a delegation of Soviet industrialists and scientists met with industrial consultants in Cleveland to help design a massive iron and steel complex in Magnitogorsk. With eyes on the future, the USSR would leave behind their agrarian past. Iron foundries, blast furnaces, rolling mills, and chemical plants would all be built on virgin land, at a tabula rasa mega-development meant to transform the Old Russia into a modern industrialized nation.

Magnitogorsk would become an ideological PR campaign as much as a massive first step to realize Stalin's dream of the USSR as a completely independent socialist power and as a "country made of metal." The Soviets found their industrial model in the booming Midwest and instructed their Cleveland consultants to design the complex in the image of Gary, Indiana, a city twenty-five miles from Chicago on the shores of Lake Michigan, planned as a company town for the United States Steel Works. At the time, Gary Works was the largest plant of its kind, capable of annual raw steel production of 7.5 million net tons. US Steel had become the world's first billion dollar company, and by virtue of this achievement, stood as the flagship of US capitalism. Obviously here lay massive ideological differences between the two states. Gary's ultimate goal as an asset to US Steel was wealth accumulation and market saturation. Socially, it was completely deprived of any transformative power besides the liquidation of its labor force into

Ice fishermen in Magnitogorsk. Gerd Ludwig/National Geographic Creative.

more capital. But as a socialist project, Magnitogorsk was imagined as the industrial foundation for the Soviet Union to literally build its utopia. Here, end goals were further ahead and much more lofty, likely more noble, yet forced the USSR into a position of constant, hypernormalized defense.

Murders and Executions /
Mergers and Acquisitions

In 1901, US Steel was formed from a gargantuan merger that combined the Carnegie Steel, Federal Steel, and National Steel companies into the largest corporation in the world which would soon manufacture a majority of the planet's steel. In the top of US Steel's founding directorate were capital magnates John D. Rockefeller, J. P. Morgan, Charles Schwab, and Andrew Carnegie. These men were behind the largest monopolies and the uniquely American frontier-capitalism combination of rail, steel, and banking. Industrial organization was evolving away from a focus on singular function and towards a more profitable, holistic integration of many functions—all while dancing on the boundaries of antitrust legislation. For the founders of US Steel, their merger was an opportunity to physically consolidate operations for maximum efficiency. A site on the northwestern shore of Indiana was chosen for its proximity to an abundant water supply for steam and cooling, to the Great Lakes and their transportation potential, to rail connections, to manufacturing centers and coal mines, to the ever-expanding American West, and to potential workers. Here, the founding of Gary as a corporate company town was drawn as a necessary integration of all disparate functions of steelmaking and finishing, including the housing, entertainment, and education of workers and their families.

Gary remembered the Pullman Strikes of 1894, which were triggered by wage decreases that carried no corresponding change in rent from company-owned housing. Pullman Town was a planned company town for the Pullman railroad car factories. It provided rowhouses for workers to rent but offered no path to ownership. Not only this, the company was notorious for its strict standards of behavior, which meant eviction if broken. As Hardy Green notes in *The Company Town,* Judge Gary advocated in spite of the Pullman example for "corporate-welfare policies—including expenditures on visiting nurses, libraries, and playgrounds—that might be regarded as paternalistic." But instead of the visible stigma of the Pullman Company's control, US Steel chose to disguise its ownership through a simulation of independence, and the Gary Land Company was founded to provide all the infrastructure for this ideal company town. Gary was to be free, if only virtually, a place where employees were encouraged to own homes and businesses were private. The company's string-pulling would be hidden. Their role became much more metaphorically "underground" but also literally; the GLC acted more as a private subsidizing agent and contractor than as a town planner, much like the Cummins Engine company in Columbus, Indiana. But where Cummins simply subsidized

architects' fees, the GLC went further to level the land, lay out the streets, pave the roads, and install sewage and water systems. In this capitalist paradise, even heat and gas would be a byproduct of the massive plants. Houses were built and sold to workers for ownership, not rent. A progressive school district was designed to split days between academic learning in classrooms and active learning in gyms, auditoriums, and workshops. As Father/Boss/Mayor, US Steel wanted to make sure it appeared that they offset their investment interests by providing for workers livelihoods, like a good boss would.

The city was laid out in a cruciform with Broadway as the vertical and Fifth Avenue as the horizontal. At the head of Gary's cross, across from the Grand Calumet River, sits the entrance to Gary Works, situating the plant as a sprawling barrier between citizens and Lake Michigan. This lakefront access hierarchy forefronts the primacy of the plant: citizen livelihood is to be in service of the plant, that is, even if people are to leave comfortable lives, it's first and foremost for the benefit of the company. To enforce the north-south linearity further and to promote southern expansion, the Gary and Interurban Railway Company was founded to build a streetcar line along Broadway to connect the official city with the privately developed, cheap frame houses for immigrants to the south, mostly built by a local real estate developer named Tom Knotts. This side of Gary is important to show, for it lays outside of US Steel's property and had none of the restrictions on alcohol or lot sizes enforced in the north, not even requirements for sewage or running water. For a brief period in the 1920s, growth occurred but it wasn't until after the Great Depression that its productive capabilities began to boom.

At its peak, in 1943, US Steel employed 340,000 workers, a wave of prosperity that continued until the 1970s. After the 1967 election of mayor Richard Hatcher, one of the first African-American mayors of a large US city, racist apprehension caused a large number of businesses and professionals to leave the city. This following decades of racial segregation, increasing deindustrialization, and a slowing steel market left Gary in a state of unemployment and poverty. In the twenty-first century, all the previous idealism associated with Gary, and the Midwest, has been essentially depleted. Gary Works cut its employee count from 32,000 in the 1970s to nearly 7,000 in the early 2000s. It's no larger today. Mayors subsequently gambled on gambling, bringing Trump riverboat casinos and Miss USA pageants, and building stadiums for unpopular teams. Thousands of properties lay vacant. In the 1990s the city claimed the title of most violent city in the country. The Gary of the booming twenties feels so far away from that city that inspired a song in the 1957 Broadway musical *The Music Man,* in which Gary is lauded as preferable to "Louisiana, Paris, France, New York, or Rome." Today, Gary has been left to reckon with the ghost of its past.

It was a noble attempt at a company town, yet setting up a community reliant on a single industry invites devastation when capitalism inevitably ebbs. Gary was an exemplar of the general view of the Midwest as an industrial boom phenomenon, founded on finite resources in a market with an inevitable bust. Looking at the rise-and-fall histories of places such as Gary, their similarity to gold-rush mining towns is unavoidable, albeit stretched across a longer span of time. It's difficult to believe that US Steel was operating benevolently when the company founded Gary was simply to maintain a nearby pool of workers. US Steel assumed a libertarian distance when times were tough. Gary is a microcosm of all US industrial centers, a case study in the national shift from manufacturing to service, as capitalism globalized working communities to compete across borders and oceans.

Utopia Rushed

In 1921, the Congress of the Soviets ratified a massive plan to electrify the USSR. They drew up plans to build some thirty power stations for a nationwide capacity of 1.5 million kilowatts, to revitalize outdated and obsolete factories, and create new industrial centers. Magnitogorsk would be the industrial foundation for a fully-metal socialism, designed to showcase Soviet ingenuity and production potential. The Soviets saw Gary as a model with revolutionary potential to synergize humankind and technology, imagining a Soviet Gary in the New Russia, freed of the confines of the market, as a platform for capitalist society to evolve into its inevitable next form and to embrace full industrialization.

At its beginning, the design of the city was an ideological battleground between opposing factions of the architectural avant-garde, leading to Magnitogorsk being one of the most thoroughly researched projects in the first five-year plan. Numerous proposals were presented, with progressive plans by an Urbanist group led by Ivan Leonidov, and a Deurbanist team led by Mikhail Okhitovich. The Urbanists imagined a collectivized "linear city" constructed along the transportation routes parallel to the metallurgy complex in the form of solitary towers loosely separated, allowing sunlight into the units and green space around the housing blocks. In contrast, the Deurbanists drew up decentralized, distributed communities of individuals with housing "pods" that could be easily moved or transported according to an individual's desire. In its purest form, Deurbanism presented a techno-folkloric vision of a socialist future distributed across the countryside in dense developments surrounded by greenery. Their reaction against a congested and unhealthy density repressive of the individual was especially innovative in its identification of centralized density as a subpar capitalist concept for the benefit of markets. Their idea of decentralized communities pushed a vision that was more than just a planned version of what already existed under capitalism and instead proposed a radical solution to the ills of modern life which were, and still are, considered necessary evils.

The highly productive conditions of this insular and urgent community are arguably reason the Soviet avant-garde is still so relevant. Experimental ideas blossom in a realm of untethered freedom; new futures require new ways of building and living. To see these ideas built, proponents required an economic foundation and political support. Neither Leonidov's nor Okhitovich's proposals were carried to construction. If the conditions for these architects were more forgiving, perhaps trial and error would have been a viable path for their work to evolve into the built environment. However, as architect and historian Kopp states in his 1970 book *Town and Revolution: Soviet Architecture and City Planning*, "the radical proposals of the 'urbanists' and 'Deurbanists' did considerable damage to the cause of city planning in general by giving the impression that the term stood for nothing but byzantine discussions with little bearing on reality." The lack of real materialized praxis meant there were few case studies or experiments to draw legitimacy to their ideas. However, this failure to try is less the architect's fault, and more understandable in the context of the massive strains the USSR was feeling at home and especially internationally. As Kopp argues later in their defense:

> The citizen of the ideal city was still unborn, because neither machines nor materials, nor funds, nor labor; nor even technicians, apart from the avant-garde, were able to build it, because the former splendors of the ruling class were still accepted as standards of taste and ambition, and, above all, because the emergence of the new man could only follow, not precede, the satisfaction of all these conditions. Too late because the era of experimentation and a certain irresponsibility

were past, because the time and means were lacking to undertake research, especially when its immediate effect would have been to slow the construction effort, and because the illusion-filled dreams of the twenties had given place to the planned necessities of the thirties.

The avant-garde proposals sparked contentious debate in the pages of avant-garde magazines and in academic circles, yet failed to overcome the critical next step of gaining political support. Pressure to deliver results and the lack of modern construction technologies forced the choice of past, proven ideas. And so the Soviet government brought in the German architect Ernst May from Frankfurt to direct construction of the Steel City. He had gained a considerable reputation for his egalitarian Frankfurt housing projects of identical, equally spaced housing blocks with simple construction methods. He understood well that he had to adapt his designs to the technical and material capabilities of the less-advanced Soviet Union. In his proposal, May drafted a linear city with green belts dividing residential and industrial areas south of the plant. Residents would live in parallel rows of identical buildings, receiving a dwelling according to proximity to work. For May and other German architects, uniformity was a truly egalitarian method of planning. For the Soviets, it presented an opportunity to keep costs low, allow for an assembly-line construction site, and make efficient use of low skilled labor.

The ethos of creating social condensers to shape a new citizen was slowly being lost to pragmatic survivalism. It was becoming increasingly clear the five-year plan prioritized industrialization above all else, even housing. There was little hope that the priority of the nation's resources would be redirected from industrialization to anything else. As Le Corbusier observed in *The Radiant City* in 1967:

> Then one fine day, authority, which is the door of reason against which all dreams, just and chimerical ones alike, must eventually knock, authority in the USSR said: 'Enough! It's all over! And stop that laughing!' The mystic belief in deurbanism had fallen flat on its face!

Upon arrival in the USSR, May found that construction had already began and that his design was barely being followed. The planned community that was supposed to showcase Soviet social engineering and superior efficiency was being detrimentally rushed. There were many reported casualties from harsh, unsafe conditions and lack of skilled labor. An uncompromising deadline and shortage of labor led to dispossessed peasants and convicts forced into labor camps. No priority was placed on the disposable workers' housing and most lived in abysmal shacks and barracks filled with lice, rats, and bed bugs. With time, city essentials such as public baths, laundries, cafeterias, nurseries, cinemas, and workers clubs were built, but too late for the thousands that suffered or perished during its construction.

Built reality was far from May's initial plans and even farther from the utopias of his Soviet contemporaries. Magnitogorsk was be a last stand for the architects who years before proposed massively transformative solutions to the big questions of what the future would look like. On May 29, 1930, the Central Committee of the Communist Party denounced utopian schemes in urban planning, and claimed for the official party line that Soviet cities became socialist "from the very moment of the October Revolution," and that maintenance for existing housing and improvements for infrastructure had utmost priority, effectively ending the avant-garde project of redefinition. Housing became at best functionalist solutions, absent of any ideology. The beginnings of Stalin's defensive and reactionary Socialist Realism began to show.

Collective Lost Dreams

The differences between Gary and Magnitogorsk are vast: one was infrastructure for increasing profit margins, the other was infrastructure upon which a social transformation could thrive. But each city was a triumph of their country's ruling ideology with beginnings drenched in visions of alternative worlds. They were conceived as backdrops for the maintenance of collectively upheld narratives of their respective societies. The psychoanalyst Jacques Lacan calls this raison d'etre the "big Other." To him, this virtual set of beliefs replaces reality with a fiction in order to provide a cohesive solution to existing contradictions, horrors, or failures. In Magnitogorsk,

this played out in the narrative of a city holding up the nation, in spite of the global US-led blocks, sabotage, and obstacles facing their socialist experiment. In Gary, it was the great potential of what capitalism can provide for its people, choosing to ignore that the very forces behind the market which allowed US Steel to boom would also allow crashes and mass disinvestment if profits were better elsewhere: in other words, the American Dream. These narratives produced a massive ideological bubble that saw the big Other become an official belief system, in spite of its adherence to reality or not. In each of these ideologically inflated cities, there was a massive gap between dream and reality. Deindustrialization in the US, and an international failure of other workers' movements to produce socialist revolutionary coalitions in the USSR caused a cancellation of the futures promised by each ideology.

The Midwest is a region whose origins were always in world building and the creation of autonomous big Others. It is a place where people have rejected the norms fabricated to structure their lives and sought to tell their own stories. You can start over here. As Phil Christman has written in his 2017 essay "On Being Midwestern: The Burden of Normality," the Midwest was in its early years of American frontier colonization a utopic blank slate for societal experimentation. It was home to communes, dreamers, and fresh starts. It was a place to create a personal world beyond the control of organized religion or despotic rule, home to New Harmony, Indiana, an attempt towards an autonomous, extraterritorial community. The tradition of isolated world building in the form of small towns, local communities, created a sort of regional localism which gave the Midwest an identity of identitylessness, with descriptions which struggle to go beyond "they are good people" and "they work hard." The stereotype of a bland, featureless swath of land is more likely attributable to a deep-rooted localism than a rootlessness, which makes identity so difficult, where local pride in family, town, and state becomes the source of identity. This social cohesion is the strength of the region and is part of the mythos of small-town, Rust Belt America, which by its own story transformed itself from wild frontier into industrial backbone through its own blood, sweat, and tears. Yet when invaded quietly by a ruthlessly globalizing economy, this insular tendency turns into a shortsighted blame game between neighbors rather than a reassessment of the new global conditions and a reorientation toward better futures.

As we look back on the Midwest to the time before deindustrialization, we risk not noticing the rose-tinted glasses sitting on our nose. We see our home as an ideal, framing photos of the towns when they had streetcars and Broadway shows, busy crowds and booming growth. Yet now, choosing to ignore what happened to these places and why they're no longer golden, allowing an idealist abstraction of the past seems vastly irresponsible. We risk the continuation of the original naivete of the American Dream. The Soviets saw in Gary a catalyst for their vision of the future. Instead, the Gary in whose image they had built Magnitogorsk became the purest representation of capitalist apathy towards humanity, as industry left and its people were forgotten. The deindustrialization of and disinvestment in the Midwest demonstrates just how little regard the free market has for community investment. If profits leave, they pack up. Regionalism in the hands of global capitalism is reduced to a marketing tool for gaining trust.

Through the lens of these visions, achieved or not, the Midwest's built landscape is a world of fiction and propaganda, ideologies in the form of industrial architecture. The construction sites had whispers of better worlds and their demolitions decades later heard only the sounds of wrecking balls and dynamite amid the silence of disillusionment. The pursuit of better worlds is key to the evolution of any society. In the cases of Gary and Magnitogorsk, their failures occurred in the process of transforming a way of life into something that resembled utopia. Magnitogorsk was the Soviet Dream, and Gary the American, each presenting a snapshot of a world where an ideal society was eternally just years ahead, always within arm's reach. ✖

George Grant Elmslie; Architect: William Gray Purcell, United States, 1880–1965. Purcell-Cutts house, 1913. Various materials. Minneapolis Institute of Art, Bequest of Anson Cutts, 90.92. Photo courtesy of Minneapolis Institute of Art.

How the Purcell-Cutts House Defined Modernity, and Me

JENNIFER KOMAR OLIVAREZ

"Houses should not be clamps to force us to the same things three hundred and sixty-five days in the year; they should not be ordering us about regardless of breeze and sunset, but they should be backgrounds for expressing ourselves in three hundred and sixty-five different ways if we are natural enough to do so."
—William Gray Purcell,
"Own House Notes," about 1915

William and Edna Purcell meant for their 1913 house in Minneapolis to foster a new kind of freedom of living for a modern family, in an era of burgeoning women's equality and waning Victorian hierarchy. William decried the "style period" houses of the early twentieth century that he felt were "planned on a jumble plan of daily life within the house and an essentially aristocratic view toward the community." William and Edna Purcell wanted a home with informal, flexible spaces equally usable by both sexes, unlike the gender-specific drawing rooms reserved for women and billiard rooms or smoking rooms populated by men of the era. (William Purcell's architecture firm of Purcell, Feick and Elmslie, partnering with George Feick and George Grant Elmslie, even employed a female draftsperson, Marion Alice Parker, in the 1910s.) Thinking of social reform as well as architectural reform, William declared in his "Own House Notes," that "What we needed to do was to lose, not so much the parlor as the parlor idea of life, and when that went the resulting change in form bore witness to a very definite occurrence."

Edna had equal investment with her husband in a house that was ahead of its time in many ways—with walls of windows, an open plan, a sunken living room, stenciled designs in every room, and integrated artwork including a fireplace mural. In a letter to Elmslie, he proclaimed the importance of the double-height ceiling "Edna is crazy to have"—they also put a priority on her own office and library. The Purcells had dreams of the house practically becoming a member of their family, allowing for a new, informal, progressive way of life—Purcell and George Grant Elmslie even referred to it as "the Little Joker"—a playful house that wasn't like its regimented foursquare or revival-style neighbors. (Purcell's firm was staunchly modern for its time—Purcell and Elmslie were purveyors of the midwestern Prairie Style second only to Frank Lloyd Wright himself.) Visitors get a sense of the house's mischievous personality when they walk up to the front door and see the art glass windows on either side proclaiming "Peek a Boo." An added bonus was that the house was sited across the alley from the home of William's grandmother Catherine Gray, who as a widow moved to Minnesota from Chicago to be close to her grandson as a continuing supportive influence.

Ironically, the family said goodbye to their dream house four years later, when the First World War changed Purcell's business fortunes. Anson and Edna Cutts purchased the house in 1919, and enjoyed this home along with their son Anson, Jr., for the next sixty-five years. After Anson, Jr. bequeathed the house in 1985 to my museum, the Minneapolis Institute of Art (Mia), it became known as the Purcell-Cutts House, and I was lucky enough to enter a relationship with it in the early 1990s. I've come to realize that over my twenty-plus year involvement with the house as tenant, caretaker, curator, and champion—and as a woman—my family and I have built an enduring and intimate bond with the house, one longer than the Purcells enjoyed. Our uses don't mirror the

Purcell family's experiences from the early twentieth century, but reflect the house's forward-looking, nature-respecting characteristics that have served, inspired, and changed families for over a century.

Almost like getting to know someone through my new career as a curator, I met the house through friends and colleagues. The house, at first blush structured and refined, was at its heart warm and intimate. At that time our department used it for events for our support group, the Decorative Arts Council, many of whom were from my parents' generation and intimidating to a twenty-five-year-old intern like myself. While they enjoyed a formal catered dinner and talked about antique furniture, I ducked out with other young staff to the maid's room off the stair landing behind its tall door, dishing about museum politics and our love lives.

When my number came up to be caretaker, I learned it had some limitations—no being a slob, cooking meals with messy ingredients, drinking red wine, or slouching in the furniture (most of it is too rectilinear for that). But over the two and a half years I lived there, I learned the potential of the house—what it would allow, even encourage, me to do. The high-ceilinged, open plan living room with dramatic pendant lighting, augmented by windows that are placed to take advantage of the sun's movement throughout the day, is perfect for informal get togethers. I arranged a couple of cocktail parties with other young museum staff from Mia and the Walker Art Center, who were often first-time visitors and thrilled to be able to gather in a house usually reserved for structured tours. It comes alive for all types of gatherings, as it did in the early 1910s when Edna Purcell would entertain friends at the piano and the audience watched and listened from the raised dining room, a domestic performance tableaux impossible in a conventional home. The flow between entry, living room, kitchen, and back porch is effortless and flexible for lively mingling. It's still best for a cocktail party today, especially at twilight with the historic lighting fixtures. If I'm there at that time of day I feel like I should have a drink in my hand. The Purcells augmented the electric lights with "several dozen candles" (definitely not allowed today) when guests arrived, and William noted that "all parts of the rooms come into quite active use at the same time."

The downtime between monthly tours also allowed me to look at and experience more closely all of the details Purcell and Elmslie's craftspeople carried out that most visitors miss on a quick spin through the house. With extended exposure to the house, I noticed details like the iridescent glass embedded in the mortar joints of the fireplace that reflect firelight. The long window seat in this spot in the living room, with its wraparound windows looking out on the front garden allowed me to spend lazy Sundays communing with nature while enjoying coffee and the Sunday paper. Sensory exploration was easy in this quiet house—punctuated by architectural pilgrims knocking on the front door, or unexplained creaks

on the stairs long after I had gotten in bed. Were the latter visits from ghosts of the longtime second owners, the Cutts family?

The house served as more than a residence—it was a matchmaker for me. I had gone on one date with a colleague of a friend, and for various reasons nothing further transpired between us over the next year. Flash forward to me moving into the house, and I ran into Enrique while at my bank changing my address. I invited him over to a cocktail party, and he brought friends and raved about the house. He promised that evening that after he took his friends home that he'd be back to the party—yeah, right, I thought. He returned, and I figured he was a keeper. He visited the house many times, helping with mundane tasks and, like me, drinking in the beautiful details. Two and a half years later we were married there.

As accommodating and welcoming as the house is, the fact that most of it is a museum meant that it wasn't practical for newlyweds. Regular tours mean little privacy, and although residents can use the house, the totality of their personal belongings are confined to the maid's room off the landing, which is not on the tour. However, moving out of the house did not mean ending my relationship with it. I continued as curator with a series of caretakers, and still do today. It's a respite from my whirlwind office to go to the house to check on a contractor, bring over a fresh fern (the Minnesota winters aren't kind to them) or meet a visiting scholar for a tour. Enrique has continued to help when needed, and both he and my daughters have made decorations for holiday tours. My younger daughter even helped with training for some experimental tours with improv actors a few years ago. They've enjoyed the house as more than just visitors, without worrying about a stuffy homeowner or security guards. These many visits have given my now teenage girls more perspective on the architecture stops I insist on during virtually every vacation and many day trips, from Frank Lloyd Wright to Eero Saarinen to Charles Rennie Mackintosh. Historic houses are now in their blood, and they have even begun to critique their interpretation on our vacation stops. (A recent observation: On a house visit, my fourteen-year-old daughter wanted to see more historical room displays and less interpretation labels so she could envision how all the rooms were used.)

My house tours have evolved, too. As a young curator, I thought it was my role to know everything about the house; to be an authority. I used to lecture visitors, even those who were experts in my own field. As a more mature professional who isn't trying to prove herself, I recognize the importance of listening and learning from others. I try to back off a bit, especially when people enter the living room space. Because it's difficult to see in the front windows when standing outside, it's hard to get a sense of the interior space, especially the double-height living room, which makes it seem bigger on the inside than it appears on the outside. I like to see visitors gasp at this phenomenon

once they've entered the living room, kind of like the TARDIS from *Doctor Who*. They extol the beauty of the windows, the fireplace with its mural of Louisiana herons flying across an evening sky past Spanish moss-covered trees, the custom-designed furniture. I also wait for—and relish—questions I've never been asked. Try to stump me! Though I've read Purcell and Elmslie's correspondence regarding the house, much of which is preserved at the University of Minnesota's Northwest Architectural Archives, I don't have all the answers. At my age, that's really okay.

The house remains my preferred office-away-from-the-office. Though my days are now filled with meetings, I relish a lunch or a visit to the house tied to an errand, tour, or interview there, especially in summer. My blood pressure drops when I can enjoy the front garden as the Purcells did, evidenced by William's candid photos of Edna and their older son James relaxing among the flowers in the planters and the puttering fountain.

The house was meant to challenge conventional (and outdated) norms, allowing for an ease of living suited to 1913. Purcell recounted the story of the skepticism of neighbors upon seeing the wall of windows planned for the front façade, remarking that "they never wholly got used to" the idea of a young family with their life exposed like that. The large window wall is an essential part of the sunroom/dining room evolution that dominated the first floor, and Purcell proudly declared in his "Own House Notes" that this part of the house offered something like universal space for universal purposes. "One can live all over the single room of the entire lower floor according to the time of day or his mood," he wrote.

As an example, he describes an evening tea table set up in August not in the formal dining room, but (gasp!) the end of the living room by the wall of windows:

> . . . open toward the east with the little pencil stream of the fountain puttering away among the pale yellow water hyacinths, was the evening table so cool looking, with two little colored chairs[,] one lilac one. The house had begun to show its desire to say things at the right time. The coolest looking tea table in town, I'm sure—most of them that night sitting in the same surroundings that felt good last winter.

Two years ago I took Purcell's advice to let the house inspire you on how to use it, when my husband and I celebrated our twentieth anniversary. By chance, a museum colleague from out of state had scheduled a pre-cocktail hour tour with the donor group she was bringing that day. I thought it would be fun to bring together my professional and personal house experiences at the end of the tour, and instructed Enrique to arrive at the tour's conclusion with champagne for a toast to the house and our special day. In that moment, we enjoyed the late afternoon light and the beautiful windows with other art lovers.

It's interesting to reflect now on my place in the house's history. It was built before women had the right to vote in the US (though they served as architects and social reformers). It resonated with Edna Purcell as a co-created modern dwelling, sparkling with her piano performances. Two long-time widows, Catherine Gray and later Edna Cutts, spent time there, and Mrs. Cutts, recognizing the house's importance, resisted renovating the house after the Second World War. My job as a curator is different—it centers on preservation and interpretation—though curators develop strong bonds with their objects and environments just like a homeowner, and this is a perfect example. The Purcell-Cutts house has been a constant inspiration through my life milestones, and I consider it something of a "second home." I put it at the center of my professional life early on, and as such my personal life has hewn closely to it as well; an art object I've curated and cared for until it's become a part of me. ⌗

"First Church of Deliverance." Photo by Gabriel X. Michael.

Beneath the Cross in Bronzeville

MARK CLEMENS

Any discussion of the preacher or his church mentions the preamble to his weekly radio service, so one may as well start there:

> You in the taverns tonight; you on the dance floor; you in the poolrooms and policy stations; you on your bed of affliction—Jesus loves you all, and Reverend Cobbs is thinking about you, and loves every one of you. It doesn't matter what you think about me, but it matters a lot what I think about you.

The preacher is the Reverend Clarence H. Cobbs and his church is Chicago's First Church of Deliverance. The service was broadcast, as it continues to be, every Sunday night from 1934 on. "You" was anyone with reason to stay home from church: racketeers and petty criminals, gamblers, drag queens, those who found the church's demands tiresome, those who preferred enjoying their money to giving it away; in short, those who found no relief or even interest in the promise of heaven but were very concerned with their needs and desires in this world. Cobbs announced, in other words, that he wanted a flock full of black sheep.

Fittingly, his church doesn't really look like a church. It's long and squat, with a facade of terra-cotta tiles, mostly cream-colored with five pistachio stripes running horizontally the length of the building. A sixth, in red, marks the top of the building. No Bible stories in stained glass, but big glass brick windows. There is no steeple; instead, twin squarish towers flank the entrance a limousine-length apart. What it does look like is the kind of old movie theater that is the pride of small towns across the Midwest. It's easy to picture a marquee unfurled between the towers, the roof below studded with high-wattage bulbs.

Cobbs came from Memphis during World War I, one of tens of thousands of southern blacks who moved to Chicago in those years—the city's black population more than quadrupled between 1910 and 1930.[63] Almost all the migrants landed in the neighborhood that called itself Bronzeville, more or less Chicago's

Harlem: a "city within a city," a long, narrow strip on the South Side. In 1928, Cobbs was riding a bus when he heard the voice of God, bidding him to start a church. The First Church of Deliverance (God revealed the name to him, he said) began the next year, with the reverend preaching from an ironing board in the living room of his mother's home. He was twenty-five years old.[64] Soon he was operating out of a storefront—common practice for the poorer churches in town.

The church belonged to the Spiritualist tradition, a syncretic strain of Pentecostalism brought to Chicago by southern migrants. Seances and other psychic effusions were common practices. Like other Spiritualist preachers, Cobbs blessed and sold flowers, medals, and candles, promising they would bring luck and healing. Unlike other storefront Spiritualists, he drew crowds, enough that in 1933 he moved the congregation into a vacant hat factory at Forty-third and Wabash. This at the outset of the Depression, which was especially grim in Bronzeville, where every other family was on relief. Every black-owned bank in the city had closed. Consider what sort of person could raise $25,000 from the poorest people in the city during this time, and then consider the ambition needed to do it in four years.

Cobbs's aspirations did not end there. He needed a church that proclaimed itself unlike other churches, that his project was something new. The most venerable black churches in the city were beautiful, but

they were not built for their current parishioners—most were churches or synagogues purchased from white congregations who left the neighborhood as Bronzeville expanded. Cobbs would instead transfigure the old factory into something tailored to his message, something never seen before.

Work began in 1939, doubling the width of the building and adding a second story for the all-important recording booth. The expanded sanctuary held over a thousand people. To house all this, Cobbs commissioned Walter Bailey to remodel the exterior. Bailey was one of the city's most prestigious black architects—the first one licensed in Illinois—and had headed the architecture department at Tuskegee University, working under Booker T. Washington. First Deliverance would be the last project he completed—he died two years later.[65]

The church's style is technically called Streamline Moderne, sort of the populist cousin to Art Deco. Think of tiled subway stations, bus depots, railcar diners, and WPA-built post offices. The illusion of high velocity is common: corners rounded in big curves as if blurred, horizontal stripes known as speed lines. Glass bricks and chrome. Clean, with little ornament. The design was almost unprecedented in Bronzeville and church architecture in general, and was an odd late-career choice for Bailey, who worked mostly in the filigreed style popular at the turn of the century. One suspects Cobbs had more than a hand in it.

It wouldn't be surprising. Cobbs grasped the tenor of modernity and how to play to it. He understood the new media, not shouting over the airwaves like a tent revivalist, but speaking softly and directly, as FDR did in his fireside chats—"he comes on in a quiet manner as the counselor," says the historian Joseph Washington.[66] For music minister, Cobbs tapped the gospel composer Kenneth Morris, who paired a Hammond organ with his choir to create the sound of gospel music for the next forty years. Cobbs liked modern art, and would drop in on the bohemians at the South Side Community Arts Center (a coterie that included poet Gwendolyn Brooks and photographer and future *Shaft* director Gordon Parks), bringing them pop and sandwiches. There he met the artist Frederick Jones, who painted two murals inside the church and carved six massive oak doors for the entrance of First Deliverance (made, it was claimed, from a hundred-year-old tree on Cobbs's summer property).[67] The doors were declared a fire hazard in 2010 and were replaced by ordinary glass ones, though the originals now stand in the church's foyer.

The church actually did have a fire, in 1945. As part of the rebuilding effort, Cobbs took the opportunity to add to the building, commissioning Jones to do the doors and murals, and adding the two towers out front. They have large glass brick windows, which catch the sun in the evening and become two sheets of reflected light. A broad, flat roof aprons both towers halfway up the building, and the resulting H creates a deep cloister. Through the doors, the sanctuary preserves some

of the movie theater look of the exterior—its 1,100 chairs are cinema-style, with spring-loaded seats. The walls are intensely bright green, almost chartreuse. Windows of opaque glass line the sides, each with a neat gold cross in the middle.

Typical for Spiritualist churches, there are lots of touches lifted from Catholicism. A traditional high altar, complete with tabernacle, sits on a dais at the front of the room. Along the wall is a devotional niche with stadium-seated red-shaded candles. The dais is a good four feet above the congregation, with white leather furniture where the speakers sit during services. Two marble lecterns stand on opposite sides, repeating the proportions of the towers indoors. Behind the altar, surrounding it on three sides, is the choir loft, its walls trimmed in chrome. All this is taken in only after staring at the ceiling, for suspended lengthwise over the congregation is an enormous cross, made of frosted glass and lit from within by dozens of red and green lights.

The whole church is organized along the horizontal. The sanctuary is a shallow U, bringing every seat as close to the altar as possible. Fred Jones's murals—the only figurative art in the building—are both long and narrow bands of color. The exterior is dominated by the speed lines that streak across the building and the low roof over the entrance. It looks like the church is trying to stretch north and south to take up more of Wabash Avenue. And in fact, it has: the buildings on either side are owned by the church, one a center for children's worship, the other a day care and community center. Across the street is a nursing home, another Cobbs venture.

Cobbs does not fit neatly into the stock clergy types. In *Black Metropolis*, their exhaustive cross section of Bronzeville in the Depression, St. Clair Drake and Horace Cayton say that Cobbs "wears clothes of the latest cut, drives a flashy car, uses slang, and is considered a good sport." There's a photo of him at home in 1941, taken by Russell Lee: he's smoking from a long cigarette holder, seated in an easy chair, his feet up. He wears an ascot and robe, and has the pencil mustache and magnificent bastard smile of Clark Gable.[68] Once he made the gossip column in *Jet* for purchasing a twenty-dollar necktie with a $1,000 bill, and during services wore vestments rumored to cost as much as the pope's.[69]

This extravagance was used to the church's advantage. Showing off his lifestyle and befriending gangsters (often holding their funerals) told potential members that getting religion Cobbs's way did not mean forsaking the world, the flesh, and the devil. Washington calls Cobbs "a man of the street, of the people . . . a man of the cloth who did not fight sin, but joined it, accepted it, cherished it." Drake and Clayton are typically blunt and class-conscious in their assessment. "It is probable," they speculate, "that in a few years even upper middle-class people will not lose status by becoming members." This proved an understatement. In the 1950s and '60s the church was a place to be seen: black celebrities from

Duke Ellington to Redd Foxx attended services when they passed through town.

As much as he relished the wealth and status that came with his position, Cobbs was no Jim Bakker-esque hypocrite. Instead he seems to have tried to prove the gospels wrong, serving God and mammon with equal fervor. He was devoted to his community and held his money in an open hand. With First Deliverance he started a blood bank, a visiting nurses service, and a home for convalescents. If congregants couldn't pay their bills, the church covered them. In the late 1960s, Cobbs discovered the R&B pioneer Billy Williams living destitute in a flophouse, and took him into his home. When Williams died and no relatives could be found to claim the body, Cobbs went down to the coroner's office and demanded it be released to his care, then performed the funeral himself and paid for the burial.[70]

While attracting the rich and aiding the poor, Cobbs was also sensitive to those on the social margins. During the mid-twentieth century, First Deliverance was part of the gay nightlife circuit in Bronzeville, with some members going directly from the 11:00 p.m. service to the local clubs. The church was known as a safe place for the gay community, where no questions were asked and no judgment preached. Questions circulated about Cobbs's own sexuality for years—he often took his male secretary on his lavish vacations, paid for by the church—though he never admitted anything in public, and in 1940 sued a newspaper who reported he was the subject of a police investigation over "rumors of a scandalous nature."[71]

The architecture of First Deliverance, then, is a sort of portrait of its flashy, modern founder. The distinctly non-ecclesial facade blurs sacred and profane, a gradient rather than the sharp transition of most churches. The church is accessible, undemanding. *Black Metropolis* describes First Deliverance as catering to "the urban sophisticate who does not wish to make the break with religion, but desires a streamlined church which allows him to take his pleasures undisturbed." It is no coincidence that *streamlined* perfectly describes the church's architecture as well as its theology.

Perhaps this is the point of all First Deliverance's horizontals: the building reaches into its neighborhood, seeking to draw in people and, like a conduit, redirect their lives (if only subtly) and send them back out to the world. Inside the church, there is little need to look up, no cathedral vault or saints in stained glass. The sanctuary has a low ceiling for a church—heaven is very close here. It seems important that there is no large cross mounted upright, not on the altar or anywhere else. Rather, the giant, lit cross hangs over the heads of the people. God is not something to be approached after performing the appropriate rites; God is already with you, just above you, raining down light.

Cobbs has been dead for almost forty years, and his church has slowly waned in size and prominence. The current pastor, James Bryson, is taking a run at restoring its old stature, using a magnetic personality, social media savvy, and a strong dose of health-and-wealth theology. At a service in 2018 dedicated to remembering Cobbs's life and work, Bryson took stock of the state of the building. "It's been neglected for a while," he said, "we just have so much work to do—the towers are wrapped in wire because they're about to fall off." The terra-cotta work is chipping and cracking, sheets of galvanized metal hold some key places together. Time has been unkind to Bronzeville since the days of Reverend Cobbs, though no more so than the city government has been. Yet First Deliverance has recently received a grant for restoration work, and at the same service Bryson revealed that a downtown bank is lining up a large donation. "We're still here," he grinned. "Turn to your neighbor and say, 'I'm still here.'" The church burbled with hundreds of people affirming their endurance.

Cobbs is still there, too. On the sanctuary wall behind the choir is a mural painted by Jones. On the left side Cobbs is depicted blessing a mother and child kneeling before him. Shafts of light pour onto the scene. On the right is Christ himself, painted with the stylized bulging forehead of Eastern Orthodox icons. With his still-bleeding hands, he embraces a family and ushers them towards Cobbs. If you would find me, he says, here's the man to see. It is an outrageous self-anointing, though not out of character for Cobbs. In their white robes the two figures are mirror images, and suggest the towers standing outside the church, the pillars it rests on. Cobbs liked to refer to the towers as the Old and the New Testament, but it may be that what they really represented, to the man himself as well as the institution he built, was the preacher and his Lord. ✠

"Saginaw St., Downtown Flint, MI." Sarah Razak/Flickr.

The Flat Lots of Flint:
A Liminal State of Mind

BOB CAMPBELL

Don't it always seem to go
That you don't know what you've got til it's gone
They paved paradise
And put up a parking lot

Joni Mitchell wasn't singing about the harmful impact of surface parking lots in Midwest downtowns. But the sentiment seems on point. These asphalt stamps on the urban core leave much to be desired in terms of placemaking. In contrast to, say, a public park, being "an essential element of and economic driver for the expanding American city," as landscape architect Frederick Law Olmsted wrote in *Public Parks and the Enlargement of Towns*, surface lots are instead artifacts of a place diminished. They are the great eraser of Midwest architecture in old industrial cities like Flint, Michigan.

"Parking lots are too much associated with loss—the loss too often, at least in retrospection, of historically significant architecture. The parking lot symbolizes a system gone wrong," wrote authors John A. Jakle and Keith A. Sculle in their 2005 book *Lots of Parking: Land Use in a Car Culture*. There is no question that Flint—General Motors' birthplace—is diminished from its heyday as an industrial powerhouse with a flourishing urban core and a population of nearly 200,000 or so. Ironically, the industry that generated so much wealth and influence for the city also helped to usher in its contraction, as the wildly popular and now-virtually indispensable automobile made it easier for people to get away and, increasingly, stay away. And when the people did return, they needed places to park their Buicks, Chevrolets, Pontiacs, and Caddies. Today, downtown Flint is pockmarked with an assortment of surface lots where a density of low- to mid-rise buildings once stood.

One such lot is a central feature of Flint's downtown. It is known simply as "the flat lot," a city-owned parking space on Saginaw Street, the city's main downtown thoroughfare. The eight-story Smith-Bridgman Department Store along with the four-story Kresge's, part of the dime-store empire that would later become known as Kmart, once anchored that city block. However, the entire three-acre chunk in the moderately sized downtown was flattened in 1984 as part of a grand redevelopment plan to leverage the city's automotive heritage to lure tourists and conventioneers. The main attraction was an indoor park named Autoworld that, according to a 1985 *Los Angeles Times* article, was "hailed as the savior of Flint's crumbling downtown district." The park and plan built around it failed, but "the flat lot" remains.

The wrecking ball closed debate on the architectural significance of the Smith-Bridgman, Kresge's, and adjacent buildings on that block long ago. But memories of their cultural significance endure—from Smith-Bridgman's magical Christmas displays to Kresge's famed lunch counter—and evoke an uplifting communal spirit as captivating as Petula Clark's voice as she serenades listeners with "Downtown."

So go downtown
Things will be great when you're downtown
No finer place for sure, downtown
Everything's waiting for you

Charming and dreamy as the lyrics are, the essence of "Downtown" feels as contemporary as a Buick "Deuce and a Quarter." For much of that way of life, and the economy that sustained it, have been radically altered in Rust Belt cities like Flint, leaving swaths of downtowns that once provided a small slice of paradise (for some, at least) paved over for parking.

✤

Yet, a funny thing happened on the way to penning a melancholic piece about the state of downtown Flint's built environment. It began in the fall of 2017 with the demolition of a decrepit parking ramp on an avenue one block west of Saginaw Street and a couple of blocks south of "the flat lot."

Once that four-level, 800-space, early-1960s structure was knocked down and the rubble cleared from the three-acre site (yes, in preparation for a new surface lot), the striking grandeur of the two-story Flint Federal Building and US Courthouse the next street over became newly evident. Built in 1931 as a US Post Office, the concrete-reinforced Beaux Arts structure is a distinctive presence on Church Street, with its gold-tinted Mankato limestone exterior, decorative spandrel panels, stylized eagle above the front entrance, and monumental stairs flanked by two colossal, cast-iron lantern urns.

From the now unobstructed view from across the way, your eyes move easily from the Federal Building to its southeast neighbor—St. Matthew's Roman Catholic Church, a Romanesque-style building constructed in 1919 of "reddish-brown brick with limestone trim accenting the door and window openings, set off by a red tile, angular roof," according to *A Guide to Flint Architecture* published by the Flint Chapter of the American Institute of Architects.

With its large, limestone rose window on the exterior wall below the gable and above the ornate arched entrance, the facade more than satisfies the requirements set forth in the *Elements of Architecture*, a 1983 book by Luxembourgian architect and urban designer Rob Krier. In the opening paragraphs of the chapter on facades, Krier wrote:

> The facade is still the most essential element capable of communicating the function and significance of a building. . . . [It] never only fulfills the 'natural requirements' determined by the organisation of the rooms behind. It talks about the cultural situation at the time when the building was built; it reveals criteria of order and ordering, and gives an account of the possibilities and ingenuity of ornamentation and decoration. A facade also gives them a collective identity as a community, and ultimately is the representation of the latter in public.

✤

The eye-opening experience of taking in the Federal Building and St. Matthew's Church anew after the parking ramp's demolition provides a fresh perspective on how "the flat lot" fits in with Flint's contemporary downtown.

Standing in the center of the lot, you can readily see the city's past, present, and future in a series of architectural gems, all chronicled in *A Guide to Flint Architecture*. Not unlike the buildings introduced above, the collection of historically significant architecture from the early twentieth century that borders the "flat lot" captures a period when Flint was a place on the rise; indeed, an "expanding American city." As a group, they are resilient, ornate, magnificent structures with textured surfaces and crowned tops, in contrast to the modular and more austere mid-twentieth-century International Style that distinguish the campuses of the Flint municipal center and Cultural Center—areas built when Flint was rising still in the period after World War II. Beginning from a position pointing north and spinning clockwise (past a parking ramp and adjoining surface lot), you will notice at:

Four o'clock: The former *Flint Journal* building—an Albert Kahn project built in 1924—where "intricate stone carvings adorn the facades," according to the Flint *Guide*. It continues:

> Above each of the arched windows along Harrison Street, the relief figures in the round medallions represent knowledge, research and literature. . . . Rectangular reliefs on either side of the round medallions represent the attributes of a free press—vigilance, wisdom, truth, accuracy and industry.

Today, the *Flint Journal* building is home to the Flint campus of Michigan State University's College of Human Medicine and sixteen loft apartments on the third and fourth floors.

Six o'clock: The Mott Foundation Building, completed in 1930, is a sixteen-story, art deco design by Smith, Hinchman and Grylls (now SmithGroupJJR), the oldest practicing architectural firm in America. A central feature of the carved limestone exterior is the fenestration of the expansive, geometrically shaped windows that also serve to bathe the cavernous second-floor interior with natural light. The decorative art deco motif—a cutting-edge design at the time of the building's construction—extends from the outside in, with stylized ornamentation throughout.

Seven o'clock: The First National Bank and Trust building—a seven-story neoclassical design by architect J. W. Cook that features a facade of white, glazed terra-cotta—constructed in 1924. As a bank, it played a significant role in Flint's development, loaning money and extending credit to "several fledgling motor companies, including Chevrolet, Dort, Monroe, and Mason." according to the Michigan Historic Site designation. Today, the building is better known as First Street Lofts, with sixteen residential units on its upper floors and the nonprofit Crim Fitness Foundation occupying the first and mezzanine levels.

Ten o'clock: The former Genesee County Savings Bank is an Italian Renaissance Revival design by the Hoggson Brothers firm completed in 1920. The broad south facade along Kearsley Street is most prominent, beginning with a sequence of seven large, two-story windows, bookended by four smaller openings for a door and windows, that were seemingly chiseled into the limestone blocks. From the inviting street-level presence, the building rises eleven stories, ending with a colonnade around the top two floors that parallels the symmetry of the ground floor, capped off with a deep cornice crown. Renovations are underway to transform the long-vacant building into a hundred-room Hilton Garden Inn, scheduled for completion in the spring of 2020. That structure shares the block with the neighboring Huntington Bank Building, a Greek Revival design handsomely detailed in granite with sculpted volutes, festoons, Grecian urns in relief on the corners, and massive twin Doric columns at the entrance. Finished in 1928, the city's iconic Weather Ball sits atop it.

If you continue toward eleven o'clock, you would come to the two-story University Pavilion. Although it began life in 1985 as the Water Street Pavilion—a festival marketplace that was part of the ill-fated downtown makeover—the modern steel-glass-and-concrete structure has found its place and a lasting presence as a part of the University of Michigan-Flint, housing the campus bookstore as well as several restaurant vendors on the first floor and administrative offices on the second.

I have wondered at times how different things might look and feel today if the Smith-Bridgman/Kresge's block was standing still, overlooking Saginaw Street's red brick pavement—particularly as residents and entrepreneurs have begun migrating back into the urban core, joining college students and longtime inhabitants in reconstituting downtown for a new generation. How might that architecture buttress the overall sense of place with the recent restorations of some other early twentieth-century buildings nearby, namely the Capitol Theatre, Dryden Building, and former Woolworth store? The most interesting cities, including those of the Midwest, have an aspirational quality and those buildings, too, might have served as incubators of some type for the imagination.

Moreover, density matters and, as noted architecture critic Paul Goldberger has said, "[B]uildings create an urban fabric—and from that comes the beginning of a civilized environment." Lecturing at the Cleveland Museum of Art in September 2010 about his then-recent book, *Why Architecture Matters*, Goldberger continued:

> Architecture is about the making of place, and the making of memory. Architecture gives us joy if we are lucky, and it gives us satisfaction and comfort, but it also connects us to our neighbors, since the architecture of a town or a city is the physical expression of common ground. It is what we share, if only because the architecture of a community is one of the few forms of experience that everyone partakes in: the sharing of place.

But, he added, the "most literal expression of the idea of common ground" is the public square.

To a significant degree, Flint's "flat lot" doubles as a public square when it is not providing parking for downtown office workers and college students during the weekday, and bar-hoppers and restaurant patrons during evenings and weekends. Even then, there are the sort of chance encounters similar to those that may occur "on a sidewalk or in a store or other traditional locale" where "the social glue of place identity is stirred and thickened," as Jakle and Sculle contend in *Lots of Parking*.

And when Flint celebrates its unique place in the automotive continuum with Back to the Bricks, a car show and cruise, and hosts the Crim Festival of Races, headlined by the internationally renowned ten-mile road race, the "flat lot"—with the five bronze statues of the town's automotive pioneers standing like sentries along its western sidewalk—becomes the central gathering spot for the tens of thousands of people who flock to those events each summer. And in that capacity, its public-square purpose is salient and absolute, in the manner described by Jakle and Sculle: "As unencumbered open space, parking lots were (and are) frequently 'colonized' for large assemblages that cut across age, gender, class, and other social lines."

But all surface parking lots are not created equal. Even though I have at long last—and largely in the course of writing this essay—reached an uneasy truce with the existence of the "flat lot," downtown Flint still has too many surface lots for my taste. To quote Goldberger:

. . . in an age when so many of our contacts are virtual, when we often live in the virtual world of computers, architecture is a constant reminder of the urgency, of the meaning, and of the value of the real. Buildings are not just inanimate objects; they are occasions for human contact, and they are shapers of human contact, which makes them a living part of our world.

To the extent that a flat-lot-cum-public-square helps draw a diversity of people back into the urban core— enabling more of us to see the beauty and potential that surrounds us, facilitating the reinvigoration of midwestern cities like Flint, then I can accept that. For now, anyway. But I still long to someday see a magnificent work of architecture rise on the flat lot, of a design befitting of its place on Flint's main street: a structure of permanence in place of the liminal monument that fills the space today. ✳

"Waterloo Public Library mural." Photo by David Marvitz.

Please Return Again

MONICA REIDA

I.

My mother and I had a problem.

We could no longer find books from the *Danny Dunn* series at the Waverly Public Library.

The card catalog system, which was a simple DOS program with copper letters on a black screen, kept telling us the books were out or on the shelves, but every trip to the new library, which looked like a simplified, modern take on Prairie Architecture, did not yield the books I wanted to read.

My family regularly made trips to Waterloo, thirty minutes southwest of Waverly. While Waverly had the only two grocery stores that matter in Iowa—Fareway and Hy-Vee—Waterloo had plentiful shopping options. On one of our weekly trips there, my mother said we would possibly go to the Waterloo Public Library.

We took the exit to go to the downtown area and pulled into the parking lot at Commercial and West Third Street; you can see the library from where your car is parked. As a child, I was able to take in the scent of freshly baked bread from the Wonder Bread factory next door; it has since been converted to a microbrewery and specialty coffee shop. I remember getting out of the car and walking along Commercial Street until we got to the steps of the library's entrance.

I had been to libraries before, including libraries in Phoenix, both Waverly Public Library locations, and the tiny Readlyn library, but the Waterloo Public Library was the first one that felt majestic. With its light stone exterior, the building looks like a riff on Italian Renaissance architecture, as if someone saw a cartoon of Venice and decided to use that as a jumping off point for the design. The first-floor windows are arched, a contrast to the rectangular windows on the second and third floors. There are stone stairs and a ramp leading up to three archways, which sit under a small terrace located in the middle of the building. There are usually banners for the library hanging in those openings, the designs changing throughout the years. In front of a balcony at the middle opening is a proud stone eagle, sitting perfectly center.

After walking through two sets of automatic doors, I stood in the darkened lobby. To the left, I saw a tapestry paying tribute to the great women of the twentieth century and a colorful mural depicting a picnic. In the painting, people dive, play music, sit on the ground with their families. On my right, I saw sunlight streaming into children's section. There, another mural depicting a day at the National Cattle Congress, keeps watch, this one showing farmers leading cows and birds to be appraised. The murals were painted in 1940 by Edgar Britton, who had been a student of Grant Wood, as part of the Works Progress Administration program of the New Deal. Even with renovations and changes to the library, they remain as vivid as they must have been when the building opened.

My mother, sister, and I walked to the children's section, where my mother walked over to a card catalog, typed in the information for the *Danny Dunn* books. We moved toward the shelves that were only a bit taller than me and there they were. After that, we decided to use the children's computers: teal, egg-shaped iMacs. They felt incredibly futuristic as I sat down and played *The Oregon Trail* under the large, boxy staircase.

I would later find out that the Waterloo Public Library was in the former post office, which was built in 1938.

The current building is the result of the merger of the east and west branches of the library in 1977. In 1979, the post office relocated to a brutalist structure on Sycamore Street and the building was converted. As a child I would often look at corners of the library, trying to figure out what purpose it had served during its time as a post office—I maintain the area behind the service desk on the first floor was used for processing mail, similar to how it was used for processing recently returned books when I was a child.

The Waterloo Public Library became our family library. It usually had the books we were interested in and, if it didn't, we could get them from interlibrary loan. It was there I finished the *Danny Dunn* series, tore through the *Basil of Baker Street* books, and received guidance from librarians after my mother said, "I've run out of book suggestions for her. She's read everything I read at her age."

II.

My parents gave my sister and I a very important rule at the Waterloo Public Library: We could check out whatever we wanted as long as we stayed within eye or earshot. This meant that we had free run of the entire children's section and they also didn't see anything wrong with us getting books from the adult section. If we were to get books from the adult nonfiction section, housed on the second floor with reference and periodicals, we had to be accompanied by one of them. There were too many dark corners far from a librarian's watch that would make it easy for someone to kidnap me, they said. This was the closest thing to a "stranger danger" talk I ever received.

It didn't help that the second floor always felt cold and dark. Maybe it was the windows or the fact the reading desks and computers were near windows that were always blocked by two-story tall banners, but there was an almost corporate feel to that floor with its fluorescent lights. Still, as I got older, I started grabbing books from adult nonfiction, accompanied by my mother. Since both the juvenile and adult nonfiction sections used the Dewey Decimal system, I knew *how* to find books, but learning *where* the books were on the second floor was tricky.

For some reason, I keep going back to the 900s, which I remember being a straight shot through the adult computer lab, past the reference desk, through the reference section, past study rooms with wood doors surrounded by green paint. The library's color scheme would change to blue around 2000 when it closed for multiple months for a renovation. A lighter carpet color was chosen and a different paint was applied. During this time, we went back to patronizing the Waverly Public Library and my mother and I were constantly frustrated by our inability to find what we were looking for.

III.

When I was ten, I went on a field trip to the Waterloo Center for the Arts, two blocks away from the Waterloo Public Library. The Waterloo Center for the Arts houses multiple galleries, an impressive collection of Haitian art, and a theater that is home to the Waterloo Community Playhouse. This field trip was to the youth art galleries. I don't remember what the exhibition was, but part of the trip involved a performance with handmade noisemakers; my group was to act out an improvised scene while someone narrated. As an incredibly dramatic, albeit shy and nervous, child, I leapt at this opportunity. When it came time to perform, I took a deep breath, stepped forward, and said, "A funny thing happened on the way to the forum."

"Waterloo Public Library." Photo by David Marvitz.

The chaperoning mothers were horrified, but I kept on. After I was done, my mother asked, "Where did you get that phrase from?" I shrugged, to which she responded by walking me over to the library. She marched up to a card catalog, entered a title, and told me to follow her over to the short shelf containing "Adult DVDs," a phrase that means something completely different at the library from what I saw at the Cedar Falls Family Video. This shelf seemed to always reside in a weird area between the children's and young adult sections and the main lobby, positioned next to the staircase. It's something I always walked past, like the shelves for paperback fiction that weren't so much a shelf as a display case, and barely noted in my mind. She flipped through the cases, pulling out one with a mugging Zero Mostel on the cover.

"You need to watch this," she said. We went home and I found myself instantly enraptured with the movie, which had the call number "DVD FUNNY."

After that, I started a regular route of going to the juvenile and young adult fiction shelves, snaking to the Adult DVDs, and then checking out my books. I worked my way through the movie musicals of the 1950s and '60s, but *A Funny Thing Happened on the Way to the Forum* and *The Music Man* were the ones I checked out regularly, especially after I fell in love with the charisma and charm of Robert Preston.

I started to borrow more books from the adult fiction section. Needing something to hold me over until new episodes of A&E's Nero Wolfe series returned, I turned to Rex Stout's books. Initially shelved along the walls surrounding the adult fiction section, at some point they were moved to shelves located behind the picnic mural. Since this was beyond what my parents considered to be the range of vision and hearing on the first floor, I told them, expecting them to accompany me. Instead, they said, "Okay, we'll meet you by the staircase."

As I walked to the shelves, the only part of the library that was completely foreign to me, the mural felt like a gateway to genre fiction—science fiction was also shelved back there—and it remains lodged in my mind as such. I found the books, bound in solid reds, greens, and oranges with white serif titles on the spine. As I walked back towards the lobby, I felt incredibly grown-up.

This feeling would only increase when I was eleven and a set designer we knew insisted I read Dante's *Inferno*. I went to the library with my family and told my mom I needed to get a book from the second floor.

"Okay," she said.

"You're supposed to go with me," I said.

"Do you know where the book is?"

"Yes."

"I trust you."

I marched up the staircase at the center of the library, my head held high. After frequent trips to the second floor with my parents, I was able to once again take the route I usually took to get to the area near the study rooms, which always grounded me. From there I could find the call numbers on the ends of the bookshelves, which led me to where I found their copy of *Inferno*, which was a Modern Library edition with Domenico di Michelino's fresco of a giant Dante Alighieri standing next to Florence and in front of purgatory and heaven, with hell off to his left. I walked down the stairs, one of the rare times as a child I felt like I was floating.

My mother only told me once that a book was too grown up, and that was when I once tried checking out a Danielle Steel novel. She had no problems with me reading *Inferno* and both her and the man who suggested I read it were elated I enjoyed it.

It also meant my mother had someone to joke with about how we needed to retire the phrase, "When hell freezes over!"

IV.

My trips to the Waterloo Public Library waned in high school. By then we had moved to Cedar Falls, and I had the Cedar Falls High School library, the Cedar Falls Public Library, and the Rod Library at the University of Northern Iowa, which was the closest to the duplex where my mom, sister, and I lived. My school's library worked in a pinch, and was how I discovered Terry Pratchett's *Discworld* series. The Cedar Falls Public Library was often something I went to out of convenience as it had a collection similar in many ways to the Waterloo Public Library. If I wanted to dive into a topic I was interested in, I hung out in the Rod Library on hot summer days, enjoying the air conditioning and old books on germ theory and statistics.

Whenever I went to the Waterloo Public Library as a teenager, it felt like visiting an old friend and seeing they have a new haircut or have had huge life changes, always for the better. There was the time when I was thirteen and I saw the selection of books in Spanish, which might have been there for a while, but this was the first time I had noticed them. About a year later, I noticed a sign for books in Bosnian. The foreign language collection was small and located next to the hold shelf, between the service desk and the bathrooms. At fourteen, I understood why the library had added these books to its circulating collection. I was aware of the growing Spanish-speaking population in the Waterloo-Cedar Falls area and in high school regularly read about ICE raids on businesses where immigrants, mostly from Mexico, were detained. The raid on a kosher meatpacking plant in Postville occurred during my junior year of high school and detainees were held on the Cattle Congress grounds, right next to where the Cedar Falls High School prom was held—the same grounds depicted in the lively, picturesque murals of the Waterloo Public Library.

Waterloo also has a large population of Bosnian refugees who resettled in the area during the Bosnian war. I treated it as a badge of pride that the library I had patronized the most had books in Bosnian, and felt like it was something that made Iowa a little better.

During my senior year of high school, I remember marching up the steps of the Waterloo Public Library, as I had done several times before, and seeing a metal sign attached to a pole outside of the library's entrance. The sign announced the distance restrictions for smokers, pursuant to the Smoke-Free Air Act. I paused on the steps and looked at the information, which was on the sign in English, Spanish, and Bosnian.

V.

I haven't been to the Waterloo Public Library since 2010, but in my mind I wander the stacks of the library regularly.

I often soothe myself by thinking of various places and routes throughout my life. It's one of the coping mechanisms I've developed to deal with occasionally crippling anxiety. These include roads in rural Michigan

and Wisconsin, the tiki bar I frequented in Milwaukee, and the Chicago Cultural Center, which is, in fact, an old library. But the two buildings I mentally wander the most are the ones tied to my own identity: Union Station in Los Angeles, and the Waterloo Public Library.

It should come as no surprise to architecture buffs that I often wander the gorgeous mash-up of art deco and Mission Revival that is Los Angeles's Union Station. But why the Waterloo Library? It's certainly more memorable than the bland modern Cedar Falls Public Library—never ask me to describe anything past the foyer of that building—but I lived in Chicago and could pick the ornate Blackstone with its murals and dome, the glimmering new Chinatown branch, or the German neoclassical Sulzer Regional Library, which doesn't feel nearly as architecturally bombastic as the Harold Washington Library downtown, despite both being designed by the firm Hammond Beeby and Babka. As a college student I spent hours in the brutalist Richard J. Daley Library at the University of Illinois at Chicago and have a soft spot for the style. And there's the Central Library in Milwaukee that's neo-Renaissance in the front—right down to the Italian mosaic floor in the rotunda—mid-century modern in the back.

But the Waterloo Public Library reminds me of my childhood. The old traditions of picnics and the National Cattle Congress are romanticized, almost like life on the frontier in the *Little House on the Prairie* books I checked out from that particular library. I know where everything is and, if I need to search for it, there's someone to help me, like neighbors looking out for each other. I can run into friends, have a chat, get book recommendations.

In my mind, the Waterloo Public Library is cozy and warm. It's like my favorite oversized cardigan, or a cup of hot chocolate on a cold midwestern winter night. While no one will ever point to it as an architectural gem, unless you're looking for a great example of something suggested by what was likely a drawing of some guy's idea of what Italian Renaissance architecture looked like, but there is something authentically midwestern about it. It is a gathering place, a place that keeps moving forward, while in some ways frozen in time, and a testament to the fact that even in the hardest of times, we get through.

It's a building, but as an institution it is required to change in order to meet the needs of those it serves. It has grown to serve a population that reads Spanish and Bosnian, added the capacity to improve cyber literacy, undergone a renovation to better process book checkouts and returns. In the most notable change since I left, the library has added a makerspace called "The Hive." This is an institution housed in a building where there are likely still people in Waterloo who remember going there back when it was the post office and federal building.

Its 2010 iteration is almost perfectly crystalized in my mind. It still has a no smoking sign outside of the entrance. There is still the tapestry hanging on the left wall between the second set of sliding doors and the security sensors. I still see the blue lobby that is always a bit dim before turning my head to see the children's section, where there will always be painted farmers gathered around painted cows. I turn my head to the left and remember every color, every face, every bird in the mural that will always be the gateway to the Mystery Section. On the second floor, there are always the magazines on the racks, people gathered at computers, unabridged dictionaries open for me to settle arguments with friends about how to spell "ketchup." I will float past the study rooms on the second floor, also framed by the color blue. And I still see the egg-shaped iMacs in the children's section, even though I know they've been replaced.

Maybe I will eventually travel back to the area I called home and step back into the library, realizing it is still the same place that was sometimes the most reliable thing in my life. I might look at the makerspace, smile, and tuck it in my brain before going to Sidecar Coffee in the old Wonder Bread factory.

Until then, I have my memories of the elegant but homey building on Commercial Street. Even if they leave the building and demolish it, I will always be able to wander this building in my mind, wrapping myself in the mazes of shelves which I will always be able to find my way out of. ✜

"Stone Temple Baptist Church." Photo by Gabriel X. Michael

Zion In Lawndale

ASHER KOHN

On a sweltering Father's Day, there are worshippers and electric fans in about equal number at ninety-two-year-old Stone Temple Baptist Church. This may be the most optimistic place in Chicago, sturdy and built to last until the Messiah comes. Until then, Stone Temple Baptist promises redemption to the prayerful on humid Sundays. But the building might also be one of Chicago's most tragic. Despite the efforts made to construct a holy land in Chicago the city obstinately refuses to be sanctified.

Chicago has twice been likened to Jerusalem—once by Jewish Europeans fleeing pogroms and once by African-Americans seeking safety in a growing city. In the early twentieth century Stone Temple Baptist was a synagogue known as Anshe Roumania; it is a sacred site. The building is crowned by the Ten Commandments, which overlook all of Lawndale south of Douglas Boulevard. The only buildings taller in the neighborhood—the Sears complex which used to employ thousands and the Homan Square police station lately accused of disappearing Black Chicagoans—stand at Stone Temple Baptist's back.

From the street it is remarkable, like a warehouse commissioned by a Venetian doge. Limestone takes up the lowest twenty feet, holding up yellow brick and multi-story pointed arches. Chicago's official landmarking report politely calls this hodge-podge of neoclassical, Moorish, and Romanesque influences "eclectic."

The interior is thick with gold trim. Only four steps lead from the pews to the bima, where the rabbi administered prayers and teenage boys read the Torah in cracking voices. Stairs lead up to the women's wings, separate and above the men as in most traditional synagogues. Sconces and stained glass light up the interior, and the occasional Star of David is the only accessory marking the space as Jewish.

It's a sanctuary constructed by a diaspora that didn't have the privilege of architectural nationalism. Anshe Roumania must have looked a little like it could fit into any city that may have had Jews, which when the synagogue was built in 1926 was still pretty much every city between Boston and Bukhara. Anshe Roumania was built by a Jewish community that had fled an eastern European monarchy where they had no citizenship, little chance of an education, and few rights that Christians were bound to respect. Many of the first families from Romania worshipped in a grocery store attic before scrimping enough to purchase a tract in Lawndale.

In Irving Cutler's history of Jewish Chicago, Lawndale is remembered as a sort of Big Rock Candy Mountain full of delis stocking pickled meat, meeting halls packed with feuding Communists and Zionists, and matzohs handed out by the 5'4" Democratic Party boss, Jacob Arvey. Families worked and gossiped and married and prayed. The synagogue—one of nearly forty in the neighborhood—brought more than 500 families to pray under its roof on the holiest days.

It was part of the infrastructure that supported the Jewish people coursing through the neighborhood. Conditions were cramped and the community was poor, but one could pray at Anshe Roumania on Saturday and then dance to a young Bennie Goodman's clarinet on Sunday. As Jewish life flickered to darkness back in the old country, Lawndale's Anshe Roumania was a hearth. Its high ceilings encompassed weddings, funerals and b'nei mitzvot.

Until, almost to the day, it wasn't. In 1950 the neighborhood was majority Jewish and 99 percent white. In 1960, it was 91 percent black. In the intervening decade the Jewish congregation by and large gave up

this Zion and took the government-funded highways up to new government-financed homes in the suburbs.

Postwar laws creating the interstate and promoting homeownership meant new avenues of wealth creation for certain families who chose to leave their ethnic enclaves. Lawndale's Jews were not just given the citizenship withheld from them in the old country, they were also given a particularly American sort of passport: whiteness.

This ascendancy meant a handshake with a mortgage officer at the bank, a seat at the land grant university, and the "public deference and titles of courtesy" which W. E. B. DuBois identified as wages of whiteness.

Fathers who worked union jobs for Sears, headquartered in Lawndale, begat sons who clerked at Sears's insurance affiliate, Allstate, in Skokie. Suburban synagogues were low-slung brick affairs, often separated from the street by a desert of parking spaces.

Kevin Coval, the poet and educator whose *Schtick* describes Jewish assimilation in Chicago, said that "whiteness is a kind of amnesia." Jewish communities quickly forgot the land promised to their grandparents and neglected the culture built on Douglas Boulevard or Roosevelt Street. The communities were given a choice of three Zions: Yiddish-speaking Lawndale, the new Hebrew-language state of Israel or Anglo-American suburbs. Chicago Jews overwhelmingly chose to pack their Chevys and drive north.

"Some of those institutions," Coval said, "we took from the community and transposed into suburban space." But Anshe Roumania is too large and too grand to be brought in a moving truck up the Edens Expressway. The building was purchased in 1954 by Reverend James Marcellus Stone, a Georgia-born and Chicago-educated minister. Reverend Stone filled the pews with families not from Constanca but from Yazoo City, Mississippi. Light came in through the six-pointed stars stained onto the windows to illuminate a new story of redemption.

It is difficult to imagine, even for an audience inured to stories of neighborhood change through gentrification, what it looked like for this urban fabric to be rapidly mended with a different color thread.

It is remarkable to think of Anshe Roumania, now named Stone Temple Baptist after its Reverend, as a beating heart of the radical project of justice. Reverend Stone organized a rally after Emmett Till, a Chicago boy, was killed in Mississippi. With the help of church ladies, he turned the lower levels into "freedom schools" to reject school segregation. His friend Martin Luther King preached from the pulpit, atop the bima, several times.

After MLK was shot on April 4, 1968, Lawndale seethed with rage. Smoke extinguished the light as wood-frame buildings around Stone Temple Baptist burned. Mayor Richard J. Daley gave his police a "shoot to kill" order on Chicagoans. Some activists would argue that this order was never lifted.

What happened next is largely defined as disinvestment. Lawndale's largest employers pulled up stakes after the fires and budget cuts drew out four teachers' union strikes from 1969 to 1975. Contract home sellers and absentee landlords neglected Lawndale's housing stock while the city could never afford to do much more than clear the rubble. The neighborhood's median income dropped by 35 percent over the next two generations.

Churches worked sometimes alongside and sometimes against radical organizations like the Black Panthers to keep children fed and minds nourished. Unlike the diversity of promises on offer to Lawndale residents of the 1940s, those who came to Lawndale during the Great Migration had to make do with the Zion the city was evaporating under their feet.

Chicago's official landmarking report ends its story on April 11, 1968, but Stone Temple Baptist has held services every Sunday since.

Omar McRoberts, a sociologist at the University of Chicago, has spoken about "the street as a religious trope" in black churches, "an evil other, against which the church is defined." This tension is underscored at Stone Temple Baptist by the open windows on a hot day—one can look out and see the scars of 1968, unremediated by an often-thoughtless city. Vacant lots mark where houses were razed, crumbling sidewalks mark where maintenance was deferred. Police cruisers now zoom by where Bundists or Black Panthers ran after-school programs. Development comes, if at all, via tax incentive programs to spur investment.

Coval, whose Young Chicago Authors program provides mentorship and training to local students, argues that the children of folks who left Lawndale have a responsibility that goes further than individual buildings due to their decision to leave behind that Zion. "We don't want to look critically at the past because that would mean we look critically at our own faults," he said, "and our own role in the maintenance in chronic structural racism."

At Stone Temple Baptist, the sanctuary is elevated from street level by two sets of stairs. It's a source of lament from older congregants, but a constant reminder of the elevated space in which one worships. There are compromises to modernity in the form of video screens, but not many. It is the same building it ever was, serving a steady role in one of many promised lands.

Stone Temple Baptist is shared space, with many ghosts sharing the pews with parishioners. The building tells one story, and in that story its audience might hear different things. Some might listen to Exodus and remember that it was in Chicago when they were first allowed to vote. Others may hear the same chapters and recall that Mayor Daley was called American Pharoah. The trick, perhaps, is being able to listen and hear both. ✺

Photo courtesy of GBA Architectural Products, gbaproducts.com.

Flex Cleveland

ERIK PIEPENBURG

The Cleveland skyline is like an old-school gay porn star. Butch. Firm. Solid. A top.

Watching over Public Square like an eagle-eyed Secret Service agent is the Terminal Tower, the city's fifty-two-story signature skyscraper, designed by Graham, Anderson, Probst and White. On the shore of Lake Erie like a geek-punk Poseidon stands I. M. Pei's geometric record player for the Rock and Roll Hall of Fame. Ameritrust Tower, the Marcel Breuer and Hamilton Smith building at East Ninth Street and Euclid Avenue doesn't give a damn what you think about its rigid brutalism. It's now part of a swank hotel and residential complex called The 9.

Then there's the building at 2600 Hamilton Avenue, a sturdy architectural gem planted firmly on the ground like a guard dog. It's a living throwback to Cleveland's industrial, working-man roots that also happens to be the biggest gay sex club in the world.

I. Sex and Much More

Walled off from a sleepy, industrial neighborhood just east of downtown is Flex, part of a nationwide chain of twenty-four-hour bathhouses. For the un-initiated, that means it's a private club where men go to socialize and have sex with each other.

It offers the usual bathhouse amenities: a pool, a well-stocked gym, a rotating calendar of porn star appearances, and private cabanas and open public areas for sex. But unlike other bathhouses around the world, Flex is massive. With over 50,000 square feet, it even has a hotel, where a presidential suite goes for $219 a night, far pricier than some traditional hotel rooms in town. Since opening in 2006, Flex has become a destination; one travel writer called it "a virtual monument to gay bathhouse culture." (A previous incarnation of the bathhouse was located downtown in a much smaller space at West Ninth and St. Clair.)

I've been to Flex a few times. On the first visit I remember being shocked at its size. Once you pay your admission and check in, you put on your tow-el—standard bathhouse attire—and enter the wet area. There's a huge pool, multi-man jacuzzi, DJ booth (music is always playing), shower area, and a steam room maze. It was only after I walked past the large gym that I realized I'd only seen half the space. I pushed through a door and found rows of hotel rooms and a kitchen where you could order food from a smiling chef. I remember catfish on the menu one Friday night.

The second floor is all about sex: There's sex in rooms, through gloryholes, on slings, and out in the open. But there is also a library-style room where you can sit and watch a movie or socialize. A roof deck lets you check out the Cleveland skyline or hobnob with a visiting porn star shooting a video to be shared on Flex's Twitter feed.

Walk around and you'll marvel at how the curved edges, horizontal lines, and street-level windows look far more Miami Beach than Cleveland. It's only when you start looking into the history of the building that you realize what a pedigreed architectural history the Flex building has.

II. A New Style

Many of Flex's structural elements are unchanged from its opening in 1939, when it was born as a Greyhound bus office and garage that introduced Cleveland to the style known as Streamline Moderne, a child of art deco characterized by nautical elements like curved corners, glass block walls, and smooth finishes. Buildings are usually rendered in aquamarine, turquoise and other colors that reference the ocean. The overall effect gives buildings a sleek, bursting-forth feeling, like a boat surging confidently on water. There are Streamline Moderne sewing machines and radios, but also diners, motels, and bus terminals.

From the street, Flex catches the eye with hallmarks of Streamline Moderne, like the rounded facade, ultramarine tiles, oversized windows, and dramatic horizontal lines that run the length of the building. The original industrial purpose of the building makes the small artistic flourishes in the architecture more meaningful.

To really understand Streamline Moderne's place in Cleveland requires a visit to the extraordinary Greyhound terminal at East Fourteenth Street and Chester Avenue, designed by the architect W. S. Arrasmith. In a 2015 feature in Cleveland's *Plain Dealer*, the reporter Alison Grant interviewed Frank Wrenick, the author of the book *The Streamline Era Greyhound Terminals*, who said the 250-foot-long facility was described by the Cleveland News as "the greatest bus terminal in the world" when it opened in 1948. The building was added to the National Register of Historic Places in 1999, and remains a Greyhound bus terminal.

It's obvious why Streamline Moderne came to Cleveland in the 1930s and 1940s. The style is associated with the locomotive design and industrial production of the period, elements strongly associated with Cleveland's past. Streamline Moderne emerged like a "path to a new day," as the Cleveland architect David Ellison told me over the phone.

"Trains and fast travel were glorified in the late twenties and the thirties," said Ellison. "After World War I, Cleveland had it with the old-fashioned stuff. Everybody was trying something new."

III. "A Place to Visit"

I tried to get in touch with the management at Flex to find out more about the renovation, but I never heard back from anyone. Maybe talking about the architectural significance of the place wasn't in keeping with the Flex brand. So I reached out to Michelle Jarboe, the crackerjack real estate reporter for the *Plain Dealer* who knows how to find out anything about any building in the city. It took her almost no time to get some fascinating documentation of Flex's former life. According to maps dated from the late 1920s through the 1930s, the entire block was Greyhound. A fire insurance map shows garages with room for over forty coaches, work pits, and washing and servicing stations. There are records of property transfers between various Greyhound entities for decades.

The man behind Flex was Charles R. Fleck, an activist and philanthropist who founded the Flex chain. A Cleveland native who died in 2012 at seventy-three,

Fleck was interested in making bathhouses more than just buildings where men could have sex. Todd Saporito, who runs the Flex franchise, said in Fleck's obituary in the *Gay People's Chronicle*, a now-shuttered Cleveland gay newspaper, that Fleck wanted Flex to be a venue where "everyone had a place to visit, even though they may have been disowned from family and friends."

According to a 2006 article in *Cleveland Scene*, an alternative weekly, Fleck spent $1.2 million on the three-acre property, with $6 million going toward building renovations. Fleck faced opposition from some public health officials in town who were worried that a bathhouse would lead to an increase in unsafe sex. Fleck told the local NPR station that Flex will "probably hand out and give away and purchase more condoms than anybody in the world."

IV. A Queer Space

Why is Flex's Streamline Moderne past so fascinating to me? Because it's old and new and queer and naughty and under the radar and so many more things that I value as a gay man. It's also a piece of gay history. After Stonewall, gay bathhouses became wildly popular with a gay community that was desperate for sexual connection in a shared sexual space. The places were gritty, for sure, but many were also majestic. The Continental Baths in New York was located in the basement of the landmark Ansonia Hotel. But the AIDS epidemic forced the closure of many gay bathhouses, eventually leaving those that remained or reopened to move into cramped and completely unremarkable spaces.

The eye-catching architecture of Flex aggrandizes, whether you think it should or not, the idea that what's happening inside is valuable, treasured, and special. The difference between going to Flex and any other bathhouse is the difference between seeing a movie at a suburban multiplex or at a restored vaudeville-era theater in Cleveland's landmark Playhouse Square. Think of it this way: Traveling to and from the mighty Grand Central Station in New York makes you and your trip feel important. To and from Penn Station, not so much. One is meaningful; the other is utilitarian.

If I ran Flex, I'd promote the hell out of the building's ancestry. I'd do so with the same pride as does Heinen's, the downtown grocery store that opened in 2015 inside a magnificently renovated 1908 bank on Euclid Avenue that was originally designed by George Browne Post, the architect behind the New York Stock Exchange.

I would also make sure that every gay man in the world knew about it. Flex—and in turn Cleveland itself—is losing out on the gay tourist dollar by not advertising itself as a one-of-a-kind-gay experience. Whether or not you visit to hook up, a trip to Flex is a chance to experience the gay past in a way that's authentic, nostalgic, and entertaining.

I could even see taking a walking tour of the place. Towel required. ▨

MIDWESTERN VERNACULAR

"House in Oak Park." Photo by Gabriel X. Michael.

"Mausoleum at Roseland Park Cemetery ." Photo by Amy Elliott Bragg.

Mausoleums

AMY ELLIOTT BRAGG

"Humanity's gift to the People of Akron: Akron is to have the grandest and most beautiful COMMUNITY MAUSOLEUM to be found in the whole world." An angel-bedecked ad in the August 5, 1911 edition of the Akron *Beacon-Journal* promoted something the people of Akron didn't even know they wanted yet: a place to be buried besides the boring old ground.

There's nothing particularly practical about stacking the dead inside of a building. Sure, you have to mow the grass around a grave, keep the ground level, tend to the headstone. But a grave doesn't need HVAC, electrical systems, roof repairs, masonry, plumbing, windows, or sofas that will be dated and faded in a decade or less—to say nothing of the special challenge of managing the decomposition of a human body when it's inside of a wall instead of under the sod.

The community mausoleum was a twentieth-century midwestern invention, a technological and architectural advancement marketed as an ancient tradition. Newspaper ads for mausoleums evoked the pyramids, Westminster Abbey, and the tomb of Mausolus at Halicarnassus—the original mausoleum and one of the Seven Wonders of the Ancient World. A community mausoleum made the kingliness of an aboveground tomb available to the common man. Through vague promises of ventilation and dryness, it offered a "dignified" alternative to the frankly yucky process of in-ground decomposition. In the first decades of the 1900s, "mausoleum men" pitched their projects around Ohio, Illinois, and Indiana small towns as magnificent landmarks that would distinguish the communities that built them, elevate the citizens who were buried in them, and enrich the investors that financed them. And it would let your relatives visit your grave in comfort year-round, not under a sad umbrella in the mud or the snow. (Maybe the weather, in the end, was the most midwestern of reasons the community mausoleum came to be.)

Some of these mausoleums are monumental works of design by the most sought-after architects of their day. Some were shabbily built and, despite promises that they would last an eternity, were torn down in less than fifty years. The movement started in rural Ohio, and in just a few years all of the biggest cities across the country had one that promised, in feverish ad copy imploring you to *save your space now before it's gone*, to be the grandest tribute to the dead ever built.

I. Shady Dealings

The first public mausoleum was built in a cemetery in tiny Ganges, Ohio, in 1907. The *News-Journal* of Mansfield, Ohio, reported that the eighty-crypt mausoleum had been "dedicated with impressive services." The prolific mausoleum builder Cecil E. Bryan later described it as "crude, cheaply constructed and in outward appearance strongly resembled some of these Ohio and Indiana hog barns . . . but the idea was born."

The modern mausoleum is a building within a building—one for the dead with its own ventilation and drainage system, hermetically sealed off from the one for the comfort, peace and untroubled noses of the living. The Ganges mausoleum was built under a patent issued in 1907 to W. I. Hood and J. W. Chesrown for a "sanitary crypt, or community mausoleum." The patent application described novel technology such as ventilation valves that would allow the noxious gases of the grave to be released into a sealed chamber and dispelled into the outside air, as well as more banal features, like long corridors to accommodate funeral-goers. Patent in hand, Hood—a former encyclopedia salesman—and Chesrown organized the National Mausoleum Company in Shelby, Ohio, which later moved its headquarters to Chicago and reincorporated as the International Mausoleum Company. The company shopped its patent around to cemeteries as a sophisticated and sanitary alternative to in-ground burial, encouraging them to license

the technology and build their own local temples to the dead.

An enterprising set saw money to be made hand over fist (or crypt over crypt): you could fit exponentially more burials per acre into a mausoleum than you could in an expanse of cemetery lawn. More patents were patented, more mausoleum companies incorporated, more breathless and billowy ads taken out in the local papers with renderings of the fabulous buildings that were ready to build—as soon as enough crypts were pre-purchased.

In just a few years, salesmen had been dispatched across the region, and mausoleums had been constructed by the score—in Morenci and St. Joseph, Michigan; in Springfield and Decatur, Illinois; and all across Ohio, in Shelby and Toledo and Youngstown and Akron and Ansonia and Elyria and more. Opportunists got into the game, like Dr. Jonathan P. Collett, who retired from his dentistry practice to found the Darke County Mausoleum Company, and the five Latchaw brothers of Findlay, Ohio, who came into mausoleum construction from various pursuits including higher education and the hardware business.

"Whenever a man has proven himself a failure in everything else, he turns to the Mausoleum," said Cecil Bryan in remarks he gave to the American

Association of Cemetery Superintendents in 1929. (Bryan, an Illinoisan who had nearly eighty mausoleums to his credit at that point, was one of the few mausoleum men who was a builder by trade.)

The traveling salesmen hawking patent licenses and pre-need crypts gave the whole business a shady vibe. (Some mausoleum men were actually scammers: in 1917, W. L. Laurence was arrested in Terre Haute for selling fraudulent stock in his mausoleum company. That same year, George B. Vore was found to have falsely represented himself as an agent of the United States Mausoleum Co. of Fremont, Ohio, the promissory notes he had collected for crypt space in a mausoleum in Dayton deemed void.) The reputation of the community mausoleum was further assailed by associations of "tombstone men" who saw it as a threat to the traditional burial business and lobbied hard to keep the mausoleum men well outside of their gates. In 1915, the president of the National Retail Monument Dealers Association, George Wemhoff, published a letter in *Granite* magazine announcing the organization of a "community mausoleum information bureau" "to educate the people to the absurdity of the promoter's claims, and to call attention to the crumbling buildings erected in recent years, and to warn the public and show what will be the outcome of this ridiculous system of burial." Repulsive stories of bad smells, leaking walls and exploding vaults—where noxious gases would build up in a too-tightly-sealed crypt and literally blow the doors off—followed the mausoleum men wherever they traveled.

And yet the community mausoleum—and its promoters—persisted. Sometimes when a cemetery would refuse to sell the land for a mausoleum, the mausoleum association would just buy up land outside of the cemetery and continue with construction as planned. These stand-alone mausoleums are unsettling to behold in their contemporary settings—like in Upper Sandusky, Ohio, where a neoclassical mausoleum hangs out behind an industrial park and across the street from a cornfield, or in Marion, also in Ohio, where you will find a mausoleum next door to a Payless ShoeSource and a pawn shop.

It may have been a made-up reason to peddle a morbid real estate scheme, but it turned out people really *did* like the idea of being buried above ground, away from the worms, at rest amid cool floes of marble. And as the idea spread, the architecture became more ambitious and monumental in scale.

In 1914, hundreds of people thronged to the dedication of the new mausoleum at Roseland Park Cemetery in the suburbs of Detroit—briefly the largest mausoleum in the country, with 1,200 crypts. Designed by locally famous architect Louis Kamper, it was so hyped that hundreds of people thronged to its dedication—where "several persons, unable to gain admission otherwise, seized ladders found near the building and climbed through rear windows," the *Detroit Free Press* reported.

Inspired by a visit to Europe, Kamper designed a neoclassical song in grey-white marble, with two stories of Doric columns, bronze balustrades along the second floor gallery, and clerestory windows brightening nave-like corridors. It's all very churchy and pure—you could host a perfectly respectable chamber music concert in there.

Later that year, Rosehill Mausoleum was dedicated in Chicago, with five times as many crypts as Roseland. Rosehill is the work of architect Sidney Lovell, the son of a butcher from Racine, Wisconsin, who started his career designing theatrical sets. After Rosehill—his first mausoleum, considered by some his master work, and the mausoleum where he is buried—Lovell made mausoleums his specialty, and designed more than fifty of them in his lifetime.

At Rosehill you may find yourself, as I did during a late summer visit (with my patient, indulgent husband and napping infant son), lost in the endless straight halls and monotonous white walls and floors. Even on a sticky-hot summer day, the corridors are cool and smell like shaved stone. Rosehill contains thirty-eight separate works of Tiffany stained glass—the largest secular collection of Tiffany glass in the country. When the sun glows through them they dapple the floors with color, the only respite from all that damn marble.

Roseland and Rosehill are great (if slightly spendy) examples of the basic classical style that mausoleum builders across the country worked with again and again for the first decade-plus of the community mausoleum movement—a central chapel, a wing of tombs on either side, and some kind of shout-out to eternity, an Egyptian lotus motif or some reliable Roman pillars.

Then, things started to get weird. And there started to be sofas.

II. The Mid-Mod Mausoleum

As the Midwest mausoleum traveled, it took on new dimensions and its architects made bolder, more contemporary moves.

California—home of the "happy death" movement, pioneered by Forest Lawn Cemetery's visionary founder Hubert Eaton and lampooned by Evelyn Waugh in his satirical novel *The Loved One*—embraced the community mausoleum and made it more fantastical, with a little help from some former midwesterners. Cecil Bryan moved to California sometime in the 1920s and created several landmark mausoleums there. At Sunnyside in Long Beach, built in 1921, a Spanish Renaissance style evokes California's colonial history, looking from a distance like a centuries-old hillside monastery. To distinguish Sunnyside beyond comparison, or maybe just for the hell of it, Bryan threw in a Foucault pendulum. When he died in 1957, Bryan had himself interred in a community mausoleum of his own design—resplendent

Mountain View, in Altadena, aglow with brightly colored stained glass and barrel-vaulted ceilings, a West Coast riff on a Renaissance palazzo.

Even more out-there is Angeles Abbey in Compton, said to be inspired by the Taj Mahal but looking more like a Grauman's Arabian movie palace, a pastiche of Mughal, Moorish and Ottoman architecture (and indeed it has been used as a set piece in numerous TV shows and movies, where it lends a touch of cheesy-exotic "1001 Nights" flair). At the time of his death in 1938, it was reported that Eli Louis Latchaw, one of the five mausoleum-building brothers from Findlay, had been "involved" in Angeles Abbey, and though his role in its construction is unclear, he was buried there.

But no one did more to modernize and fantabulize the twentieth-century community mausoleum than Detroit-based architect Alvin Harley.

Like most mausoleum men, Harley didn't set out to make mausoleums. After an apprenticeship with Detroit's best-known architect, Albert Kahn, Harley established his own firm in 1908, and had a modest but respectable practice designing homes for wealthy automotive industry executives and some small downtown hotels.

Harley got his big break in the mausoleum business when he was commissioned by Clarence Sanger, one of the founders of White Chapel Cemetery in Troy, Michigan, to create the cemetery's community mausoleum, the Temple of Memories. Sanger liked Harley's initial sketches for the mausoleum, but sent them back for revisions with the directions: "I want the finished project to cost twice as much. White Chapel must be the ultimate." Harley designed an art deco marvel with a six-story central tower capped by a pyramidal ceiling and skylight. (The exterior of the mausoleum also features a beautiful bas relief of Mother Earth by a young woman sculptor, Hester Bremer.) Construction on the Temple of Memories began in 1929, and it was reported that year that it would cost $29 million to build (in today's dollars, adjusted for inflation). Compare that to the $7 million it cost to construct Rosehill, and you get a sense of just how expensive an impression Sanger was hoping to create.

But it would not be the ultimate, or the most expensive, or the most impressive Harley mausoleum. After making his name with the Temple of Memories, and finding that community mausoleums made for brisk business in the otherwise slumpy post-Depression years, Harley sent his nephew Frank off on a road trip to rustle up cemetery business across the country. Harley's firm became the nation's go-to mausoleum builders.

Two mausoleums in greater Chicago are Harley's twin crown jewels—his most significant mausoleum designs and two of the country's best. In the city of Justice, the bright white neo-formalist Resurrection Mausoleum is an homage to classical mausoleum design somehow both stripped bare and tricked out:

"Resurrection Mausoleum ." Photo by Amy Elliott Bragg.

the shapes are simple, the lines clean and sharp, but there are larger-than-life-sized statues of saints in every nook and niche, and the entire building is wrapped in a monumental work of colored glass by then-Milwaukee-based Conrad Pickel studios—at 22,000 square feet, it's the largest stained glass window in the world, according to the Guinness Book of World Records. The mausoleum was completed in 1969.

But the mother of all mega-mausoleums is Queen of Heaven, in nearby Hillside, its initial phase completed in 1957 with subsequent additions in 1960 and 1964. Queen of Heaven contains over 30,000 crypts and is the largest Catholic mausoleum in the world. (As of this writing there are still 9,000 left, if you want in.) It cost an astonishing $35 million in today's dollars to construct—financed completely by the advance sale of crypts, which cost an average of $10,000.

You would never know from its stately neo-Gothic exterior, but inside Queen of Heaven you will find literally miles of over-the-top mid-century modern design. There's a map of Catholic population distribution around the world—the numbered tiles are movable so the data can be updated, though the last time anyone bothered to do so was in 1997—and a timeline of Christianity starting with *the creation of the universe* sprawled across two walls. There are several life-sized dioramas, including one of the grotto of Lourdes with a water feature. It is not the only water feature in the building! There are glittering mosaics of Catholic icons, big sculptures everywhere, and countless eye-popping panes of stained glass. All of the design work, done mostly by Chicago-based Studio Daprato, is contemporary bordering on whimsical—expressive and bold-colored as a production of *Godspell,* it was meant to make people forget their grief and think joyfully about the afterlife to come. As a bonus, it would appeal to poor kiddos being dragged along to the mausoleum to visit departed relatives, as an ad in the *Chicago Tribune* promised. And like all of my favorite modern community mausoleums, Queen of Heaven has an excellent collection of furniture—sofas, loveseats, armchairs, ottomans, side tables, lamps and lampshades, all custom-made and color-coordinated.

What I love about mid-century modern community mausoleums is how unconcerned with eternity they are. Harley and his contemporaries were breaking the mold of traditional, inherently conservative mortuary architecture. Why shouldn't there be carpeting, wood paneling, and couches in the halls of the dead? Wasn't the whole point to make people comfortable? But in making mausoleums that were cutting-edge for their time, they were also making mausoleums that were *of a time,* and so to visit today is to feel like stepping into a fancy grandma's parlor. (For better or worse, no one ever sits on those sofas, so they're still in excellent shape.)

In 1958, Harley celebrated the fiftieth anniversary of his architecture firm. The *Detroit Free Press* interviewed and photographed him to mark the occasion.

(He looked great! The reporter even called him "handsome.")

"Harley doesn't call [his] style 'modern,'" the columnist wrote. "They're 'in step with the spirit of the times.' 'We're in the throes of tremendous change,' [Harley] says. 'It takes centuries to develop a style such as Romanesque or Gothic, and a lot of poor stuff is produced before it becomes a good period of architecture. Today's 'modern' may look as old as Methuselah in 10 years. It's the use of new materials that influences our thinking today.'"

III. Built to Last?

Mausoleums, born of hustlers, are today as ubiquitous an option for your eternal rest as ground burial and cremation, and cost about the same. And while rural Ohio cemeteries probably weren't having any land use problems when their mausoleums were constructed, a century later our cemeteries—like our cities—are certainly more crowded, and building vertically solves a real problem for some superintendents.

Some are still moving the form forward. Lakewood Cemetery in Minneapolis, a newer mausoleum, built by HGA Architects and Engineers in 2012, was thoughtfully designed to blend into the cemetery's low-rolling hills, and to harmonize with the cemetery's existing buildings (including a modest

modernist Harley mausoleum built in 1965). With an interior of slim grey-granite brick, mahogany, bronze Chicago school-inspired grillework, and—not kidding—*Edison bulbs,* the space is both gorgeous and looks like an Instagrammable boutique hotel.

But it remains to be seen whether mausoleums, an idea invented a little over one hundred years ago, will indeed be monuments to eternity. Many mausoleums that were built in the 1910s were abandoned—some razed—after all of the owners died out and perpetual care funds dried up.

In 2013, Landmarks Illinois named the state's community mausoleums one of its most endangered historic resources, recognizing buildings including the Cecil Bryan-designed Beecher Mausoleum in Beecher, the Fernwood Mausoleum in Roodhouse, and the American Mausoleum in Peoria. Illinois's first mausoleum, built in 1908 at Greenwood Cemetery in Decatur, was torn down in 1967. Community preservation groups have organized around the Beecher Mausoleum, Green Lawn Abbey in Columbus, Ohio, and the Fairview Mausoleum in DeKalb, Illinois (which was restored and rededicated in 2014).

An extreme example of the impermanence of the community mausoleum is at Union Cemetery in Nimishillen Township, Ohio, where the mausoleum has a caved-in roof, collapsing walls, and trees growing through the floor. It languishes in perpetuity, since its owners have all died or otherwise disappeared, and no one knows who's responsible for its maintenance or demolition or the remains that lay within.

But there are other, slower examples too. The ceiling at Kamper's Roseland Park is water-damaged, signaling a gradual but insistent decay. Harley's couches will inevitably need to be reupholstered, or replaced.

When you think about it, the Mausoleum at Halicarnassus is a ruin, too. No one knows where Mausolus is. Maybe eternity is relative. ✠

"View from window." Photo by Audrey Kletscher Helbling, mnprairieroots.com.

Iowa Rest Areas as Cultural Landscape:
A Journey in Haiku

RANDY BROWN

My first architectural haiku was the result of an ad-lib during an editorial meeting. I was then the editor of a *Better Homes and Gardens*-brand quarterly consumer magazine, one that focused on high-end new home design and construction. My boss, located at the head of a long conference table, had just suggested that with my next issue, we place more emphasis on photos and captions, and less on dreamy, long-form homeowner narratives.

As a journalism major in college in the late 1980s, I'd worked a summertime stint at Gannett News Service. "Got it," I told the room. "We'll write it so short, it'll be in haiku." The chirpy, happy brevity of *USA Today* took over my tongue, and I found myself counting five-seven-five syllables syllables on my fingers.

You can have this house:
a beautiful Cape cottage.
Won't they be jealous?

Reader, he laughed! I was not fired. It even became something of a running joke in future conferences— in telling the story of a place, can you distill it into fragment of seventeen syllables?

I got my first magazine gig as editor of a national trade magazine published in Cedar Rapids, Iowa. The family-owned multimedia company had just acquired a magazine called *Maintenance Executive*. Once you got past the tongue-twister title, the purchase made sense. The company already owned *Buildings* magazine, a facilities management title published since 1906. I was tasked with taking *Maintenance Executive* up-market, expanding its audience of chief custodians to include people who managed large-scale facilities operations: college and healthcare and corporate campuses, four- and five-star hotels, governmental office complexes, and military bases. We added content on groundskeeping, housekeeping, physical plant, security.

In my editorial role, I learned to analyze the effectiveness of an organization by visiting the spaces behind the scenes. The places that no one thinks about. Kitchens. Parking garages. Restrooms. In much the same way that a film major learns to deconstruct movies, I learned to peel apart buildings by systems and layers. While my friends jokingly prompted me for restroom ratings ("I give it a thumbs-up and five plungers!"), I smiled at this acquired wisdom: Cleanliness is an indicator of organizational godliness.

In other words, people judge you by the restrooms you keep.

When I was coming of age in Iowa, the rest areas that dotted the interstate highways were simple brick-and-tile designs first executed in the 1960s, plumbed shelters barely discernible from their rustic campground counterparts. There are still a few of these around, although my kids—now tweenagers—prefer to avoid them in favor of more modern amenities.

Beginning in 1998, the Iowa Department of Transportation embarked on a journey of restoration and renewal, constructing what are now eighteen "new generation" rest areas along three midwestern interstates. Interstate 80 bisects the state east-west through the capital of Des Moines. Interstate 35 bisects north-south, also through Des Moines. Interstate 29 runs north-south along the "West Coast" of Iowa, the Missouri River. As a tourist, as a taxpayer, even as an Iowa National Guard citizen-soldier, I have travelled them all.

In the new rest area designs, planners consolidated three previously separate archetypes—restroom buildings, open-air vending machine shelters, and "welcome centers" for the distribution of tourism pamphlets—under a single standardized roof and floor plan.

The new rest area buildings are institutionally postmodern—amalgams of textured concrete blocks, colored standing-seam metal roofs, and exposed interior beams. High, shed-style roofs announce themselves on the landscape, while clerestory windows invite in the daylight. Friendly glass-box airlock entries—with hands-free automatic sliding doors, of course—create optimal visibility into the interior, day or night. Openness is perceived comfort, and also security.

Men's and women's restrooms are placed opposite each other, across a central hall. Similar to many airport layouts, there are two entries to each restroom; half of each restroom may be temporarily cordoned off, in order that cleaning may take place without denying availability to the public.

In its own way, Iowa is an industrial state. There is very little "natural" area. More than 92 percent of Iowa land is in agricultural production, much of it by corporations. Family farms still exist, but rural areas are depopulating. As of the 2010 census, two-thirds of the state's 3 million citizens live in urban areas. Where two-lane highways and farm-to-market roads once connected passers-through to small towns with local flavors, interstates allow travelers to largely bypass that experience. Instead, they now race through rolling fields and flatland tapestries at seventy miles per hour—corn, soybeans, windmills, corn, fast food, truck stop, corn, *repeat.*

In this blur of franchise signs, the Iowa rest area takes its place as a new archetype—its functions, its location, even its midwestern "brand" are instantly recognizable. Instead of burgers and fuel, the new rest areas are designed to sell Iowa. Each of the eighteen new installations is organized around a different story, including themes of art and architecture, education, science, business, literature, and history.

For each location, multidisciplinary teams of artists, architects, engineers, and landscape architects provided opportunities to jog the mind, as well as to stretch one's legs. If you've ever visited a Walt Disney amusement park property, and discovered a "hidden" Mickey Mouse silhouette embedded in the landscape, interior design, or architecture of a place, the mental effect is similar: A wandering mind considers a small object or detail, and, upon contemplation, may be rewarded with a pleasurable jolt of recognition. Artists and architects talk about such moments as being in "dialogue" or "conversation" with the people who view their works.

One rest area near Iowa City, for example, celebrates writing and literature. Iowa City is a UNESCO City of Literature and home to the Iowa Writers' Workshop, a world-renowned graduate program in creative writing. On site, the lighting bollards along the sidewalks are shaped like eraser-tipped yellow pencils. Looming in a courtyard like a giant sundial, a stylized fountain pen nib serves as a focal point. Meanwhile, while viewed at a particular angle from that plaza, the letters "IOWA" are revealed to splash in black across the building's face.

Another rest area, and another example: At a Civil War-themed location near Dows, pointed sculptures shaped like trash-can-sized Minié bullets punctuate the landscape. Nearby, a leisurely looping walkway evokes a cemetery or garden, and invites visitors to stroll past quotations from Civil War veterans, presented on a series of "headstones."

At some rest areas, located right next to the dispensers of free Iowa road maps, the Iowa DOT distributes souvenir postcards, which describe and depict that particular rest area's theme. ("Collect them all! Trade with your friends!") There are also posters describing the DOT sites, digitally distributed via the department's website.

To the mindful traveler, then, each Iowa rest area presents as something of a puzzle box: Why this material? Why this sculpture? Why this architectural detail? Unpacking each clue reveals something about the site's theme, and about the state and story of Iowa. Take five minutes, or take an hour. Take a rest. Take a moment.

I joke that I finally found a vocation that pays less than newspaper journalist: that of architectural poet.

My haiku aren't always great works of art. I'd much rather use the form to trick people who say they don't read poetry into reading poetry. I'd also like to create moments of mindfulness—opportunities for contemplation and dialogue. Haiku is a handy and familiar tool for both objectives. Most of us, after all, still learn how to write haiku in grade school: Three lines, seventeen syllables, usually unpunctuated. The first line is five syllables, then seven, then five. Bonus points if you mention nature. A surprise of some sort is ideal, like a frog—*hop!*

A haibun is a combination form: First, a piece of prose—often related to travel—followed by a haiku. While not commenting on each other, the prose and the poem are interconnected. Tension and conversation are created in the spaces between. Another related form, the haiga, pairs a piece of visual art—a print or a photo, for example, or perhaps, even a building—and a haiku.

Like architectural details, the new Iowa rest areas are themselves fragments of a whole, scattered across the terrain. After traveling around the state, as a companion to this essay, I sought to weave together the eighteen themed rest areas as a single, cultural landscape. Each visit was an opportunity to distill sights, sounds, and other site content into haiku form. I'll admit, it started out as something of a joke.

An exercise in architectural cheek.

In the spaces between the poems, however, I found a version of Iowa.

Thank goodness, it was clean.

I-35, north/southbound, near Dows, north central Iowa
Rest area theme: The American Civil War
Drying ears of corn
shaped like artillery shells
await harvest—pop!

I-35, southbound, near Story City, central Iowa
Rest area theme: Celebration of Transportation
"Flyover Country,"
the "Heartland," and the "Crossroads"
are all the same place.

I-35 southbound, near Elkhart, central Iowa
Rest area theme: Technology that Feeds the World
Genetics! Tractors!
Unravel and multiply!
Increase our bounty.

I-35 northbound, near Elkhart, central Iowa
Rest area theme: Technology that Changed the World
Whether plowing rows
or linear equations:
Build a better tool.

"Adair (IA)—WB, rest area." Photo by Belle Montano-Zygmunt.

I-35 north/southbound, near Lamoni, south central Iowa
Rest area theme: The Natural Environment

Not just prairies,
but woodlands, riverbanks, and where
rivers used to be.

I-29 southbound, near Sergeant Bluff, west central Iowa
Rest area theme: The Corps of Discovery

Sacagawea
deserves more than a mural
outside a restroom.

I-80 westbound, near Davenport, eastern Iowa
Rest area theme: Mississippi River

"One cannot enter
the same river twice," but I
bet you can cross them.

I-380, northbound, near Cedar Rapids
Rest area theme: "The View from Our Window: Grant Wood in Iowa"

A pointed window.
A woman, man, and pitchfork.
You think you know us?

I-80 eastbound, near Tiffin, eastern Iowa
Rest area theme: "It has 'IOWA' written all over it."

Launched by the Cold War,
the Writers' Workshop became
our greatest export.

"Grant Wood Iowa Rest Stop." Photo by Audrey Kletscher Helbling, mnprairieroots.com.

I-80 westbound, near Tiffin, eastern Iowa
Rest area theme: Education

One-room schoolhouses
were once our only standard.
Now we write the tests.

I-80 eastbound, near Wilton, eastern Iowa
Rest area theme: Underground Railroad

Hiding in plain sight,
quilts were made like semaphores
telling of escape.

I-80 westbound, near Wilton, eastern Iowa
Rest area theme: Harvest

Our slogan was once
"Iowa: a Place to Grow."
We were younger then.

I-80 westbound, near Mitchellville, central Iowa
Rest area theme: Town and Country

Where dirt meets pavement
farmers and bankers exchange
fruits of their labors.

I-80 eastbound, near Grinnell, central Iowa
Rest area theme: Pioneers

Like the mound-builders,
we shape the earth into words
that we recognize.

I-80 westbound, near Grinnell, central Iowa
Rest area theme: Century and Heritage Farms

We planted ourselves;
tore open the prairie crust
and grew families.

I-80 eastbound, near Adair
Rest area theme: "The Greatest Story Never Told"

Henry A. Wallace,
breeder of corn and chickens!
And . . . Vice President?!

I-80 westbound, near Adair
Rest area theme: Wind Farming

Spinning white flowers
electrify our landscape.
The wind sows; we reap.

I-80 eastbound, near Underwood
Rest area theme: Loess Hills

Fine-ground glacial flour
deposited by the wind;
sacred and fragile

Photo courtesy of University of Minnesota Archives, University of Minnesota–Twin Cities.

Groundscraper City:

Touring the Subterranean Structures of Minneapolis-St. Paul, 1978-1983

ANDY STURDEVANT

On a typically chilly upper midwestern afternoon on April 5, 1980, after a day of seminars and presentations, a group of about twenty architects, engineers, geologists, urban planners, and policy experts, all clad in winter jackets, piled into a charter bus outside the old Leamington Hotel in downtown Minneapolis. They were headed out on a two-part tour of four notable underground structures in the Twin Cities, all of them constructed within the past five years.

Early April is still winter in Minnesota. The bus was unheated, but the interiors of the four buildings were considerably more comfortable. As the deeper earth surrounding them maintained a subterranean temperature of fifty degrees year-round, each structure required only minimal heating to reach room temperature. "Energy savings of up to 75% are possible in underground space," the conference literature cheerfully reminded the attendees.

These four buildings represented a new wave of progressive architecture making its home in the region. The Upper Midwest was a perfect test site—both geologically and politically—for trying out big ideas about how underground architecture could reflect a new type of environmentally conscious post-oil society. The state legislature, under the guidance of a bipartisan commission on natural resources, had kicked off a boom in underground structure construction in the state with a number of funding recommendations for study of the topic, and later, a handful of building projects. This included a dedicated Underground Space Center at the University of Minnesota, that were co-sponsoring the event. The attendees were there to see what these structures looked like up close, to poke and pry and ask questions.

Most on the bus were already involved with the underground space movement, but in-person visits were an important tool for introducing underground buildings into the mainstream of American architecture. The director of the Underground Space Center, Ray Sterling, wrote that year that "such firsthand inspections often serve as a major turning point in people's perceptions and assessments of earth sheltered housing." The hope is that the conference-goers would return home and take with them the lessons that Minnesota engineers, architects and planners had learned the hard way. If it could work in Minneapolis, maybe, it could work anywhere.

If you're a person who finds yourself interested in utopian architectural plans of the Whole Earth Catalog era, there are vast sections of the design-focused internet devoted to intriguing scrapped ideas, gauzy proof-of-concept illustrations, and faded snapshots of lone geodesic domes out in the high desert. Unlike so many of those plans, however, progressive architectural and engineering ideas originating in Minnesota in the 1970s and '80s exist outside gouache painting renderings and out in the world, on a fairly large scale. These underground buildings still exist. Together, they represent an ecological and architectural legacy that is, by design, hidden from view.

For the most part, it's possible to recreate the 1980 tour of earth-sheltered structures in the Twin Cities almost four decades later. At least six noteworthy earth-sheltered structures from this era remain in the twin cities of Minneapolis and St. Paul and their immediate first-ring suburbs; of the three that don't, two were demolished in the 2010s, and one collapsed in the 1980s.

Retracing this tour today provides some insights into how an earlier generation, galvanized by the energy crises of the 1970s and a distant but quickly approaching sense of ecological disaster, hoped to address energy and environmental issues that have still not been resolved in the four decades since. "During the late twentieth century it became evident that human activity has the capacity to alter the natural history of the world, destabilizing the global climate and poisoning the natural environment," wrote Minnesota architect David J. Bennett in those years. "Some new directions have to be tried." In the 1970s and '80s in Minnesota, that direction was down.

If you're a person who finds yourself interested in utopian

Williamson Hall, on the East Bank of the University of Minnesota, is the first stop. When it opened in 1977, the awards had been piling on for a few years: before it even opened, the design won a special commendation from *Progressive Architecture* in New York. It later received special commendations from regional landscape architecture organizations.

The building was constructed as a facility for the office of admissions and records, the campus bookstore, and the Minnesota Book Center. It's a diagonal, angular structure, bold in appearance but also quite reticent, peeking up through the ground in parts, but ceding the spotlight to the old stone piles that surround it.

The bookstore is now gone and with it, public access to the open, light-filled atrium that was meant to provide social space for thousands of students. The building today still houses the office of admissions, along with the offices for the physics and astronomy department. The underground configuration solved a number of problems for the university in the mid-1970s. For one, it preserved the sightlines in an important stretch of the campus's most historic section, creating thousands of square feet of usable space without cluttering up an already crowded part of campus.

More importantly, though, it served as a showcase for how the university could rise to meet the challenges of the era, and conserve energy at a time when fossil fuel seemed to be running out. Not only was it earth-sheltered for maximum energy efficiency, but with support from the Department of Energy, it was arrayed with a system of solar collectors not dissimilar from those President Carter had installed on the roof of the White House. Those would, unfortunately, be made obsolete as photovoltaic technology improved over the next few years. By the mid-1980s, oil prices had dropped again, and most Americans forgot there

had ever been an energy crisis. From the perspective of the early part of the decade, it began to look a little like a relic of a bizarre, pre-"Morning in America" era of heedless countercultural experimentation. Students called it "Lake Williamson," as the windows in the atrium frequently leaked, pooling water on the floors.

Williamson remains, though, looking more or less as it did in 1977. Its lead architect David J. Bennett, speaking with the soft Brooklyn accent of his childhood in Manhattan Beach, complains today that it was "butchered," but remains proud of the building. Bennett's website, a vast compendium of images and text relating to his work and architectural practice, highlights it prominently. Of all of these underground structures, it's the most easily accessible today—you can just walk in during regular campus hours. When you enter the elevator on the lower concourse, you find a pleasingly counter-intuitive, upside-down format for the buttons: B is at the top, going down to 1, 2, and then 3. A walk through the concourse leads out onto the sunken courtyard, surrounded by concrete and a lush layer of plants, and giving you an opportunity to crane your neck upwards slightly for a brochure-ready view of the ring of historic buildings looming over you.

It feels a little like standing in an excavation for a future that never quite happened. The poured concrete forms, forty years later, call to mind not historical structures, but instead the dystopian science fiction of that period. It's the hard-edged, modernist vistas of *A Clockwork Orange* or Truffaut's adaptation of *Fahrenheit 451,* which of course made heavy use of the existing brutalist architecture of postwar London.

It's a little funny and a little gloomy that the only context we have for experiencing these types of structures today is science fiction. Walking through the concourse out into the courtyard, it calls to mind what some writers like Mark Fisher have dubbed "hauntology"—an uneasy nostalgia for lost futures, a new society promised and hinted at in those idealistic years, but never fully achieved.

Underground architecture was, in this context, not connected to utopian (or, if you prefer, dystopian) ideals tumbling down from a distant centralized planning committee about how the future should be. It was, instead, built into the earth of the Midwest as a regional movement. Bennett recalls that what fascinated him was integrating buildings into the landscape of Minnesota. "It irritated me that the attitude of landscaping was decorative," he said. "The earth was just a platform, and everyone celebrated the objects and forgot the relationship with platform was somewhat tenuous." To this end, Bennett worked with the university landscape architect Clinton Hewitt to create a system of containers containing a species of native deciduous vine plant. In the summertime, the vines grew rapidly, shading the interior space. In the winter, it retreated, allowing light to stream in and warm the common spaces. "The whole idea," he explains, "was to make an integrated system."

Bennett had moved to the Midwest from his native New York, in part because of the lure of the Prairie School. "What was unique about the Prairie School," he says, "is that the architects looked at the land, and the geometry and geology, and said what we need to do is develop buildings that express the land—the horizontality. It's a uniquely Middle Western concept."

He pauses and smiles wryly. "I learned something that only naive young people learn—culture is a function not only of place, but also of time. The Prairie School was done. All I'd hoped to find were not there." What he found instead was a community of like-minded architects and planners, including fellow East Coast transplant and dean of the architecture school Ralph Rapson—even if the Midwesterners he worked with found his Brooklyn-bred forthrightness and aggressiveness as a young man perplexing. "I had not anticipated it, but I suddenly found myself in a very supportive, collaborative environment. In New York, you had to fight like hell to do something that wasn't a penis. All the students wanted to do the next Chrysler Building."

At the time, Bennett wrote about the work in an expressly midwestern way, with innovations like underground architecture following in the tradition of the Chicago and St. Louis architects of the previous century. In a 1983 issue of *Architecture Minnesota*, Bennett asserted that "we are equipped to deal with our unique climate in a unique way," and that "what is required of us is to shake off our timidity, re-assert our self-confidence and instead of purchasing an ersatz culture from elsewhere, risk creating one of our own."

The next stop is the Seward Townhomes, on the other side of Interstate 94, at the corner of Ninth Street and Twenty-fourth Avenue. As in many large metropolitan areas, the promise of the interstates in the 1950s and '60s was to connect automotive commuters to the centers of population quickly and efficiently. Even as late as the 1970s, the interstates still had a vaguely futuristic, technologically sophisticated sheen to them—Minneapolis's favorite son Prince's first synth-funk band was called 94 West. They did connect the two downtowns, but they also resulted in the mass displacement of established neighborhoods—particularly neighborhoods of color—and brought with them noise, pollution, and a shredded urban fabric.

In 1979, Mary Tingerthal was a recent college graduate working as manager of home improvement programs for the Minnesota Housing Authority. In addition to her regular work with the agency, she'd also volunteered to help administer a Minnesota legislature-funded demonstration program on earth-sheltered housing, managing a number of design contests for structures around the state, mainly just out of the urban core. Work around earth-sheltered structures became a large part of her job.

She was on this 1980 tour, as well—one of many across the US she attended through the late 1970s and early 1980s. "It was a brief but intense phenomenon," she recalls cheerfully. "They trotted us around between conferences all over—Colorado, New England. I'd talk to people about considerations when they were getting mortgages. I never expected to be involved with this, and never more than as an interesting thing I'd do at work."

But the connection became quite personal for Tingerthal when she moved into one of the Seward Townhomes: "I was so swept up! I wanted my own earth-sheltered housing." Since it was for sale in the open market, there were no conflicts of interest, and so she bought one of the units. She lived there for nearly a decade, first one her own, and then with her husband, ultimately selling it to a nurse at the nearby university hospital.

The townhomes were meant to be a showpiece for earth-sheltered architecture, and to correct some of the damage the interstate had done to the urban fabric. The townhomes face I-94 and are, by all accounts, exceptionally quiet considering the amount of traffic just feet away. The reason why the site was developed in the way it was, with such a willingness to try out new ideas, is that no one else wanted to develop a site so close to the freeway. They'd rendered the site almost unusable.

Walking the sidewalk in front of the Seward Townhomes today, you're confronted with that distinctly seventies-era mixture of hard-edged concrete and billowing greenery spilling out of planters. The entrances are set back into the earth, appearing almost as if on the side of a hill. One of the reasons why underground architecture took hold in the imagination of the Upper Midwest of the time is that it drew heavily on popular narratives about and self-perceptions of the region: the Underground Space Center at the University of Minnesota was funded in part after a late 1970s trip to Sweden to visit underground structures there, and an enthusiastic group of returning academics and Minnesota legislators drew direct connections, as so often happens in the Upper Midwest, between the culture and geology of Scandinavia and Minnesota. Early writing about underground structures in Minnesota took lengths to point out that it was nothing new in the region—the sod houses of prairie homesteaders and pioneers in particular were invoked early and often, guarantors that this new way of thinking wasn't too out there, bur rooted in centuries-old midwestern traditions.

It's true, though, that underground architecture is uniquely suited to the landscape of Minnesota, both above and below ground, where the unique geology of the region layers soft sandstone and hard limestone in a way conducive to subterranean construction. Public-private partnerships such as the townhomes were meant to show that such buildings could fit into the landscape, and create modern, energy-efficient structures that were suited for the climate, as well. Heating and cooling an aboveground house requires

accommodations for an external temperate that can swing between a hundred degrees and negative thirty degrees. An underground structure, however, surrounded by fifty-degree earth at depths of twenty feet or more, needs only to be heated by twenty degrees to room temperature, and doesn't need to be cooled at all, once solar energy is taken into consideration. In the period of time between the 1973 oil embargo and the 1979 energy crisis, such a model looked very attractive, even viewed strictly from an economic perspective.

The roof of the Seward Townhomes no longer has visible earth-berms, as it did in 1980, when the conference attendees walked through it. The residents, in response to leakage problems, sued the contractor and had a conventional roof built over the sterilized earth cover—if moisture problems aren't addressed early in the process, or your builder cuts any corners, it's much harder to make repairs later. In this case, repairs put an end to the moisture problems.

"It absolutely worked," Mary says of her home. "It was really quite quiet. And my energy bills in January were astoundingly low. I learned a lot about concepts of energy conservation, about taking advantage of passive solar. That's a part of the lasting legacy—how passive solar can fit into a design. It's a natural marriage."

These units are some of the quietest structures in this noisy part of the city. They're private homes, but if you have a chance to step inside one of the units sometime, do it. The way the light streams down at an almost forty-five degree angle through the south-facing windows in the afternoon, and the stillness that surrounds you, is quite sublime. It is a little like stepping into a machine engineered to keep its occupants concealed within a perfectly balanced and nearly monastic state of light, warmth, and silence.

The third stop, at 474 Concordia Avenue, is an unremarkable-looking brick box housing the Minnesota Safety Council. The building that once lay below this site was known as the Criteria-Control Data Corporation Building, or the Terratech Center. Control Data Corporation (CDC) was a leading supercomputer manufacturing firm in the 1970s and '80s, and when the Terratech Center opened in 1981, it was hailed in the pages of the *New York Times* as "the most ambitious of the nation's corporate groundscrapers."

Nineteen eighty-five was not a great year for underground spaces. "The decade of business and finance," sighs Ray Sterling. "Everybody sort of forgot about worrying about energy—there seemed to be money and energy, and the whole second half of the decade went towards how to maximize your profits and financial status than the environment and energy." Bennett echoes this thought: "All the greedy people wanted to buy as much as they could, burn as much as they could, and go home with their loot." Energy-related funding for the Underground Space Center had dried up by the mid-1980s, and the center

shifted its focus to other equally important though less visible applications—management of underground utilities, for example.

It remains unclear what happened to the underground building at 474 Concordia, but after a particularly heavy rain, the steel culvert structure in the building's north-facing wall collapsed, and a forty-nine-year-old CDC librarian named Maxine Ann Murray was killed in her sleep. Murray was sleeping on a couch outside the apartment she also lived in; the building incorporated some living space along with the office space and a fruit and vegetable garden in a greenhouse. The architect, Jerry Allen, was interviewed in the paper the following day. He was quoted as saying he had no idea what had happened.

When the site was redeveloped a few years later, the current aboveground design was chosen, and the space in the earth was filled in. Two other underground structures built in the late 1970s in the Twin Cities met less traumatic but no less conclusive fates: the underground Walker Library in Uptown Minneapolis closed in 2014 for two years of renovations, and the visitor center at Fort Snelling historic site a few years later. Both were built to preserve sightlines, conserve energy and—maybe just a touch here—to show off a little by big clients eager to get in a on a hot trend, even if it didn't make a lot of sense for the sites.

"It had no neighborhood presence," said Jennifer Yoos, an architect working on the redesign of the library, which opened atop the site of the old earth-sheltered building in 2016. "People didn't know it was there."

The visitor center at Fort Snelling, though it succeeded in preserving the sightlines along the bluff it was built into, apparently had moisture issues from the beginning. The writer of a 2007 report on the facility threw their hands up in something approaching disgust when addressing the core issues: "There is no clear evidence whether the ongoing water infiltration is due to static pressure in the bluff, the location of the building on an underground spring, the fact that the building roof is the lowest point on the site, or more likely a combination of issues." As of the beginning of 2019, the old center is scheduled to be shuttered and abandoned in favor of a repurposed cavalry barracks elsewhere on the site.

The final building on our trip, the Girl Scouts Building at 400 South Robert Street in St. Paul, is an example of how some of these structures have survived, and are hiding in plain sight. The building has been renovated twice since it was constructed in 1979—an expansion in 2001 that surrounded much of the original earth-sheltered features, and a total remodel in 2017 that added several thousand square feet, but further obscured what remained of the original design. Unless you note the earth-sheltered windows on the south side of the building, which offer a glimpse into a subterranean concourse, you'd never realize it was

anything other than a standard administrative building on a commercial strip of St. Paul.

The vision of the late Girl Scout Council of St. Croix Valley Executive Director Thea Childs drove the fundraising and then construction of the building, then known as In Town Center. Coming not from academia but from the nonprofit sector, Childs was an idealist and passionate environmentalist who wanted a site that could serve as a model to other organizations, and to the girls her organization served. It was, she said, "a teaching tool," complete with color-coordinated pipes that could be used to educate girls on alternative energy and conservation. A waterless, Scandinavian-designed composting toilet called the Clivus Multrum was installed, after a period of initial resistance from the plumbers union, who had lingering professional concerns about installing a waterless toilet. Featuring a green roof with solar and wind power features, the centerpiece of the building was a two-story earth-sheltered atrium that served as a living library of plant life. In the original design, you entered the building through the atrium, into an airy, light-filled and humid greenhouse oriented around a water feature and fountain. The atrium was also home, apparently, to a number of pink flamingos, who made their home among tropical fishes and prairie grass.

The flamingos, fountain and Clivus Multrum are all gone now, along with many of the original features. The bravura bank of windows lighting and heating the atrium is today a suite of cubicles in the rear of the building, but it still retains the sleek, angular glass and blonde wood contours that suggest its 1970s roots. Over time, the solar and wind features atrophied and were removed, piecemeal, from the structure. One of the few remaining elements of the original design is tucked away in the boiler room: the pipes still retain their bright blue, green and red color-coding. The pipes that run over the atrium, however, have been repainted a flat gray.

In some respects, a tour of this kind is not a great format for appreciating these types of buildings. As helpful as it is to see each building in its environment, singling out specific structures also privileges the uniqueness of each site, as opposed to how they might work as part of a larger system. Underground buildings work best when they're part of a system, suited for the site and working in concert with the surrounding urban and natural environments. And of course, it doesn't work everywhere, even in landscapes best suited for them.

"We might promote the consideration of underground space use," Ray Sterling says of the work of the Underground Space Center, "but we were not in the business of promoting it for building without regard to whether it made sense or not. I think you'll find some of the examples around Minnesota in that mix—some which were fairly successful or appropriate for the site, and some which were . . ." He pauses. "Well, people just liked the *idea*, and shoehorned it into a site."

That stigma of trendiness can be difficult to shake as time goes by. "It's a challenge to get that balance," Sterling tells me. "Where I think they really make the most sense is where the ecological and environmental aspects work with the energy aspects and the site to form a natural success. Because if you're only interested in an energy-efficient building, it's reasonably true that you can heavily insulate it and put in solar, and you can get a building that uses a very small amount of energy, and you can do that without building underground. But when you take a site where you want to preserve the characteristics of the site, or not intrude on the natural environment, and you want a good energy performance to fit with the landscape, then using the underground space and putting all or part of the building underground starts to have more success factors associated with it."

The mechanics of earth-sheltered buildings aside, the emphasis on energy performance during the period has had a long and lasting effect on architecture. Solar power and earth-sheltering went hand-in-hand, and even when the latter fell by the wayside, the innovations in solar energy and energy efficiency developed alongside earth-sheltering remained, and gradually entered the mainstream conversation after decades. Minnesota adopted some of the earliest energy efficiency standards for new buildings, and many of those standards came out of the work pioneered at the time.

"It raised awareness of the impact of design and siting of residential buildings on energy performance," says

Tingerthal. "In terms of green building standard, I think it got a practical start then. We financed thousands of affordable units of residential housing, and they were all required to be built in accordance with those standards. It's now a part of what we do."

Near Williamson Hall, built three years after the 1980 conference, stands the Civil Engineering Building, also designed by Bennett and also an award-winner, edging out the Epcot Center for 1983's Outstanding Achievement Award from the American Society of Civil Engineers. It's a truly remarkable building, an inverted high-rise plunging seven stories in the earth. When it's written about, what's most frequently highlighted are its most fantastical features—a passive lighting system that would spread light into the bottom stories, though now inert through an evident lack of interest in maintenance from the university; as well as a device called the Ektascope, meant to provide a 3D view of the outside courtyard optically reflected in a screen on the bottom floor, and intended to mitigate the psychological discomfort that comes with being below ground. Today, it's a black mirror.

But fantastical as those features are, they're not the primary draw of the building. Despite some ongoing challenges with moisture and leakage, the building remains one of the most energy-efficient on campus. Standing on the bottom floor, seven stories below the limestone cap, in an artificially lighted hallway looking at an elevator bank where the numbers run backwards, there's a quiet, odd feeling of being

displaced from a future that didn't turn out as radically optimistic as planned for the Upper Midwest.

Perhaps it didn't. However, there's also a parallel feeling that, decades removed from the specific political and ecological discussions of the period, nonetheless still registers as powerfully, viscerally midwestern. These are buildings created to harness the most basic characteristics of the surrounding landscape and the larger environment. Those lessons remain. ▦

"New Glarus Brewing Company." Photo by Walter Kadlubowski.

Form Follows Values:
New Glarus Brewing Company's Hilltop Brewery

BILL SAVAGE

Beer geeks from all over make pilgrimages to the small town of New Glarus, Wisconsin (population 2,172), to the New Glarus Brewing Company's Hilltop Brewery. The beer produced there can only be purchased in Wisconsin, but the brewery's reputation for taste, variety, and quality reaches around the world. Some specialty brews are available only at the brewery itself, and so if you're the sort of person who likes to dissect the relative values of IPAs and APAs, ABVs and IBUs, or if your instinct in any brewpub is to order the flight and try all their beers, you might well make your way there.

If you do, you will visit a rare sort of place, one where the architecture expresses a set of personal, cultural, and corporate values above and beyond the mundane necessities of the industrial-scale brewing and selling of beer.

On the east side of Highway 69, just south of town, you enter the Hilltop Brewery complex. On the left, hops are cultivated; on the right, what looks like a red farmhouse is actually a wastewater treatment facility, designed to fit into the roadside scenery of dairy country. Continue from the entry up a curvy two-lane road at a cool ten miles per hour. The narrow ribbon of asphalt snakes its way up the hill, never in a straight line for long. Motorcyclists get extra warnings to take care and go slow, as even a not-very-wide turn would put their Harleys in the oncoming lane. Trees and hedges line the right side of the road, while on the left the hillside plunges sharply downward. Everything about the road says: Slow Down.

This design was not dictated by the geography of the hill, or by some efficiency expert. New Glarus could have built a bus-friendly switchback to funnel as many people up as fast as possible. Instead, New Glarus president and cofounder Deborah Carey told me that she wanted every visitor to slow down and have an "ah-ha! moment" upon arrival.

At the top of the road, parking lots open up on both sides, and the brewery's complex of buildings rises ahead. To your left, what look like two large barns—one forest green, the other firehouse red—loom, housing the production facilities. Dead ahead, rough-hewn stone stairs curve around boulders, rain barrels, shrubbery, flowers, and trees up to the entrance to the taproom and store, and part of the company's office complex. A half-timbered multi-storied building rises to the right. It is built into the side of the hill, and houses the rest of the offices and the large chilled cave-like room where bulk purchases of beer can be made.

This building seems like it's from somewhere else, even some-when else. It's semi-symmetrical, centered on an entryway with a wide overhang, with a clock tower above. To the overhang's left at ground level, three wide doors gabled by canopies lead to the retail spaces where people back up their minivans and load up cases of beer to deliver to people unlucky enough to not live in Wisconsin. On the upper levels, the building features a symmetrical array of dormer windows; all have steep rooflines.

The whole ensemble looks as though a bit of Bavaria, or the Swiss canton of Glarus, has been airlifted and dropped into this Green County hillside.

Quasi-European kitsch is commonplace in Wisconsin, of course, from Mars Cheese Castle in Kenosha to countless other highway off-ramp "Cheese Sausage Gifts" emporia, cheap strip-mall architecture where some ramparts are put on top of the same structures that could house any fast food joint or gas station in any parking lot off any interstate.

But the Hilltop Brewery doesn't feel that way; it has an idiosyncratic and consistently imagined aura about it, a sense that it's not just about commerce. It's instantly obvious that the place surely cost much more to build than it needed to be, and interesting stories must lurk behind every bit of it.

Drew Cochrane, New Glarus's COO and general counsel, gave me a behind-the-scenes tour; I also interviewed Deborah Carey by phone to get these stories. Along with the documentary about the brewery, *Tale of the Spotted Cow*, these are my sources for all facts herein. (All aesthetic judgments, speculations, and opinions are mine alone.)

Daniel Carey, the brewmaster, and his wife Deb originally opened a small brewery in the town of New Glarus in 1993, in a former warehouse by the river. As they expanded, they considered moving to other nearby small towns, but decided to buy out the farm on this hilltop instead. Deb wanted something unique, and unlike the standard industrial brewing plant. Architects were dragging their feet a bit, so Deb finally designed it herself. Beyond the Teutonic aesthetics, her design exhibits practical businesslike symmetry: the production facility to the south can expand in that direction, and the offices, taproom, and retail space could expand to the north, without either impinging on the other.

Walk up the stone stairway that curves almost as much as the road you just drove. When the hilltop was being leveled so the complex could be built at all, a worker noted that the stone was coming away in regular slabs, and suggested to Deb that they could reuse it. Such a conversation between worker and boss is common here; employees of the brewery get vested in co-ownership ("Employee owned" boasts all their beer packaging) and the company's collaborative culture encourages everyone to make suggestions up the corporate ladder. And so instead of carting the stone off to a landfill, it got reused on the spot. The environmental consciousness suggested by the wastewater treatment plant at the foot of the hill continues to its summit.

At the top of the stairs, an archway covers a walkway between two buildings with three passages: the door on the left leads to the small gift shop and tap room. There you can get your T-shirts, caps, coasters, glassware, bottle openers, and a beer, along with a selection of local cheeses and, if you're lucky, a stick of fresh landjaeger sausage. The room is small, and leads to the self-guided tour into the production side, as well as a museum of the brewery's history.

To the right, another door leads into an overflow meeting room and seating area designed like a tap-room in a monastic brewery, with an ornate back bar salvaged from a closed tavern, below more office space for the ever-growing staff.

Go straight through the archway and you enter a courtyard where the architectural exuberance continues. The courtyard is framed on two sides by the office buildings: to the east, the top half of the mass-purchase building, with another clock and a carillon of church bells. Some old brewery equipment functions as an elaborate water fountain, utterly necessary for the summer afternoons when as many as 1,500 people visit the brewery and need to hydrate in the heat. Scattered around are picnic benches set among half a dozen seemingly ruined old buildings.

They are not ruins, but "follies," fake ruins. It was once popular to build such things in England, where nothing classes up a country estate like a faux-Norman tower fallen into Romantic rubble. The follies occupy several levels, with bench seating built in or picnic tables, some shaded by trees, and all offering a spectacular view to the west of the rolling hills, forests, and farms of Green County.

The story: as the brewery expanded (and kept winning awards, which attracted even more pilgrims), drinkers at the gift shop tended to congregate in that archway, blocking access and creating no small amount of chaos, like the people at an apartment party who won't leave the kitchen. Deb tried to put picnic tables out, but the muddy grass didn't inspire people to spread out. So, they paved the courtyard and sought out these follies, from Redwood Stone Follies in Somerset, England.

That company, though, like New Glarus, doesn't just build stuff to order. They asked for a narrative to create the designs around, so Deb spun a vision of a 300-year-old abandoned country brewery and manor house. The faux-ruined buildings tell an implicit story, with a farmhouse, a silo, a stable and other functional buildings scattered throughout. Now they function to shelter drinkers, and to please the eye, and the doorway is only crowded when it rains.

It's also notable what New Glarus does not have: there's no restaurant, and while they do sell beer on site, there's no large indoor drinking space for bad weather. In summer months, visitors can double the population of the town, Cochrane tells me. But instead of selling food, the brewery encourages their customers to patronize the restaurants in the town itself. Everyone who buys a beer gets a token good for one of their beers at pretty much every restaurant in the village. The brewery then pays those bars for the beers bought with these tokens.

In other words, the Careys value community over raw profit. Just as the exuberant flourish of their architecture is not particularly cost-effective, but expresses an aesthetic value—don't just drink our unique and tasty beer: drink our beer someplace unique and beautiful—the company consistently makes business decisions that many accountants might advise against.

The brewery's physical design has an intellectual parallel in Spotted Cow, New Glarus's signature brand, a farmhouse ale. Daniel Carey, whom Deb describes as having "yeast in his veins," came up with the recipe in an act of historic imagination. What would the Swiss immigrant settlers in the New Glarus area have brewed in the mid-nineteenth century? They lacked the ice and lagering capacity for classic middle-European style pilsners, but a farmhouse ale would work.

Deb wanted to call the beer "Spotted Cow" after the dairy herds commonly seen on central Wisconsin hillsides. Distributors and marketing experts shook their heads: could you picture old timers in some small resort town lakeside tavern or Wisconsin VFW hall ordering something with that name? Nowadays, after the Big Bang of the craft brewing expansion, beer names are commonly quirky or obscure, but back then beers were usually named after breweries, and sometimes after the beer's style, not after some whimsical vision of farm animals frolicking in roadside pastures.

Nevertheless, Spotted Cow it would be, and Deb designed a label featuring a cow leaping over a map of Wisconsin. With much hard work, the beer took off and is now their flagship brand, so popular that a bar in New York City took to illegally importing it, until it got busted by the local liquor board.

This persistence of vision is obvious in the design of the place, but it's also evident in their corporate values. Both Careys were raised poor, and both worked their way up in the world. But they did not forget where they came from; above and beyond the employee stock option plan, they pay good wages, their employees get health care, as well as vacation time and proper holidays.

New Glarus believes that if you do what's good for the community, and good for your workers, you will make good beer, and prosper.

These corporate values are also on display in the industrial side of the plant, on the self-guided tour.

Brewing is a labor intensive process. Cochrane pointed out to me that the majority of that time and labor is spent cleaning equipment and just moving or shifting things from point A to point B. So, even with all the pay and benefits, working in a brewery can be physically demanding, and that's a health issue, one that New Glarus addresses in a way accountants would not approve of.

For instance, one of the most physically demanding manual jobs in the production area is moving cases of empty bottles off shipping palettes and putting them on the conveyer belts that feed into the bottling system. This job, when done by hand, requires workers to reach high over their head and down to their feet, twisting and torquing: a killer job, one that can cause repetitive stress injuries or back trouble.

So, New Glarus spent $500,000 on a robot to de-pallet the cases, and you can spot it on your tour just beyond the glass walls by the bottling line. The workers who'd done that job didn't get fired: they simply moved on to other things.

Automation at New Glarus is not a labor-saving device, it is a *laborer-saving* device.

They also have a robot to flip kegs of Spotted Cow; since it has live yeast in it, they ship it upside down, so the retailer has to turn the keg over to tap it, mixing the yeast more evenly throughout. That robot is, of course, called the "Cow Tipper."

I've always suspected that this rural entertainment—bored teenagers roaming dairy country under the cover of night, knocking over sleeping cows—was more mythic than real. But the architecture of the New Glarus Hilltop Brewery mixes the mythic and the practical in a way that makes me question my dubiety. If a beer called Spotted Cow can inspire interstate smuggling, and a brewery can look like it was flown in from Switzerland, maybe anything is possible. ✵

"Trubek House." Photo by Anne Trubek.

From Spectacular to Vernacular

DAVID M. TRUBEK

It all started with Frank Lloyd Wright, or rather with James Dresser, one of Wright's protégés. In 1953, along with a few other University of Wisconsin students, I moved into a house designed by Dresser, a young architect fresh out of Taliesin.

The house was spectacular. It sits on the brow of a cliff in Shorewood, a Madison suburb: we dubbed it the Cliff House. Built of Wright's characteristic Wisconsin limestone, the house has a soaring roof, wide overhanging eaves, vast plate glass windows, and a massive fireplace. The roof comes to a peak above a glass-enclosed tower echoing the "prow" or hands-in-prayer style of Wright's nearby Unitarian Meeting House, which I passed almost every day.

It was in this house that I fell in love with architecture. But what were an ill-assorted bunch of students doing in a spectacular Wright-inspired house in an upmarket suburb? It turned out the house had flaws that made it hard to sell. Dresser, handling it for the owners who had to leave Madison unexpectedly,

couldn't find a buyer and was desperate to have it occupied over the bitter Wisconsin winter. Students would fill the gap.

Flaws indeed! The hot air heating system was inefficient, the huge expanse of single pane glass did not retain the heat, and the fireplace could not make up for the difference. We had to wear overcoats in the house on the coldest days. But it still was spectacular: it was like living in someone's first novel—the brilliant passages made up for the structural weaknesses.

My love affair with Wright and architecture continued through my college years. Thanks to Dresser, we were able to visit Wright's campus and compound at Taliesin East several times and see Wright himself in action. There are few places more beautiful than Taliesin, with its graceful integration of buildings and landscape set in rolling hills on the edge of the Wisconsin River. Just visiting there was a primer in architecture. And Wright, ruling like a lord over his 800-acre demesne, was equally spectacular. I saw him once at dinner with his acolytes where he sat on a high-back throne while almost everyone else sat on backless benches.

I learned about the Prairie Style of architecture, Wright's major early career breakthrough, and poured over pictures of his Prairie Style houses in Oak Park, Illinois. The Prairie Style, an authentically midwestern contribution to domestic architecture, was developed by a network of regional architects called the Prairie School. It featured substantial houses with open floor plans, low pitched roofs, overhanging eaves, rows of casement windows, and rich articulations of horizontal geometry, echoing the midwestern prairie. The growth of this style coincided with a great economic boom in the Midwest around the turn of the century, and the growing recognition of the region's importance, paired with a desire to establish an identity separate from the handed-down standbys East Coast cultural arbiters offered. Many of the buildings were commissioned by a rising upper middle class that wanted to show they were both sophisticated and midwestern.

I read Wright's books. I became a fan of his organic architecture and an admirer of the heroic architect. I looked for buildings by Wright and by Wright-influenced Prairie School architects in Madison.

This experience cemented my love affair with architecture, but I wasn't good at drawing and I struggled with math: I feared I lacked the skills to make it a career. So I became a passionate amateur devouring books and looking at buildings wherever I went. In later years, I

studied the buildings at Yale University when I taught there, and Brazilian architecture when I was stationed in the US Embassy in Rio de Janeiro. All along, I kept my loyalty to Wright, sneering at the faux Gothic of Yale and questioning the baroque modernism of Brasilia. I knew I couldn't design buildings. But could I commission one someday? Maybe something spectacular like Taliesin? I carried those dreams with me as I went on to a career in government and academia.

And then one day an opportunity arose. In 1970, I found myself the owner of a beachfront lot on the harbor in Nantucket Island. Having decided to build a summer home, I saw the opportunity to realize my dream of commissioning something spectacular. Little did I know that this would take me away from Wright's world-famous, totalizing and exacting design philosophy, and toward the world of the vernacular: the architecture of the everyday, often made without professional architects.

The location was certainly worthy of great architecture. The four-acre plot looked out over the harbor to Coatue, a narrow spit that separates the harbor from Nantucket Sound. But our budget demanded something modest. We did invite Alice and George Wislocki, my wife's sister and her husband, to build a companion house. But this was not going to be "Taliesin by the Sea": we could afford just two smallish beach cottages.

Who could we find who would use this opportunity to make a major contribution to architecture? How could I find a famous architect willing to build two small houses on a remote island? At that point the Gods of Architecture smiled on us. We had first come to Nantucket to visit our New Haven neighbors Marian Scully and her husband Vincent, the dean of American architectural historians. I decided to turn to Vince for help. He suggested we approach Bob Venturi, whose early buildings and writings helped usher in the postmodern movement. At the time, Venturi was only beginning to gain the reputation he later enjoyed. Bob initially was reluctant: he may have been hoping for bigger and more profitable commissions in less remote places. But Vince finally convinced Bob to take it on. Vince was one of Venturi's earliest champions, and may have helped him see the opportunity presented by clients who were willing to underwrite creativity and experimentation.

And so we embarked on an adventure. It was our version of a "Nantucket Sleighride"—the experience of harpooning a whale in tiny whaleboats. Stung by the harpoon, the great beast swims rapidly away and the sailors in their tiny boat, and are dragged along behind the leviathan: they must have felt completely in its power. Pulled along by our Great Architectural Project, we, with the Wislockis, travelled to Nantucket with Bob, his wife Denise Scott Brown, and his partner John Rauch. We raced around the island, looking at the Nantucket scene with special attention to the Shingle Style beach homes of the late nineteenth century and the earlier vernacular fisherman's cottages in Wauwinet. We said a few things about program and

waited as they developed designs and built models for review. The designs that emerged drew heavily on elements of the local architecture, both the simple cottages and the larger Shingle Style houses. We approved the plans—who wouldn't?—hired a builder, and within a year the Trubek and Wislocki Houses

"House in Madison, Wisconsin." Photo courtesy of David Trubek.

took shape. Venturi described the larger Trubek House as "complex and contradictory": one facade reminds you of the Shingle Style homes on the island but on a smaller scale and with a Palladian touch; the reverse facade side looks like a blown-up version of a Wauwinet fisherman's cottage. The smaller Wislocki House (which Bob dubbed "ugly and ordinary") drew more consistently on the local vernacular. They form a pair, turning slightly toward each other and, while each road-facing facade is asymmetric, when seen together they offer a sense of symmetry.

Soon these two small homes began to attract interest in architectural circles: they were featured in the *New York Times*, appeared on the cover of Vincent Scully's *The Shingle Style Today* and were mentioned in other books. By drawing on the vernacular traditions of Nantucket, Venturi had created something spectacular. No one could have put it better than Vincent Scully:

> With the Trubek and Wislocki Houses we are in the presence of what modern architects have always said they most wanted: a true vernacular architecture—common, buildable, traditional in the deepest sense, and of piercing symbolic power.[72]

If the Cliff House and the trips to Taliesin with James Dresser were my first courses in architecture and my introduction to architects, the Nantucket experience was my doctorate. With Venturi, I encountered an architectural sensibility and a personal style very different from Wright. Both stressed the importance of context, but Wright was more concerned with the natural context while Venturi paid more attention to the built environment. Wright was more interested in the form of the building than the way it fit into the city around it—compare the Guggenheim Museum in New York by Wright (a freestanding sculptural form at odds with its surrounding) with the Sainsbury Wing of the National Gallery in London by Venturi that delicately orchestrates the transition from the original building. And where Wright made it clear to everyone that he was a genius and a font of wisdom, Venturi adopted almost an antiheroic image.

Inspired by my contact with Venturi, I read and reread his *Complexity and Contradiction in Architecture*. Once you have read that masterpiece, you will never look at the built environment in the same way. You learn to see contradiction as well as harmony, find symmetry in the relation of asymmetric elements, and look more closely at a building and its built context. And once you have learned to appreciate the vernacular as well as the spectacular, you can understand why Venturi once said, "Main Street is almost all right."

It wasn't long after the Nantucket houses were completed that I returned to the Midwest and started a new phase of my Midwest architecture journey. In 1973 I found myself owning a quintessentially and authentically vernacular building—an American Foursquare house.

I did not go looking for a "Foursquare"—a term that did not exist at the time. We just needed a large home and this was the best one on the market when my wife and I and three daughters moved back to Madison. The house suited us. It had plenty of bedrooms. Through the use of pocket doors, the first floor was relatively open although not as open as the best Prairie Style houses. It was in good architectural company—down the street were Prairie Style buildings by Wright and George Maher and the Louis Sullivan-designed first Bradley House. That company may explain why the owners had tried to fancy up our Foursquare with eclectic decorative touches like a balustrade and ogee arches on the porch, but it remained a vernacular house, the basic design probably derived from a builder's pattern book.

Sometime after we moved in, I came to realize just how common Foursquares were. Venturi had helped me appreciate the value of the vernacular, and as I walked around Madison, I kept running into houses that shared many characteristics with ours. Like ours they had (at least originally) a square footprint, a large front porch, two stories plus an attic, and a low-pitched hip roof with dormers and wide, overhanging eaves. I assumed that like ours they had four rooms on each floor—"four above four" was the expression. I counted more than a dozen within easy walking distance of our house. Later I found that the Wisconsin Historical Society's Architecture and History Inventory (AHI) lists 197 Foursquares in Madison.

If the Prairie School was the upscale architectural expression of the growth of the Midwest, Foursquares played an important role on the other end of the building spectrum. The heyday of the Foursquare in the first two decades of the twentieth century overlaps with that of the Prairie School. If a Prairie School house was a symbol of a rising regional upper middle class, the Foursquare offered relatively cheap and commodious housing for less affluent residents. It was an economical building type and lent itself to mass production: companies like Sears Roebuck produced them by the thousands in kits. You could order your Foursquare by mail and it would arrive in a box full of hundreds of numbered pieces to be assembled like IKEA furniture or a giant Lego toy.

While it influenced architects around the world, the Prairie School was centered in the Midwest and the great bulk of buildings by Prairie School architects are in the region. Foursquares, on the other hand, can be found all over the US. But the type does seem to have been particularly popular in the Midwest: for example, the Wisconsin Historical Society's statewide AHI data base has 3782 Foursquares and is far from complete. A search of the Oak Park Illinois Historic District database for Foursquares shows over 1000 out of a total of little more than 3000 homes in the area.

While we cannot claim the Foursquare type for the Midwest, there is a Foursquare version that does seem to be regional. The Old House Journal and other sources indicate Foursquares can be found in many

"House in Oak Park." Photo by Gabriel X. Michael.

styles: the most common include Craftsman, Colonial Revival, Arts and Crafts, and Prairie Style. Writing in *Old House Journal*, Patricia Piore describes the Prairie variant:

> Many Foursquares throughout the Midwest incorporated the "modern" motifs of the region: horizontal banding, porch with a slab roof, geometric ornament, and "Prairie" art glass after Frank Lloyd Wright.[73]

Those with Prairie Style influences are sometimes called "Prairie Box," and that sure sounds midwestern. It seems reasonable to assume that the confluence of the Prairie Style and Foursquare houses happened mostly in the Midwest. You could find Prairie School buildings everywhere in the region, and they must have influenced owners and builders of these vernacular houses. Look at Oak Park, where Wright got his start, and where the Prairie School originated. In the Oak Park Historical District, not only is there a high percentage of Foursquares, but many of the Foursquares are listed as Prairie Style.

Take for example the house at 721 Belleforte Ave in Oak Park: this is a classic example of a humble Foursquare dressed up in Prairie Style. Constructed by a builder in 1915, this house is a common Foursquare type with obvious Prairie elements including massive pillars, horizontal banding, stucco, hipped roof, and overhanging eaves. With this building—and many other Prairie Style Foursquares around the region— the vernacular meets the spectacular: we could almost say "Main Street is almost all Wright."[74] ☒

Clockwise from top left: Armco-Ferro-Mayflower House; Florida Tropical House; House of Tomorrow; Cypress Log Cabin. Historic American Buildings Survey.

Yesterday's Tomorrow:
The Afterlife of the Century of Progress Homes of Tomorrow

LINDSAY FULLERTON

Perched on the edge of Lake Michigan and surrounded by the bucolic Indiana Dunes National Lakeshore, five retro-futuristic houses hover mirage-like above the shoreline. Constructed with flat roofs, boxy exteriors and fanciful colors, this assembly of homes is unlike any of the structures in the surrounding area. Some in striking hues, their geometric forms arrestingly contrast with the neighboring dunes and verdant forest. Seemingly out of place, they are also out of time: these are the last remaining major structures from Chicago's 1933 Century of Progress World's Fair.

Civic boosters began planning the Century of Progress World's Fair in the 1920s to celebrate Chicago's forthcoming 1933 centennial. However, organizers of the Fair, drawn mostly from Chicago's business elite, felt that it needed another more universal theme,

and they settled on the scientific and technological progress of the previous century. The Fair's President, Rufus C. Dawes, stated the theme "dramatizes the achievements of mankind, made possible through the applications of science to industry."[75] Fair organizers also sought to highlight scientific progress and technology, in the belief that these systems could help alleviate the Great Depression, which was at its depths in 1933. Organizers' emphasis on scientific and technological progress carried through to all exhibits and the modern architectural designs of Fair buildings. While the Fair presented a vision of the American dream predicated on the utilization of the latest technologies, during the height of the Great Depression many of the presented innovations remained out of reach for the average visitor. And so while Fair organizers' celebration of the latest and the greatest would be trumpeted by industry for years to come, its innovations—particularly the Homes of Tomorrow—remain symbols of stark inequalities during and after the Fair.

The Century of Progress Fair also marked the forty-year anniversary of the 1893 World's Columbian Exposition in Chicago. While the Century of Progress organizers hoped to emulate to epoch-defining success of the 1893 Chicago Fair, they did not seek to copy its architectural style. Whereas the 1893 Fair was a neoclassical "White City," the Century of Progress organizers and architectural committee adopted art deco and modern architecture, with sleek, geometric designs, painted in a palette of bright colors and accented by neon tubes and electric floodlights.

The Homes of Tomorrow Exhibit, to which these five houses once belonged, was a showcase of technological progress in home construction and architecture, featuring mass-produced and prefabricated elements made of new materials, with the latest in appliances and furnishings. According to the official 1933 Fair Guidebook, the exhibit's "group of eleven houses are designed to show progress in architecture, comfort and economy." In 1933, companies like Masonite and Good Housekeeping sponsored homes in the hopes of featuring their wares and attracting new customers. Though affordability was a stated goal of the exhibit, it is unlikely that many of the innovations presented would be affordable to fairgoers. In the midst of the Great Depression, many of the homes were more aspirational than attainable. Eight of the homes in

the exhibit embraced modernist design and the latest innovations in construction: state-of-the-art, man-made materials and prefabricated, mass-produced elements.[76] The homes also featured a plethora of laudatory advertising brochures and pamphlets for visitors to take home. These brochures included information on how consumers could obtain the home's materials or trimmings. Organizers added more homes for the second year of the Fair in 1934, and the original homes received new furniture and other updates.

Despite its architectural and cultural impact, the Century of Progress disappeared from Chicago's landscape. As in most World's Fairs, the organizers chose to construct temporary buildings, which were quickly demolished after the end of the Fair in 1934. However, real estate developer Robert Bartlett spirited away five model homes before they could meet a similar fate: the Cypress Log Cabin, the Wieboldt-Rostone House, the Armco-Ferro House, the House of Tomorrow, and the Florida Tropical House. These homes now stand just fifty miles from their original site on the fairgrounds along the shores of Lake Michigan between Twelfth and Thirty-ninth Streets and Northerly Island, the man-made peninsula jutting into the lake.

After the close of the Fair in 1934, Robert Bartlett bought a total of sixteen exhibited structures as a publicity stunt in the hopes that they would attract people to his nascent lakefront resort community in northwestern Indiana. "The reason we bought these model homes," Bartlett said, "is that they represent what we find are the most outstanding examples of modern home building, combining beauty and practical value."[77] Of the five houses that still stand, Bartlett moved four from Chicago across Lake Michigan to the Indiana Dunes by barge, while the Cypress Log Cabin was moved by truck. Bartlett bought other structures from the Fair for what would be become the lakeside Beverly Shores community, including a sixth Home of Tomorrow, the Modern Country Home (no longer standing), as well as structures from the Fair's Colonial Village. The only remaining structure of the colonial group is a replica of Boston's Old North Church, which is now a private residence.

Among the houses on the shores of Lake Michigan, the House of Tomorrow, designed by modernist architect George Frederick Keck, was the most forward-thinking. The 1933 Official Guidebook describes it as a "'laboratory' house, for the purpose of determining the attitude of World's Fair visitors to the idea of an utterly different home." Exhibit organizers did not position the House of Tomorrow as attainable or affordable, and it was instead intended to show the most cutting-edge technologies— per the guidebook—"price has been no object when building this house." While the rest of the model homes were free to visit, the House of Tomorrow's separate ten-cent admission charge highlighted its special appeal and exclusivity. The steel frame structure boasted concrete floors, a flat roof, floor-to-ceiling glass windows on each of its twelve sides, and all utilities and wiring were concealed away from view in the center part of the house.

The top two stories consisted of living space, while the first floor included a hangar for a personal aircraft, the ultimate in modern luxury.

Bolstered by the success of the House of Tomorrow, Keck debuted a second house in a different section of the Fair in 1934. The Crystal House showcased many similar novelties to the House of Tomorrow, but featured a rectangular shape, along with many more mass-produced and prefabricated elements. Though a future where the average citizen owned an airplane did not come to pass, other innovations featured in the House of Tomorrow did, including passive solar heating, open floor plans, air-conditioning, flat roofs, and prefabricated units. The House of Tomorrow also featured cutting-edge appliances that are now commonplace: the dishwasher and the "iceless" refrigerator. However, further modifications of the House of Tomorrow over the years significantly altered its appearance, covering over many of its windows, making it nearly unrecognizable from its original form. After their success at the Fair, George and his brother William continued to design homes throughout the Chicagoland area, using some elements and innovations from the House of Tomorrow, though modified and adapted for the needs of the typical homeowner, and coupled with a use of prefabricated elements championed by the Crystal House. The use of mass-produced elements in home construction highlighted at the Fair increased dramatically after World War II with its attendant increase in demand for housing.

The Armco-Ferro and Rostone Houses are both significant for the use of modular, prefabricated elements in pioneering new materials. Armco Steel (American Rolling Steel Company) and Ferro Enamel Corporation developed the Armco-Ferro House, designed by Architect Robert Smith Jr., to showcase their "Frameless Steel House" with an exterior covered in a new building material: mass-produced steel panels coated with porcelain enamel. Armco-Ferro produced the prefabricated panels in uniform heights, but with various widths that builders could easily assemble into structures. Promotional materials advertise durable, customizable frameless steel houses that are "built like your car." Of those homes remaining in Indiana, this house fit most closely the Fair organizers' stated goal of being affordable, though not for everyone (the 1933 construction cost was $4,500, which is approximately $86,000 in 2018).[78] All interior furnishings were also mass-produced and the official brochure stated that the furniture "Is not costly and you will be able to buy it in department and furniture stores all over the country." Armco-Ferro took great pains to show that their affordable houses, though factory-made, could still be customizable.

In the Rostone house, Rostone Inc. (manufacturer of its new, eponymous building material) showcased its mass-produced stone product made up of quarry waste, shale, and alkali. Prefabricated in standardized sizes, Rostone had a stone-like appearance, but with the benefit of being available in a variety of sizes and colors at low cost. To create the house's structure, pre-sized Rostone panels were bolted onto a steel frame, which Rostone claimed could be arranged in almost any configuration. Again, customization was key: "Do not, however, confuse it with the so-called 'mass production' houses which are supposed to made only in a certain few set designs" urged the official Rostone brochure. The structure, designed by Indiana architect Walter Scholer exhibits a modernist style with Mediterranean touches, and was clad entirely in tan Rostone panels, featuring an expansive rooftop deck and solarium. The company also featured Rostone in the interior of the building and the fireplace. Though at the time of installation, Rostone claimed its new material would last decades, by the 1950s, the panels had begun to fail. While the proprietary materials used in the Armco-Ferro and Rostone houses were not commercial successes, they are credited with paving the way for later homes that utilized prefabricated, mass-produced materials after World War II and beyond, such as Lustron homes.

Featuring a striking modern design, the Florida Tropical House was primarily selling a glamorous lifestyle that would have likely been out of reach for the average fairgoer. The state of Florida sponsored the house to advertise the exotic image of the state, in the hopes of attracting residents and investment. Architect Robert Law Weed designed the flamingo-pink, art deco style stucco house to reflect Florida's tropical climate and landscape. To further cultivate the tropical image, an essay in the house's official brochure described Florida as a place "of sunny skies, blue waters, colorful flowers, swaying palms, the odor of orange blossoms and vistas of attractive homes set in tropical bowers, a land of contentment . . ." The house featured a large, open living space, including a two-story living room, and a large roof terrace with expansive lake views. The art deco architecture displayed by the Florida Tropical House was a contemporary of the still-preserved architectural gems of Miami Beach, where Weed designed many other buildings in a similar style.

If the House of Tomorrow cuts the most striking figure, the Cypress Log Cabin, set back from the shore, blends into nature with its traditional silhouette. The Southern Cypress Manufacturers Association of Jacksonville, Florida, funded the Cypress Log Cabin, designed by architect Murray D. Hetherington as a "mountain lodge or rustic vacation cabin in the woodlands," per its official brochure. The home was not designed to display the latest architectural trends, but was instead intended as a showcase for all things cypress, a wood native to swampy areas in the American South. The home showcased cypress's versatility and durability, from exterior siding, blinds and flooring, to more fanciful touches like footbridges, carved animal heads, lamps, and furniture (which were not moved to Indiana). However, in keeping with the scientific emphasis of the Fair, cypress' technical advantages are also touted in the home's official brochure, including "a natural preservative [in] its innermost cell" that has to be imitated in other woods through the addition of creosote.

Ever since the Beverly Shores area was connected to Chicago by rail, it has been an attractive location for developers and well-heeled Chicagoans both past and present. Chicago real estate scion Frederick H. Bartlett (brother of Robert) purchased three-thousand acres of land where the houses now stand in 1927 with the intention to turn them into a resort. The stock market crash of 1929 thwarted these plans, and in 1933 Frederick sold the land to his brother. Robert Bartlett rapidly started developing the purchased land into a resort community with a series of freshly-built stucco homes, and other amenities including a hotel and a theater. However, the country was still in the depths of the Great Depression while the Robert Bartlett development was underway. Even after Robert's acquisition of the Century of Progress homes, lots sold at a slower pace than anticipated, and World War II stalled the project further. Robert Bartlett withdrew from the project in 1946, and the few hundred residents voted to incorporate themselves into the town of Beverly Shores in 1947.[79]

Over the years, many of the original Fair structures in Indiana were destroyed. Years of battering wind and water took their toll on the remaining homes, and they passed through many owners, falling into various states of disrepair and modification. Beyond cosmetic differences, erosion of the lakeshore further threatened the very existence of the structures. The federal government established the Indiana Dunes National Lakeshore on the site in 1966, though the homes at the time were still in private hands. The Fair homes eventually gained a new life when the National Park Service acquired them in 1980, and the houses made it to the National Register of Historic Places in 1986. The Fair houses changed hands again in the early 2000s, when four of the five homes were leased by Landmarks Indiana (a historical preservation nonprofit) from the National Park Service, and then sub-leased to private citizens for thirty-year terms.[80] As of 2019, these new owners are working to restore the Fair homes to their original state, with their own financing. The House of Tomorrow, left in the gravest state of disrepair, is still seeking an occupant who will rehabilitate the structure.

Today, as they hug the windswept shore of the Indiana Dunes, the Homes of Tomorrow stand as an embodiment of the Fair organizers' and participating companies' touting of the consumption of science and technology, even in the depths of the Great Depression. It is perhaps fitting, then, that the Homes of Tomorrow only survive today as the result of a publicity stunt to help sell more houses. Whether in Chicago, or after their move to Indiana, the Homes of Tomorrow assured visitors that a brighter future for both themselves and the nation could be theirs for a price. However, despite the grandiose promises of their brochures, the Century of Progress homes remained symbols of an out of reach dream for many. ✠

"White Dove building." Photo by Bivens Photography.

Ruin and Porn

RYAN SCAVNICKY

"A flaw ain't shit but a unique identifying mark. Everybody got a flaw. If you got a big belly, rub that motherfucker. Love it. I don't care what's wrong with you or how fucked up you think you are, somebody love your ass. So if your buck toothed? Bitch, relax. I bet there's a man in the house right now don't want nothing less than a bitch who can bite an apple through a picket fence."
—Adele Givens, *Queens of Comedy*

Cleveland is already sexy. Not to everyone, but being sexy to everyone isn't really desirable, is it? When we try to be universally sexy, we look to compensate for what we feel we lack. We get a haircut, join a gym, or get a Brazilian butt lift. We can either conform our image to the universal-basic-MTV-and-yoga-pants-at-Starbucks sexy, or we can accentuate our unique character. In doing so, one can become the object of someone's fetish. Fetish sexy is much more interesting because it contains within it some hidden or less understood desire. The Rust Belt is plagued by economic and ecological issues, but as an architectural site it is widely considered a collection of relatively bland landscapes dotted with signature projects by a few international architects. However, Cleveland, unbeknownst to itself and to the world, is at an apex of generating one of the most desirable spaces in the architectural vocabulary. It's not just that these spaces exist, but that they are being augmented and proliferated across digital space, where material, texture, scent, and sound are consumed by the power of the image. To make this legible, we have to take a close look at the industry leading the way of creating space that frames contemporary desire.

This industry is not architecture, but pornography. As always, it is one of the major industries dealing with the future of visual and interactive experiences. Virtual and augmented reality engines are currently being tested and perfected. The industry itself has moved from simply producing porn to facilitating pornographic experiences. Much like YouTube has done for video, most of the production itself is generated by a user base. The most popular category is "amateur," wherein—whatever the sexual act—the film appears to have been made outside of the studio by an everyday person in a recognizable space relatable to one's own specific desires.

Now, the most interesting shift in the industry to stem from this decentralization is the resulting Cambrian explosion of fetish categories considered desirable by various amateur directors. Porn production studios explored location early as an added aphrodisiac but never to the extent of today's sexuality market. Often enough, these locations amplify the acts themselves. This is achieved by placing the act in a greater social context. This happens in two ways. Either the act is housed somewhere in secret, relieving the viewer of the constant dread of being caught in real life, or the opposite, wherein the social disapproval of the act affords risqué locations which increase the excitement behind the acts themselves.

For example, the desire for gay sex to achieve social acceptance leads to its portrayal in a lily-white suburban home. Meanwhile, on another website, the front seat of an automobile hosts hijinks which satisfy an urge one may sublimate with road rage during rush hour traffic. Another recently popular location can architecturally set the stage for a wide variety of fetishes—anything from a massage parlor with a secret menu, a bondage dungeon, or a wrestling arena with unspeakable victory celebrations. Framing these kinky sex scenes, to my surprise, is the familiar exposed brick, concrete floor, and rusted steel structure of a warehouse, an aesthetic I associate with the Rust Belt, well represented in Cleveland.

In asking producers in the industry why they pick such spaces, I've been informed that the warehouse is a kind of catch-all aesthetic for sexual acts. It has no distinct fetish associated with it, yet it presents a highly desirable backdrop. Many backgrounds are similarly desired regardless of the acts they host—a hot tub, sports car, or rooftop garden all become actors in the scene to augment the social implications of the viewer's desire. Cleveland is home to an overabundance of this warehouse aesthetic that is considered risqué and desirable. Unfortunately recent construction like the Flats East Bank project exemplify an easily-rejected, half-baked simulation of this aesthetic. The project's most obvious design failure is it's curved plan and resulting facade, which is highly inconsistent with the warehouses it's imitating. (Nevermind the sea of parking lots.) Cleveland's newer buildings often reek of the desperate desire for universal acceptance rather than confident mania. It is as bland as suburban homes yet packaged as authentic Cleveland.

Another way of fetishizing the aesthetic territories of abandonment, rust, grime, and industrial might is through a genre of photography appropriately named "ruin porn." Nomenclature aside, this photographic category typically features a first person tour of an empty building. The movement became a documentary of the scars and relics of industrial abandonment. The resulting photographs uncover forgotten memories and forsaken relationships, yet reflect a sense of serenity and repose. The often viral photos mark an era when young Americans raised in McMansion suburban hell became entrapped by the rich imagery of despondent cities given new life through the internet.

A collapsed steel beam would elegantly cross the frame of the photograph, while the ensuing hole in the roof gave way to a bright sun shining down upon a floor covered with rubble. It wasn't just about the melancholy, but the hope one found at the availability and possibilities these photographers uncovered. These buildings only needed love.

For those of us in Rust Belt suburbs, those photographs were taken only a short drive from the sterile environment that surrounded us. Looking at ruin porn photography felt like watching *The Truman Show* for the first time. What I knew as home was dramatically revealed to be a stage set where everyone was simply acting. As a suburban-raised Clevelander I discovered that my friends and neighbors were collectively keeping a big secret: that at the heart of our pristine collection of suburbs was a putrid wasteland to be avoided completely. As a result of the burbs, the teenage angst of my generation found its way to school shootings, suicide, and drug abuse. But there were also little plots to escape the stage set, launching a grassroots return to Cleveland's gritty punk dive bars and lowly breweries in a desperate search for the remote possibility of authenticity. Yet we now find this mass return to the city is already being commodified by apartment blocks as faceless as the suburban situation we tried to leave behind. While this is typically evidence of gentrification and displacement in many large cities, with the right foresight it is possible to plan city growth in an equitable manner. Cleveland has shown that it can stay on top of it through

implements like the Evergreen Cooperatives: nationally recognized models of sustainable growth through worker and community-owned development.

Most cities have an old manufacturing area, including Vienna and Paris. Historically, the repurposing of industrial spaces for raves or gay bars has existed because those fetishes had to be kept secret. So they happened where space was cheap and out of the way which, for well-planned cities, existed out of sight. The houses and trees that once lined the streets of neighborhoods surrounding the manufacturing areas in Cleveland are nearly fully eroded due to the massive loss in population. The result is that in Cleveland those spaces are very much out and in the open, almost unavoidable and exposed by adjacent vacancy. And specifically, Cleveland's vast quantities of industrial spaces uniquely bend between Fordism and global post-Fordism. Many of Cleveland's companies hit a sweet spot of local manufacturing yet never fully conglomerated into a General Motors or US Steel. The resulting mutations on Cleveland's stock of warehouses is in a unique position to argue itself as among the most diversely constructed, creating repurposed magic. For example, the 78th Street Studios building in the Detroit-Shoreway neighborhood is the result of a rather haptic expansion of manufacturing and office spaces, producing four interconnected buildings totaling 170,000 square feet. This complex is now filled with a dizzying mix of spatial hierarchies, occupied strictly by artists' studios and galleries. In Midtown, the Mueller Lofts offer cozy living spaces in the ornate home of the "Alligator Clip" still used in electronics. This level of detail and spatial variety is lost on the tilt-up mega warehouses of today, which would prove aesthetically and spatially inadequate for any of these conversions. The fetishization of old industrial space is a vital and underutilized aesthetic territory that Cleveland can and should claim.

What makes these buildings so desirable has little to do with manufacturing, but the specific set of lyrical qualities imbued. For example, Rust Belt industrial areas feel almost quaint in comparison with the mega-production coming out of contemporary industrial facilities found in Shenzhen or Beijing. But those factories in China and elsewhere are built to handle a newer form of production. Tens of thousands of orange jumpsuits in a grid across a mighty space is a different aesthetic altogether, and it has influenced its own set of photographic explorations echoing a different, and very powerful kind of sublime. Modern industrial sublime can be seen in the large photographs of Andreas Gursky. Cleveland, however, is more like the work of Gursky's contemporary, Gregory Crewdson. Crewdson eschews the modern for the weird, complex angst and multifaceted narratives made possible by America's heartland. Crewdson's photographs often have audiences asking "what happened here?" just as a warehouse conversion holds an embedded history that provokes the imagination. Cleveland is filled with bespoke buildings created before the cheap airplane-hangar suburban warehouses of today. Its heavy manufacturing history was supplemented by just enough cultural capital and craftsmanship to produce buildings that are beautifully detailed yet pockmarked by years of abuse in a way that is often beautiful and surprising. I took my fiancé on a Valentine's day picnic in an abandoned arms factory, saw my cousin get married in what was the first American Greetings card production facility, and I went to a Catholic mass where the first electric carriage was manufactured. Some find synergy in marrying their past use with the present. In one example, the altar of said church was split down the middle by an inlaid rail line used to roll molten steel across the room to be poured. To capitalize on this culturally requires more than to embrace the fetish of grit and grime of the current urban core. In fact the greatest challenge moving forward is in reproducing and sharing the feeling one gets when confronted with the weight of that urban core.

This is a challenge because Cleveland seems to fight against the fetishization of its professed authenticity. For example, in the inner-ring neighborhood of Ohio City, entertainment areas have flourished over the last ten years as Americans reinvent craft beer. Drinking a pint in this rejuvenated Cleveland wouldn't be the same without the gritty backdrop of the city, in much the same way a hand job isn't risky if the door is locked. When popular urban brewpubs begin expanding outward into the suburbs this aesthetic becomes hotly contested. How can a brand new building attempt to replicate this aesthetic? Is a pint of Great Lakes Dortmunder Ale in Crocker Park Lifestyle Center the same as it is on West Twenty-fifth?

In researching the spread of the simulated industrial chic, it is important to look in and around Ohio, but also to look in the last place that would want to be associated with harsh winters, blue collar jobs, and sports debacles: Scottsdale, Arizona. Located in the historic old town of Scottsdale is a midwestern bar that opened its first southwest location called Two Brothers Brewing. This is a brewpub in an area marked by single story structures architecturally gesturing to western vernacular and drenched with imagery of the Sonoran Desert. But inside Two Brothers one discovers an open floor plan with tall brick walls, exposed steel structure, a concrete floor, and of course exposed ductwork. They even had the audacity to match up the grout in the faux brick wall covering as it turns the corner in the restrooms. This bar is a simulation of an abandoned manufacturing facility that has been converted to a lively brewery. A simulation of a fulfilled emptiness; a flaw that found its fetish. In the porn terms from before, this is the version of the story where fetish sex is acceptable and safe. It is normal. Whatever the motivation behind this brewpub, the warehouse aesthetic is spreading, yet ambiguous and unclaimed. There is something in the Rust Belt that isn't entirely reproducible yet a new building can get close enough for most to desire and enjoy it. That is a successful branding recipe.

As displayed by ruin porn photography, empty structures also entice the imagination to consider what it would fill that structure with. Porn directors do so in truly creative ways, but I'll leave that up to your imagination. This leads us to an interesting conclusion: an old warehouse is a desirable backdrop because it is cute, much in the same way a kitten or a baby is cute because we want to hold, feed, and care for it. Cute defines the ability of capital to exploit our maternal instinct. Interestingly enough, Rust Belt warehouses aren't exactly flying off of the shelves. In fact, Cleveland is lagging behind. Maybe it's the weather, but maybe it's just a confidence issue.

Architecture is at its best when it is indiscernible from fantasy. Digital media and culture cause physical place to mean less and less, making the aesthetic and experiential affordances of a place increasingly valuable. As hegemonic barriers of sexuality fall, the fetish sites of old become important history.

This is an architectural call to arms. What Cleveland needs is not discovering some lost authenticity but encouraging others to seek a simulation of what is thought of as authenticity. We need to convert empty warehouses, yes, but also new construction must find a way to be a little less straight and a little more kinky, in both senses of the word. We need brick that is a little crumbled, beams and columns that twist and turn, and pieces of leftover machinery with a curious presence. What would happen to Cleveland if suddenly a lot more people were asking themselves, "What could I do with a big empty warehouse?" ✠

An Abridged History of the Tallest Buildings in the Midwest

COREY SMITH

We can sketch them out, the records we almost have. For instance, the horizon behind the horizon. If you watch a sunset, then climb up a ladder, you can see another sunset, at least for a moment.

For instance, all the buildings that we imagined could be here.

When I talk about imaginary buildings I'm talking about ghosts, all the former selves who got off the train at an early stop and stayed there, the selves that you forgot about but found one afternoon looking at the old books you keep at your parents' house. I'm talking about myths, slight religion, the images that fill guidebooks and postcards and the lips of strangers. These are dreams, don't mistake them for what's real.

I want to tell you a small history about tall buildings.

I. *The Illinois*

The first tallest building in the Midwest is imaginary. Proposed by Frank Lloyd Wright in 1956, on "Frank Lloyd Wright Day in Chicago" as declared by Mayor Daley.

There is a public ceremony at the Sherman House Hotel Ballroom. Wright is in attendance and brings a banner that stretches from the ceiling to the floor— twenty-two feet. It's a sketch for a new project. No one has asked him to do this. There is no funding, no site, no public support. It's a drawing of a skyscraper. The skyscraper is a mile high. The tallest building in the world. 528 stories, 130,000 tenants, 56 atomic elevators, garages for 15,000 cars, two helipads for 50 helicopters each. The skyscraper is called the Illinois.

I love to hear that name. The Illinois. It's monstrous, it's stupefying, it's ridiculous.

Opposite: "Architect Frank Lloyd Wright Speaking at Press Conference." Bettmann/Getty Images.

❈

There is something I love about my home and it is that when I tell my mom that I'm reading about Toledo, she asks back to me, "Why?"

And I am as guilty of this as anyone, selling ourselves short. I'm trying to relearn how to answer that question. Because Toledo is beautiful and is the place I was born. Because Chicago is beautiful and is the place that I live. The mayor of Chicago says "Global City" like it's a defensive maneuver and I'm still trying to figure this place out—I bought a dress but I don't know how to wear it, I found ambition but I don't know how to see it through.

❈

The innovation that Wright proposed was a new method of building that he called the "Taproot System," where a skyscraper would stand because of a very long mast shoved into the earth and all the floors would cantilever off of it. This is actually pretty close to how grasses in the prairie stand so tall. It resembles Organic Architecture, that magical phrase that Wright invoked so often—building *into* the earth, not just *on* it.

And yet, as of this writing, the current tallest building in the world is just over half a mile high. A mile-high Illinois is a fever dream.

❈

It's a publicity stunt, is the problem. Let's not read too much into the logistics of the situation. We're here for a history and here it is: Wright hated cities and advocated for his singularly weird vision of suburban sprawl. Wright was a socialite, a publicity fiend, he loved the needlessly provocative and so let's not trust him on logistics. Instead, let's read into the poetry of the situation.

The Midwest does not contain mountains. Flatness is our water. We are students of subtle deviations in the landscape. "Illinois" is a word that comes from a verb meaning "to speak the regular way." Our tallest building is an icon of holy smallness, holy unchanging, holy gridded streets flung into the air.

Outside of the invisible building, we stand waiting for everything that has ever been written down to come true.

II. The Spire

The second tallest building in the Midwest is the opposite of a building and the opposite of a building is a hole in the ground.

The story I've been told goes like this: there was a plan that everyone was secretly looking a little forward to, which involved the construction of a new tallest building called the Chicago Spire. It would wrest the title of "Tallest Building in America" away from New York City and back to Chicago, and Chicago has always had a little chip on its shoulder about New York City, so it would be a symbolic victory and it would feel good.

The Chicago Spire was planned to be a little less tall than the Burj Kalifa in Dubai—so it wouldn't quite be the tallest building in the *world*, but it would make up for it at least by being the tallest in the Western Hemisphere.

The plan was ill fated, though.

Construction began in 2007 and it was a hole pressed into the ground downtown. It was construction workers and it was photo-ops and it was foundations and it was suddenly 2008 and the economy slumped. It was a hole in the ground. Suddenly the plan was lost capital and lost political will and a public embarrassment, a shorthand for the housing crisis and municipal dysfunction and the fact that we couldn't even get *this* done, the thing that Chicago is known for—giant buildings in the sky. What's more is that they had finished the hole for the foundation but *only* that, so we were left with a bitter reminder floating next to the high rises of downtown, like an ex-lover's coffee cup quietly staking out space on your end table. An inverse monument. The screeching of the highway nearby.

There is something a little too diminutive, too folksy or one-dimensional to say that the Midwest is filled with *humility* and *no-nonsense people*. In my experience, the region is much messier than that—queer and dystopic and racist and transcendent and urban and strained. It's a boring narrative, the one we've inherited. What's worse is how untrue it is.

Instead of *heartland values*, I'm captivated by the much more honest *midwestern fatalism*—an oscillation between unrestrained regional boosterism and a learned sense of flyover country, the feeling that everyone has entirely passed us by.

There are different strands of this. Molly, in Detroit, still incredulous at people moving there. Michelle, in Toledo, confused by a new coffee shop going in. They both give Chicago a healthy dose of big city skepticism. Fair enough. But Chicago has its own particular version. I have learned the sigh that translates to: "They moved to LA and it was better for their career."

A hole in the ground doesn't get you anywhere in the city, especially not Chicago, a place that looks at shifts in altitude like they're distasteful. It reminds me of walking in the prairie in Kansas and how few trees there are. A prairie balks at a tree, doesn't reject it outright, but is a little hesitant about it. The prairie only lets a few trees grow, only letting a little bit of shade creep in, and we can't have too many trees grow in a prairie anyway, it wrecks the whole ecosystem, it doesn't make sense with all the tallgrass and the beetles and the bison and the ants and the tiny little prairie stream curling through the acres and acres of space that seems not to have human beings, not anywhere, not as far as you can see, not to the horizon, and, you think, not past that. (There are horizons and then there are horizons beyond that if you shift your perspective to be higher up, and that is the opposite of a conversation, although just as intimate.)

Not that a massively tall spire dropped into the Chicago skyline would mean anything for our designation as flyover country. But I do think there is something interesting and unrestrained and bizarre about the optimism of a tall building in a place as flat as here.

It also feels important to note that our construction isn't the Chicago Spire, it's the Chicago Hole and the fatalist in me thinks that it was always supposed to be that way. This is something I have grown to treasure inside of me. I have learned to love this tender, anxious animal.

In 2018 they announced that someone is going to fill the hole that the Chicago Spire was supposed to fill. Two new skyscrapers. Not the tallest in the world, but at the very least something to put there. At this point, we are a little sad to see the hole go away. There is something comforting about a hole in the ground.

III. The Mast

I'm going to confess to you something—there are places I've never seen and Blanchard, North Dakota, is one of them. Blanchard has become something of a Mecca in my mind, a place of intense midwestern holiness. The site of pilgrimage is just a little bit west of town—the KVLY-TV mast

The KVLY-TV mast is the tallest thing in all of the Western Hemisphere, and, as of this writing, the fifth tallest thing in the world. It is not a building.

The third tallest building in the Midwest is not a building.

You look hard enough at anything and you'll find the limits of language crawling within it—arguments over

KVLY-TV Mast. Ratsbew/Wikipedia.com.

classification and Guinness records and definitions of increasingly specific varieties—but there is a particularly tragic bureaucracy that concerns itself with what a building is. I've always imagined all those bureaucrats and architects and project managers all got together one evening and, over cigarettes and oranges, eventually decided that a building is *something that stands*.

The KVLY-TV mast doesn't *stand*, it sort of *hangs*, supported by beams stretching down to the ground. This disqualifies it from being considered a building, and because of this technicality, almost no one knows about North Dakota's fifth tallest thing in the world. Almost everyone knows about Dubai. Our record is impressive, but we haven't been good about publicity. The tree outside of my bedroom window bears fruit that I know is safe to eat, but I've never reached out to try its berries.

Tallest buildings get remembered, written up, archived, talked about and there is beauty in choosing something as arbitrary as *tallness*. But I'm ignoring the most fundamental question—when the tall building gets built, who gets to go in? Who does it serve? Skylines are iconic. But icons are only so useful. Images aren't houses. Myths can't nourish.

When I talk about imaginary buildings, I'm imagining us looking up at them. I'm fantasizing about the train stop that's not mine and the ghosts who live in my old books. When I talk about imaginary buildings, I'm

talking about the tattoo of the Chicago skyline on the bicep of a stranger, the flag of my home state pinned to the wall, the symbols of place, the mythologies of region. These are useful, but only so much. A tall building deserves our praise no more than an anthill does. Let us sing praise to the anthill. Let us hold skepticism and zealotry in our hearts. Let us say no to floors, no to helicopters, no to systems, no to continuous horizontality, no to spires, no to glory, no to names, no to self-effacement, no to homogeneity, no to buildings, no to what's not real, only a straight line up and a straight line across, only holy unchanging and holy grid flung into the air, only the Midwest, only the people, only the fifth tallest thing in the world.

Consider *heliocentrism*, a word for frame of reference. If you can put the sun at the center of the solar system you can put anything—any point in North Dakota—as the center. And if you climb up a television mast at dusk, you can see the sunset over and over again.

We've got the stupid plans in the drawer for the tallest building in the world. We've got a hole in the ground for it. We can sketch them out, the dreams we keep, the records we almost have.

Signals from the KVLY-TV mast are sent up all over the sky, out into space, most of them small, entirely and lovingly mundane. ▨

Contributors

Michael R. Allen wrote and edited *Ecology of Absence*, a blog chronicling abandonment, historic preservation and austerity urbanism across the Midwest, between 2003 and 2013. Currently he is Senior Lecturer in Architecture, Landscape Architecture and Urban Design at Washington University in St. Louis and Director of the Preservation Research Office. Allen's writing about architecture and cultural landscapes has appeared in the *St. Louis Post-Dispatch*, *Temporary Art Review*, *CityLab*, *Next City*, *Disegno* and *Forty-Five Journal*.

Bryan Boyer is cofounder and partner at Dash Marshall, an architecture and strategic design studio working with people who care about cities. He runs the Civic Futures practice, which focuses on the intersection of new technology, urban environments, and institutions. You may find Bryan's amateur geo-ornithology on Instagram by following #eaglepants.

Randy Brown is a former editor of national consumer and trade magazines, including Better Homes and Gardens's *Beautiful New Homes* magazine and the now-defunct *Maintenance Executive*. He holds a 2006 Master of Science degree in architectural studies from Iowa State University and is the author of the 2015 poetry collection *Welcome to FOB Haiku: War Poems from Inside the Wire*.

Milenko Budimir, a lifelong Ohioan, is an editor for an engineering trade publication and an adjunct philosophy instructor. His interest in architecture, travel, and history made writing about Louis Sullivan's Ohio bank buildings a natural fit. He even tweets occasionally @MilenkoBudimir.

Bob Campbell was born and raised in Flint, Michigan, and now parks his car weekdays in "the flat lot." His creative nonfiction has appeared in *Belt Magazine, Gravel Magazine*, and *Forge Literary Magazine*. His debut novel, *Motown Man*, will be published this fall by Urban Farmhouse Press.

Dante A. Ciampaglia is a writer and editor in Brooklyn, New York, whose work has been published by *Metropolis*, *Architectural Record*, the *Paris Review*, and the *Daily Beast*, among others. A native Pittsburgher who spent his first twenty-seven years in the Steel City, Dante has a complicated relationship with the place that, to paraphrase Jimmy Breslin, he loves and hates equally.

Mark Clemens, a lifelong midwesterner, lives outside Chicago. He was awarded the 2018 Bodley Head/FT Essay Prize and has previously written on the architecture of the region for *Midwestern Gothic*.

Sophie Durbin is a multidisciplinary artist based in Minneapolis, Minnesota. Her favorite structures to analyze are churches and small municipal offices. She has only lived in states that touch Great Lakes.

Amy Elliott Bragg is a Detroit-based writer, editor, and cemetery creep. Her work has explored the origins of the cremation movement in the US, the birth of Detroit's historic preservation movement and why Michigan is on Eastern Time, among other curiosities. She first became interested in mausoleums when her beloved aunt and uncle were interred in the mausoleum at St. Hedwig Cemetery in Dearborn Heights, Michigan.

Matthew R. Francis is a physicist, science writer, and connoisseur of jaunty hats. He has written about physics, astronomy, mathematics, and the culture of science for more than thirty publications. This is his first foray into writing about architecture, which may explain why he thinks Wilson Hall looks like the Atari logo.

Joe Frank grew up on the South Side of Chicago in a cluster of I.M. Pei and Harry Weese row houses. Before becoming a lawyer, he was a reporter for the *City News Bureau of Chicago*, the *Ledger* (Lakeland, Florida), and the *St. Petersburg Times*. He practices corporate bankruptcy law in Chicago and represented the development company that tried to build the Chicago Spire.

Lynn Freehill-Maye is a Central Illinois native who writes about travel, food, sustainability, and design. Her work has been published, in print or online, by the *New Yorker*, the *New York Times*, the Atlantic's *CityLab*, and other publications.

Lindsay Fullerton is an independent scholar whose work on social media and the history of technology has appeared in *Critical Studies in Media Communication, Culture & Critique*, and the *International Journal of Communication*. A third-generation Chicagoan, her current book project about the 1933-34 Century of Progress World's Fair in Chicago engages her longstanding interest in the history of World's Fairs and her home city. Currently based near Cleveland, Lindsay holds a B.S. from the University of Pennsylvania and a Ph.D. in Media, Technology, and Society from Northwestern University.

Jordan Hicks is an architect and writer exploring spaces and structures that communicate order and generate immersive experiences. He currently works at Studio Gang Architects. Jordan lives with his partner, fiction writer Amanda Goldblatt, in Chicago's Logan Square neighborhood.

Asher Kohn is an urban planner and writer who was raised in the suburbs of Chicago. His work focuses on land use and demographic change.

Alexandra Lange is a historian and design critic. She is the architecture critic for *Curbed* and her work has appeared in *New York*, the *New Yorker*, the *New York Times*, the *Atlantic, Architect*, and many other publications. In 2018 she published the book *The Design of Childhood: How the Material World Shapes Independent Kids* (Bloomsbury USA). In 2019 she was awarded the AIGA Steven Heller Prize for Cultural Commentary.

Jennifer Komar Olivarez served as a curator in the Decorative Arts department of the Minneapolis Institute of Art (Mia) for twenty-five years, specializing in architecture, craft, and design, particularly from the nineteenth to twenty-first centuries. As Head of Exhibition Planning and Strategy at Mia since February 2016, she engages the public with innovative exhibitions and dynamic programs generated in conjunction with the curatorial team. Since 1994 she has overseen the museum's 1913 Prairie School-style Purcell-Cutts House, authored *Progressive Design in the Midwest: The Purcell-Cutts House and the Prairie School Collection at The Minneapolis Institute of Arts* (2000) and curated the Mia exhibition *The Progressive Pencil: George Elmslie's Prairie School Designs* (2013).

Eric Lawler received a Bachelor of Science in Architecture from the Ball State University College of Architecture and Planning in Muncie, Indiana. He currently lives and works in Los Angeles, California as an architectural designer and Hoosier expat.

Allison C. Meier is a Brooklyn-based writer on art, history, and culture. Growing up in Oklahoma, her interest in architecture was sparked by exploring the hidden passageways of Bruce Goff's Shin'en Kan and the triangular balconies of Frank Lloyd Wright's Price Tower. She moonlights as a cemetery tour guide.

Zach Mortice is a Chicago-based design journalist who focuses on landscape architecture and architecture. If you listen closely to his interview tapes, you can hear the percussive roars and metal-on-metal squeals of the Red Line El as it rumbles by his apartment. You can follow him on Twitter and Instagram @zachmortice, or at zachmortice.com.

Daniel Naegele is an architect and architectural historian who has taught at Iowa State University for eighteen years. He holds degrees in architecture from the Architectural Association in London, from Yale, and from the University of Pennsylvania where he completed his dissertation under the supervision of the renowned British scholar, Joseph Rykwert. He recently published *The Letters of Colin Rowe* and *Naegele's Guide to the Only Good Architecture in Iowa*. Presently, he's completing *Waiting for the Site to Show Up: Frank Lloyd Wright's Popular Press House for Lowell Walter*.

Monica Obniski is the Demmer Curator of Twentieth and Twenty-First Century Design at the Milwaukee Art Museum, where she is responsible for decorative arts and design installations, exhibitions, and programming. She has held curatorial positions at the Art Institute of Chicago and the Metropolitan Museum of Art, and received an M.A. in the History of Decorative Arts and Design from the Bard Graduate Center, and a Ph.D. from the University of Illinois at Chicago. Her current projects include an international traveling exhibition and publication that is co-organized with the Los Angeles County Museum of Art for 2020-21 called *Scandinavian Design & the United States, 1890-1980,* and a show exploring Lillian and Willis Leenhouts's practice as architectural activism.

Amanda Page is a writer living in Columbus, Ohio, with two senior dogs. She divides her time between Ohio and Scotland, where she hosts an annual writing retreat on the Isle of Skye.

Erik Piepenburg is the features editor at Serino Coyne, a live entertainment advertising agency in New York City. He has been a journalist for over twenty years, mostly at the *New York Times*, where he covered theater as a writer, editor and digital producer. He is originally and proudly from Cleveland, where he grew up very gay on the West Side.

Monica Reida makes a point of visiting the public libraries in every city she visits and while the Waterloo Public Library holds a special place in her heart, she is also a huge fan of the central St. Louis Public Library. Her writing has appeared in *Barista Magazine, OnMilwaukee, NewCity,* and *Gapers Block,* where she was the politics editor from 2013-15. She lives in Milwaukee.

Jonathan Rinck studied art history at the University of St. Andrews, Scotland, and teaches at Spring Arbor University in Michigan. Memorable Sunday brunches at Earl Young's iconic Weathervane Inn were always a highlight of childhood family vacations to "Charlevoix the Beautiful."

Samantha Sanders is a freelance writer and editor whose work has appeared in the *Awl, Catapult, Writer's Digest,* and *Artists Magazine.* Born and raised in Cincinnati, she has lived in Seattle, Los Angeles, and now makes her home in Brooklyn.

Bill Savage teaches in the English department at Northwestern University and at the Newberry Library of Chicago. There, his class "The City that Drinks: the Chicago Saloon in Literature and Film" focuses on Midwest tavern culture from the nineteenth century to today. He will never drive more than two hours out of his way to stop at the New Glarus Brewing Company.

Ryan Scavnicky is the founder of Extra Office, a practice engaged in contemporary culture, aesthetics, and media to seek new agencies for critical architecture. He currently serves as the Visiting Teaching Fellow at the School of Architecture at Taliesin, an experimental graduate school located in the Sonoran Desert. He received his Masters of Science in Design Theory and Pedagogy from SCI-Arc.

Corey Smith is a composer, performer, and writer based in Chicago, Illinois. His ongoing project, THE NEW PRAIRIE SCHOOL, is a sequence of performances, video works, and essays about architecture and the Midwest.

Andy Sturdevant is a writer and artist living in Minneapolis. He has written about art, architecture and history for a variety of Twin Cities-based publications, including *ArchitectureMN, City Pages* and *MinnPost.* He is the author of three books of nonfiction, and also runs Birchwood Palace Industries, a small press that publishes art books and printed novelties.

David M. Trubek is a retired UW-Madison professor and amateur architecture buff. A visit to Taliesen East and an encounter with Frank Lloyd Wright during his college days was the beginning of a lifelong architectural pilgrimage that has included exposure to both high styles and the vernacular in the Midwest and around the world.

Notes

Out of Earth: The Cahokia Mounds and the Radix of Midwestern Monuments

1 Jerome E. Dobson and Joshua S. Campbell, "The Flatness of US States," *Geographical Review* 104, no. 1 (2014): 19.

2 This section gives a very brief overview of Native American mounds. It is a fascinating history, and there is much more of interest than I can touch upon here. For a good introduction, see George R. Milner, *The Moundbuilders* (London: Thanks & Hudson Ltd, 2004).

3 See Biloine Whiting Young and Melvin L. Fowler, *Cahokia: The Great Native American Metropolis* (Urbana and Chicago: The University of Illinois Press, 2000), 30-32 for an examination of these nineteenth-century "theories" and their political ramifications.

4 As these cultures are long since vanished, we do not know the names by which they called themselves. The Adena are named after an Ohio property where a mound was excavated around 1900; the Hopewell are named for a specific mound group. See Milner, 54-56.

5 A recent public radio piece highlighted this history. See Jesse Dukes "Map Quest: Searching for Chicago's Lizard Mound," *Curious City*, WBEZ, April 15, 2018. Online at http://interactive. wbez.org/curiouscity/lakeview-effigy-mound/?_ga=2.167415166. 1987246893.1523801561-823055192.1466264372.

6 Nineteenth century viewers described the orb as an egg (Milner, 79-80). More recent theories posit that the orb references the moon, and the swallowing explains its phases.

7 Milner, 92.

8 See Timothy R. Pauketat, *Cahokia: Ancient America's Great City on the Mississippi* (New York: Viking, 2009) 26, Milner, 135 and Young and Fowler, 310-311.

9 For a fascinating design study of how landfills can act as monuments, see Rania Ghosn and El Hadi Jazairy, *Geographies of Trash* (New York and Barcelona: Actar, 2015).

10 The engineering of the mound is a fascinating negotiation of drainage, angle of repose, and buttressing. See Young and Fowler, 284-285.

11 Ibid.

12 See Pautekat, 127-128 and Fowler and Young, 286.

13 Pautekat, 37-38.

Making Nature Present: Frank Lloyd Wright's Magazine House in Iowa
Many thanks to Joy Kestenbaum, in New York City, for her assistance with these notes.

14 "Opus 497," *The Ladies' Home Journal*, vol. 62, no. 6 (June 1945), 138-139, 141.

15 As quoted in *Frank Lloyd Wright*, Part 1, a documentary film by Ken Burns and Lynn Novick, 1998.

16 Lowell Walter was born in Independence, Iowa in 1896, and was raised in Quasqueton, Iowa. In 1913, he went to Des Moines to seek his fortune. There he married Agnes Nielsen of Humboldt, Iowa. From 1917 until 1944, they owned and operated the Iowa Road Builders Company. They invested in Buchanan County farmland, at one time owning more than 5,000 acres. Walter died in August 1981.

17 The letter is dated January 25, 1945 and can be found in "1945 Correspondence, Folder 1" in the Lowell E. Walter Collection of the State Archives at the Iowa State Historical Department in Des Moines. Included with this letter was Walter's three-part sketch featuring:
- Single-line plans of the house he envisioned
- A hand-drawn site plan locating the house in relation to the river (the lot is 80' N x 292' W x 385' E x 137' S on river)
- A second site plan locating the prospective house in relationship to a creek that flows to the river, and showing the drive to the prospective house.

18 Telegram from Taliesin West, Scottsdale, Arizona, Frank Lloyd Wright to Lowell Walter, February 3, 1945. "1945 Correspondence, Folder 1," Lowell E. Walter Collection, State Archives, Iowa State Historical Department, Des Moines.

19 Letter, Lowell Walter to Frank Lloyd Wright, December 28, 1949. "1949 Correspondence (July-December), Folder 6," Lowell E. Walter Collection, State Archives, Iowa State Historical Department, Des Moines.

20 Letter, Frank Lloyd Wright to Lowell Walter, January 2, 1950. "1950 Correspondence (January-March), Folder 7," Lowell E. Walter Collection, State Archives, Iowa State Historical Department, Des Moines.

21 Volunteers of Quasqueton's Veterans Memorial Park Committee led tours. Adults were charged 50 cents and children a quarter with all proceeds going to the Veteran Memorial Park. 4,178 visitors toured the home those two Sundays. Lowell Walter, who conducted some of the tours himself, prepared a handout intended, he said, "to answer the many questions asked by the visitor." He titled the detailed account, "Lowell Walter House Dwelling: Cedar Rock." Want to know how many bricks are in the house?

Louis Sullivan in Central Ohio

22 Twombly, Robert. *Louis Sullivan: His Life and Work.* The University of Chicago Press, 1987.

23 Tebben, Joseph R. *The Old Home: Louis Sullivan's Newark Bank.* The McDonald & Woodward Publishing Company, 2014.

24 Tebben, *Old Home,* 12.

25 Tebben, *Old Home,* 49.

26 Jeffries, Anna. "Sullivan restoration to begin soon; fundraising continues." *Newark Advocate*, 9 June, 2016.

27 "People's Federal Savings & Loan Assn.–1918." Shelby County Historical Archive, https://archive.is/20010308031100/http://www.shelbycountyhistory.org/schs/downtown/peoplefederalp2.htm.

Lillian Leenhouts's Milwaukee Eco-Socialism

28 Oral History Interview with Robin Leenhouts, 2007, Willis and Lillian Leenhouts Architects Records, University of Wisconsin-Milwaukee Libraries, Archives Department.

29 Lillian S. Leenhouts, Portfolio for AIA Fellowship Nomination, 1975.

30 For more on this project, see Madeline M. Riordan, "Grassroots and Community Activism Within Milwaukee's Black Community: A Response to Central City Renewal and Revitalization Efforts in the Walnut Street Area, 1960s to 1980s," MA Thesis, Urban Studies, University of Wisconsin-Milwaukee.

31 Oral history interview with Robin Leenhouts, 2007, Willis and Lillian Leenhouts Architects Records, University of Wisconsin-Milwaukee Libraries, Archives Department.

32 Ibid.

33 See https://www.citylab.com/equity/2016/08/how-wisconsin-became-the-home-of-black-incarceration/496130/ and http://www.wuwm.com/post/how-did-metro-milwaukee-become-so-segregated#stream/0, for example.

34 These letters may be found in Willis and Lillian Leenhouts Architects Records, 1936-1990, University of Wisconsin-Milwaukee Libraries, Archives Department, UWM MSS 223, Box 4 Folder 20. The cost for one set was $25 (with additional sets priced at $5 each).

35 The solar house built directly to the east of the Leenhouts home (and completed nearly two years before it) was built from these plans.

36 Lillian S. Leenhouts, "Twenty-Two Years in a Pollution Conscious House & More Plants in One for Tomorrow," *Botanical Club of Wisconsin* newsletter v. 4 (January 1972), 11.

37 "Architects at Home," *Wisconsin Architect.* (January 1967).

38 Lillian S. Leenhouts, "Twenty-Two Years in a Pollution Conscious House & More Plants in One for Tomorrow," *Botanical Club of Wisconsin* newsletter v. 4 (January 1972), 12.

39 Daniel Barber has recently written about one of these—solar energy. Daniel A. Barber, *A House in the Sun: Modern Architecture and Solar Energy in the Cold War.* New York: Oxford University Press, 2016.

40 "You Can So Have a Solar House in a Cold Climate," *House Beautiful* 90 (June 1948): 84-91.

41 "A Solar House Designed to the Compass," *House Beautiful* 87 (November 1945): 128-133.

42 "Notes for Time and Energy, A New Aesthetic of Architecture," 1978, 3/15.

43 According to the Passive House Institute, the five principles are: thermal bridge free design, superior windows, ventilation with heat recovery, quality insulation and airtight construction. https://passivehouse.com/02_informations/02_passive-house-requirements/02_passive-house-requirements.htm.

Building a Quirky Science Lab in the Middle of an Illinois Cornfield: The Architecture of Fermilab

44 Fermilab History, http://history.fnal.gov/dome.html.

45 Fermilab History, http://history.fnal.gov/neutrino.html#photos.

46 Lillian Hoddeson, Adrienne W. Kolb, and Catherine Westfall, *Fermilab: Physics, the Frontier, and Megascience* (University of Chicago Press, 2008). This book is somewhat hagiographic (having been written by in-house Fermilab historians) but contains a lot of information about the details of construction and the struggles over funding.

47 Henry Petrowski, "Robert Wilson: Fermilab's Master Physicist, Sculptor, and Engineer," *American Scientist* 103 (May-June 2015), 170. DOI: 10.1511/2015.114.170.

48 Obituary for Alan H. Rider: "Accomplished architect, Hastings grad dies in D.C.," *Hastings Banner* (Hastings, MI), July 15, 2009. http://hastingsbanner.com/accomplished-architect-hastings-grad-dies-in-dc-p1697-86.htm.

49 Alan H. Rider, "The Architect's Point of View" (1976), republished on Fermilab history site: https://history.fnal.gov/design.html.

50 Hoddeson, Kolb, and Westfall.

51 Robert R. Wilson and Adrienne Kolb, "Building Fermilab: A User's Paradise" in Lillian Hoddeson et al. (eds.), *The Rise of the Standard Model* (Cambridge University Press, 1997).

52 Paul Halpern, *Collider* (John Wiley & Sons, 2009).

53 Wilson and Kolb.

54 I've visited Fermilab on three occasions (in 2004, 2012, and 2016), but my trip in 2012 for a book project that never came to fruition was the one where I got the behind-the-scenes look at the facility I describe here.

Finding the Sacred in the Secrets of Christ Church Lutheran, Minneapolis

55 Ledgard, Henry F. *Minnesota Modern*. University of Minnesota Press, 2015.

56 Saarinen, Eliel. *The Search for Form in Art and Architecture*. 1948. (Dover, 1985), 315.

57 Anderson, Rolf T. *Christ Church Lutheran*. National Register of Historic Places Registration Form. Minneapolis, Minnesota. (February 9, 2008), 12.

58 Saarinen, Eliel. *The Search for Form in Art and Architecture*. 1948. (Dover, 1985), 316.

59 Anderson, Rolf T. *Christ Church Lutheran*. National Register of Historic Places Registration Form. Minneapolis, Minnesota. (February 9, 2008), 13.

60 Mattes, Mark C. *Martin Luther's Theology of Beauty: A Reappraisal*. (Baker Academic, 2017), 144.

61 "Lutherans Work to Shed Stuffy Image and Kick-Start Change." *Star Tribune*. Minneapolis, MN, July 3, 2017.

62 Mattes, Mark C. *Martin Luther's Theology of Beauty: A Reappraisal*. (Baker Academic, 2017), 123.

Beneath the Cross in Bronzeville

63 This and all statistics in this essay, as well as most of the historical context of early twentieth-century Bronzeville, comes from St. Clair Drake and Horace Cayton's monumental and still-indispensable *Black Metropolis: A Study of Negro Life in a Northern City* (1945. University of Chicago Press, 1993).

64 This story comes from First Deliverance's own account of its history, found at https://fcdchicago.org/church-history/.

65 A detailed overview of the architecture of First Deliverance,

including sketches of the careers of Walter Bailey and Rev. Cobbs, can be found in the Commission on Chicago Landmarks' 1994 report on the church, available online: https://ia600702.us.archive.org/5/items/CityOfChicagoLandmarkDesignationReports/FirstChurchOfDeliverance.pdf. Further information comes from Kymberly Pinder's *Painting the Gospel: Black Public Art and Religion in Chicago* (University of Illinois Press, 2016).

66 Washington's rather skeptical view of the Spiritualist tradition, including Cobbs, is in *Black Sects and Cults* (Anchor, 1973).

67 See Pinder, *Painting the Gospel*, for a biography of Jones and his relationship to the South Side Community Arts Center.

68 I encountered this and many other wonderful photos in *Bronzeville: Black Chicago in Pictures, 1941-1943*, edited by Maren Stange (New Press, 2003).

69 "New York Beat." *Jet*, September 11, 1952. Cobbs appeared in dozens of issues of *Jet* and *Ebony* from the 1950s through the 1970s, many of which can be read in full through Google Books.

70 "Billy Williams Sings Blues in His Death." *Jet*, November 2, 1972.

71 Best, Wallace D. *Passionately Human, No Less Divine: Religion and Culture in Black Chicago, 1915-1952*. (Princeton University Press, 2005).

From Spectacular to Vernacular

72 Scully, *The Shingle Style Today*, 36.

73 *Old House Journal* Online, September 7, 2010.

74 I am grateful for help from Jim Draeger of the Wisconsin Historical Society, my colleague and Wright enthusiast Stewart Macaulay, Anna Andrzejewski of the UW Art History Department, and Julian Edgoose an architecture buff who now owns our Madison Foursquare.

Yesterday's Tomorrow: The Afterlife of the Century of Progress Homes of Tomorrow

75 *Official Book of the Fair Giving Pre-Exposition Information 1932-3 of A Century of Progress International Exposition Chicago 1933* (1932).

76 For a more thorough discussion of the innovations of each home, see Lisa D. Schrenk, *Building a Century of Progress: The Architecture of Chicago's 1933-4 World's Fair*. University of Minnesota Press: 2007.

77 Chase, Al. "Fair's Model Homes Go To Beverly Shores: Buildings Will Be Placed In Permanent Exhibit." *Chicago Daily Tribune*: November 17, 1934.

78 *Official Guidebook of the Fair 1933*. (1933).

79 More information on the area, houses, and national park can be found in Robin A. Carlascio and Theresa K. Badovich's 2014 book, *Saving a Century of Progress*.

80 More information can be found on the Indiana Dunes National Lakeshore website: https://www.nps.gov/indu/index.htm.

Acknowledgements

This book truly has been a collaborative effort. Martha Bayne, Alexandra Lange, Zach Mortice, and Anne Trubek all vetted and edited the essays. That was a pleasure, thanks to the dozens of writers who offered unique, thoughtful insights into Midwest architecture. Meredith Pangrace is responsible for the gorgeous interior design, and David Wilson for the cover. Many thanks to photographers, particularly Gabriel X. Michael, for crawling under fences and atop buildings to capture just the right detail or angle. Dan Crissman and Rebekkah Rubin offered crucial editorial help. We hope you enjoy the process of reading and viewing this book as much as all of us did putting it together.